Praise for *When Jesus Became God*

"A splendidly dramatic story . . . Rubenstein has turned one of the great fights of history into an engrossing story."
—Jack Miles, author of *God: A Biography*

"Succeeds in bringing fully alive a moment in history when matters of faith were capable of inspiring authentic passion in ordinary men and women." —Jonathan Kirsch, author of *The Harlot by the Side of the Road*

"[Rubenstein] has taken one of the major religious controversies of the early Christian church, a controversy that consumed its energies for most of the fourth century, and turned it into a flesh-and-blood encounter of real people that reads like an adventure story."
—*The Christian Science Monitor*

"A vivid, engaging account of the times . . . readers will find an engaging and informative guide to a turbulent period in Christian history and will take from it an enhanced sense of the complexity and controversy that makes up all human endeavors." —*Boston Book Review*

"Early church history has never been so fascinating. . . . The author breathes life into the personalities that dominate this era in history. . . . A book that is like a novel in its ability to grab a reader's attention."
—*The Dallas Morning News*

"Any half-alert Catholic realizes that the church is an intensely political organization. What I saw even more clearly in this book was how even basic theology, doctrine and dogma were dictated by secular politics."
—*National Catholic Reporter*

"One of the most compelling stories of Church history, insightfully told . . . Perceptive well-written Church history." —*Kirkus Reviews*

"Rubenstein's lively historical drama offers a panoramic view of early Christianity as it developed against the backdrop of the Roman Empire of the fourth century." —*Publishers Weekly* (starred)

WHEN JESUS
BECAME GOD

WHEN JESUS BECAME GOD

The Struggle to Define Christianity during the Last Days of Rome

Richard E. Rubenstein

A Harvest Book

HARCOURT, INC.

Orlando   Austin   New York   San Diego   Toronto   London

FOR HANNAH AND SHANA,

WITH LOVE AND ADMIRATION

www.HarcourtBooks.com

Library of Congress Cataloging-in-Publication Data
Rubenstein, Richard E.
When Jesus became God : the epic struggle over Christ's divinity
in the last days of Rome / by Richard E. Rubenstein.—1st ed.
p.   cm.
Includes bibliographical references and index.
ISBN-13 978-0-15-100368-6   ISBN-10 0-15-100368-8
ISBN-13 978-0-15-601315-4 (pbk.)   ISBN-10 0-15-601315-0 (pbk.)
1. Jesus Christ—Divinity—History of doctrines—Early
church, ca. 30–600. 2. Arianism. I. Title.
BT216.R83   1999
273′.4—dc21   98-52097

Text set in Fairfield Medium
Designed by Camilla Filancia

Printed in the United States of America
First Harvest edition 2000
I K M O Q P N L J

Again and again in the writings of the Eastern Fathers there appears this singular devotion to the dignity of man, an attitude which survives in the Offertory in the Mass: "O God, who didst marvelously create the dignity of human nature. . . ."

ROBERT PAYNE
The Fathers of the Eastern Church

THE ROMAN WORLD
IN THE FOURTH CENTURY

Contents

Preface

THIS BOOK was conceived in an unusual setting.

The year was 1976. I had just arrived with my family in Aix-en-Provence, France, where I was to spend a sabbatical year teaching at the university. We had rented a house for the year from Michel Vovelle, a well-known French historian who was just packing up to leave for a sabbatical year of his own at Princeton. The lease was for a certain rent, quite reasonable, but with a proviso that if I wanted to use Professor Vovelle's private library, the rent would be a bit higher. After greeting him—a man with whom one felt immediately at ease—I asked to see the library.

It was a rectangular room decorated in simple Provençal style, running the whole length of the house. A tall, built-in bookshelf crammed with volumes covered one long wall. The wall opposite was fully windowed, windows thrown open to admit the warm September air. From Professor Vovelle's desk one could see a garden with shrubs and an olive tree. Just beyond the garden a stream murmured and splashed as if auditioning for the part of "gurgling brook" in some Arcadian drama. My normally frugal wife took in the room at one glance and whispered, "Rent it!"

We signed the amended lease, and that evening I explored the contents of the bookshelves. There were small collections on dozens of subjects, reflecting my landlord's wide-ranging interests, but a great many books dealt with theology and Church history. I recalled that Michel Vovelle was widely known for his work on the "de-Christianization" of France prior to the French Revolution, a sensitive blend of social and religious history that had helped define the new French scholarship. A number of titles piqued my interest, and I was sitting at the desk riffling through half a dozen books when he returned to pick up his remaining suitcases.

"So, already you are studying," he remarked amiably.

"Yes. I'm very happy to have the use of your library. By the way, what do you know about the Arian controversy? I've just been reading about it."

"Ah, '*l'affaire Arius*,'" he replied. "You must learn all about it. Was Jesus Christ God on earth, or was he something else? Three hundred years after the Crucifixion, Christians still had not made up their minds about this. The Arian controversy! It is the most interesting debate in the West until the struggle between Stalin and Trotsky."

I was hooked. That year, I read most of Vovelle's books on "*l'affaire Arius*," and for years afterward, interrupted by other writing projects and life-altering events, I continued to investigate the fascinating story. The sources of information were plentiful, although most books and articles were aimed at a narrow audience of scholars interested in the history of Catholic doctrine. Almost everything I wanted to read was written in English or French, languages that I understand, and I was able to discuss the meaning of certain important Greek terms with experts in that language. Church historians, theologians, and clergy were happy to answer my questions, as were scholars interested in the later Roman Empire.

Several times I began writing the book that I had already entitled *When Jesus Became God*, but something always prevented me from continuing. The problem was not just competing interests. I suppose it was self-doubt. What business did an American

Jew have writing about the divinity of Jesus Christ? How could I presume to meddle in sensitive matters concerning other people's faith? Beneath these questions dwelled another, more difficult to answer. What drew me so strongly to explore the subject of Jesus' identity and mission?

Answers began to emerge during a second sabbatical year, this time on the island of Malta, a nation of about 350,000 people of whom more than 300,000 are Roman Catholics. The head of the University of Malta's sociology department, where I taught courses on conflict resolution, was a wise, amiable, energetic Catholic priest named Joe Inguanez. Father Joe looked at me a bit quizzically when I asked him to help me locate materials on Arianism at the university library. The library *did* have an unusually fine collection on early Church history, he said. But why did I want to study that particular heresy?

The explanation I proffered was accurate but impersonal. I have spent most of my professional life writing about violent social conflicts. To conflict analysts, intense religious conflict is still a great mystery. Virtually none of us predicted the current upsurge in violent doctrinal disputes around the world. The current civil war in Algeria, the struggle between ultraorthodox nationalist Jews and other groups in Israel, even the conflicts over abortion and homosexuality in the West strike many observers as weird throwbacks to a more primitive age. "Religious fanaticism" is offered as their cause, as if that phrase could explain why people are motivated at some times and places (but not others) to kill each other over differences of belief.

I told Father Joe that my interest was in exploring the *sources* of religious conflict and the methods people have used to resolve it. I wanted to examine a dispute familiar enough to westerners to involve them deeply, but distant enough to permit some detached reflection. The Arian controversy, which was probably the most serious struggle between Christians before the Protestant Reformation, seemed to fit the bill perfectly. . . .

Joe nodded, but he knew that my account was incomplete. "And?"

"And there's something else," I responded with some hesitation. "I am a Jew born and raised in a Christian country. Jesus has been a part of my mental world since I was old enough to think. On the one hand, I have always found him an enormously attractive figure, challenging and inspiring. On the other . . ."

Joe's raised eyebrows demanded that I continue.

"When I was little, growing up in a mixed Jewish-Catholic neighborhood, most of my playmates were Italian-American boys. They were friends, but I learned to stay in my own house on Good Friday, since after hearing the sermon at St. Joseph's Church, some of them would come looking for me to punish me for killing Christ. Once they caught me out on the street and knocked me down. 'But Jesus was a Jew!' I shouted through my tears. That idea, which they had never contemplated, infuriated them. It earned me a few extra kicks and punches."

Joe looked so sorrowful that I hastened to explain. "That's one side of the story. Sometimes it seems that Jesus has meant nothing but trouble for us. But the other side is that he can't be ignored. I don't worship Jesus, who—I'm sorry, Joe—I believe to have been a man, not God's Son. But what a man! I think that if his followers *hadn't* caused us so much trouble, we would consider him at least a *tzaddik,* a great sage. Perhaps even a prophet."

"Yes," Joe said after a pause. "It would be hard to love Christ if you were always being injured in His name."

"Yes." One reason the Arian controversy interests me, I remarked, is that because before it ended, Jews and Christians could talk to each other and argue among themselves about crucial issues like the divinity of Jesus, the meaning of salvation, basic ethical standards . . . everything. They disagreed strongly about many things, but there was still a closeness between them. They participated in the same moral culture. When the controversy ended—when Jesus became God—that closeness faded.

To Christians God became a Trinity. Heresy became a crime. Judaism became a form of infidelity. And Jews living in Christian countries learned not to think very much about Jesus and his message.

Joe absorbed this with quiet understanding. "But the doctrine of the Holy Trinity did not cause these problems," he noted.

"No," I said, "but it reflected and encapsulated them. I want to write about this controversy because it tells us so much about where we come from and what divides us. The story may even suggest how violent divisions can someday be healed. And, somehow, I believe that the figure of Jesus will play an important role in that healing. I think his life teaches us what it really means to be members of the human family."

Joe and I sat together in silence for a few minutes. The quiet was refreshing. "Later," he said, taking a missal from his backpack, "I'll show you the collection on heresies in our library. Right now, if you don't mind, I think I'll say my prayers."

And he did.

Acknowledgments

THIS IS a work of storytelling and interpretation that relies on the research of experts in several fields, including classical studies, the history of Late Antiquity, Church history, theology, and conflict studies. The past two decades have seen a great renewal of scholarly interest in the Arian controversy. As a result, I was able to profit from the labors of a number of outstanding researchers and writers. Those whose work proved especially useful and inspiring include Peter Brown of Princeton, whose understanding of late Roman society and its religious sensibilities is unequalled; Timothy D. Barnes of Harvard, the outstanding historian of the Constantinian period; and the late R. P. C. Hanson of the University of Durham, whose massive *Search for the Christian Doctrine of God* provided an education in Arian and Nicene theology. My interpretation of Arius's thinking owes much to the pioneering work of Robert C. Gregg and Dennis E. Groh, as well as the philosophical insights of Rowan D. Williams. Obviously, neither these scholars nor the others cited in the endnotes and bibliography of this book are responsible for the uses to which I have put their research.

My work on this book was greatly facilitated by the support of George Mason University, which enabled me to spend a sabbatical semester doing research at the University of Malta. I am most grateful to Father Peter Serracino Inglott, rector of the university; Leslie Agius, director of the Foundation for International Studies; Father Joe Inguanez, head of the Department of Sociology; and the staff of the university's fine library for their friendship and assistance. I should emphasize that these distinguished clergy and educators bear no responsibility for my rather unorthodox (although, I hope, not disrespectful) interpretation of the Arian controversy.

My colleagues and students at George Mason's Institute for Conflict Analysis and Resolution helped me think more clearly about religious conflict and why it is so difficult to resolve. Thanks, in particular, to Kevin Avruch, Marc Gopin, Daryl Landau, and Rex van der Riet for their counsel and assistance, and to Maureen Connors of Fenwick Library for her valuable help in locating research materials. James R. Price of the Schriver Center of the University of Maryland, Baltimore County further stimulated my thinking with his own wise observations.

I am most grateful to literary agents Gail Ross and Howard Yoon for their skillful assistance, and to Jane Isay and Lorie Stoopack of Harcourt Brace for their moral support and fine editorial judgment. Special thanks to my dear daughters, Hannah and Shana Rubenstein, for putting up so gracefully with my demanding work schedule and writerly moods. Finally, I want to thank Susan Ryerson, whose most valuable contribution, among many others, may have been to deliver a message acknowledged long ago by the poet Sir Philip Sidney:

"'Fool!' said my muse to me, 'look in thy heart, and write.'"

RICHARD E. RUBENSTEIN
Fairfax, Virginia

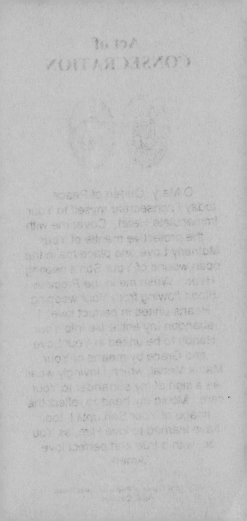

Act of
CONSECRATION

O Mary, Queen of Peace,
today I consecrate myself to Your
Immaculate Heart. Cover me with
the protective mantle of Your
Motherly Love and place me in the
open wound of Your Son's beating
Heart. Wash me in the Precious
Blood flowing from Your weeping
Hearts united in perfect love. I
abandon my entire life into Your
Hands to be united in Your Love
and Grace by means of Your
Matrix Medal, which I lovingly wear
as a sign of my surrender to Your
care. Mould my heart to reflect the
image of Your Son until I, too,
have learned to love Him, as You
do, with a true and perfect love.
Amen.

©Our Lady Queen of Peace House of Prayer,
Achill, Co Mayo

One

An Incident in Alexandria

December 24, 361. Midmorning.

By THE TIME the men at the front of the mob smashed through the prison gates, the crowd had grown until it overflowed the square like water pouring over the sides of a full jar. Even for Alexandria, where riots were as common as Mediterranean gales, this demonstration was unusually large. More unusual still, the mixed crowd formed a unified mass. Instead of fighting among themselves as they so often did, pagan and Christian rioters stood side by side, bellowing for blood.

A roar of approval greeted the splintering of the gates. Minutes later the invaders reemerged from the prison bearing their trussed-up quarry on their shoulders like hunters returning from the desert with a prize antelope or lion. Three prisoners, their hands and feet still chained against the possibility of escape, were their catch. As the demonstrators began to toss them about the square like toys, the helpless captives squealed in pain and terror.

Two of these unfortunates were high government officials. They had earned the crowd's hatred by carrying out the Roman emperor's orders to close pagan temples, expel "heretical" Christians from the churches, and punish protesters.[1] The mob's prime target, however—the third man in manacles—was a figure of greater importance than any civil servant. This was

George of Cappadocia, the metropolitan bishop of Alexandria and titular head of Egypt's huge Christian community.

Bishop George owed his recent preeminence and present agony to Constantius II, the son and successor of the first Christian emperor, Constantine the Great. Like Constantius, he was an Arian: a Christian who believed that Jesus Christ was the Son of God, but not God Himself. A tradesman's son, George had accumulated a fortune as a military contractor in Constantinople before taking Holy Orders. He was widely known for his religious zeal and owned one of the finest private libraries in the empire. After he became a bishop in Cappadocia, the emperor asked him to instruct the young members of the imperial family in the Christian faith. A few years later, after sending the current bishop of Alexandria, a local man named Athanasius, into exile, he brought George in from Asia Minor to replace him.

The appointment was a disaster from the start. Replacing a native Alexandrian with a Cappadocian "foreigner" who could not even speak Coptic, the language of the common people, was Constantius's first mistake. His second was to name as bishop a militant Arian who considered it his duty to persecute both pagans and Christians opposed to his theology. And his third error was to allow the formidable Athanasius to escape to the sanctuary of a friendly monastery in the Egyptian wilderness. From his desert hideout, the popular ex-bishop made a series of lightning undercover visits to the city to encourage his supporters there, adding a bandit's glamour to his reputation for dedication and brilliance.

Poor George! Even with the aid of imperial troops he could not establish control over Alexandria's turbulent Christian community. About one year after he took office he was attacked by an anti-Arian mob at the Church of Dionysius and barely escaped with his life. After that, he spent most of his time in the Balkans and Asia Minor attending a series of Church councils called by the emperor to resolve the controversy over Christ's divinity that was tearing the Church apart. When these councils declared his Arian beliefs orthodox and Constantius promised him unqualified support, George decided to return to his post in Alexandria. What he did not know, however, was that his imperial patron had become seriously ill. Four days after he returned to Alexandria, Constantius died of a fever . . . and the city exploded.

As soon as messengers arrived with the news of the emperor's demise, Athanasius's supporters seized control of all Alexandria's churches. They captured George and several imperial officers, put them in chains, and turned them over to the director of the city prison. Now, almost one month later, a larger, more diverse crowd had returned to exact further punishment. It is not entirely clear what provoked their attack on the prison, but the stimulus may have been a piece of further news: the new emperor, Constantius's nephew Julian, had announced that he was not an Arian, not even (as everyone had assumed) a Christian, but a worshipper of the old gods. A pagan! Clearly, the prisoners were fair game.

Punishment was duly administered. George and his fellow prisoners died in the prison square, presumably as a result of lethal beatings. A fifth-century historian reports that after the rioters killed their victims, they paraded their corpses through the middle of the city. George's body was on a camel, but the other men were dragged with ropes, "and, when they had maltreated their corpses in this way, about the seventh hour [one o'clock] they burned them."[2] Burning the bodies was not only an insult to the deceased, but a way of ensuring that their remains would not become relics to be preserved and venerated by their followers.

In one respect, at least, the new emperor might have been expected to be upset by this lynching. Julian had been one of the royal children tutored by George of Cappadocia when he was a boy and nominally a Christian! Nevertheless, his reaction was limited to a mild reprimand: the "enemy of the gods" should have been properly tried and legally executed.[3] No one was ever prosecuted for the murders. Less than two months later, Bishop Athanasius returned in triumph to his city and his episcopal throne.

A LYNCH MOB'S behavior is always primitive. Yet the Alexandrians who paraded their murdered bishop's corpse around the city inhabited one of the most prosperous and civilized regions on earth. In Late Antiquity, the urban settlements ranging in great arc from Greece and Asia Minor (Turkey) through Syria, Lebanon, and Palestine to Egypt and Libya were the heart of the Roman world. Trade and commerce, art and learning flourished in this "archipelago of cities,"[4] drawing political power inexorably in their wake. The Greek-speaking Eastern Empire boasted three great metropolises—Alexandria, Antioch, and Constantinople— as well as hundreds of smaller but highly developed towns. By comparison, the Latin West was an economic and cultural backwater, and Rome herself (although still considered the "first city" for historical reasons) a city in sad decline.

Alexandria! Imagine a city of one million souls spread out for about ten miles along the Mediterranean coast, its great harbor crowned by a four-hundred-foot lighthouse: the Pharos, one of the Seven Wonders of the World. From the top of the Pharos, it was said, one could look through a transparent stone and see ships far out at sea, invisible to the naked eye. What sort of lens this might have been is unknown, since the lighthouse was later destroyed in a series of earthquakes. But there is no doubt that Alexandria commanded the talent to fashion it. For centuries the city had served not only as the Mediterranean world's busiest port, but as its premier center of science and learning. The metropolis founded by Alexander the Great was home to Greek geniuses like Archimedes and Euclid, Jewish sages like Philo, and the greatest early Christian thinkers, St. Clement and Origen. It was also the site of the world-renowned Great Library (burned during Caesar's wars) and the somewhat smaller Serapeum, donated by Cleopatra and destroyed by militant Christians at the close of the fourth century.

In the waterfront city, diverse cultures mixed, clashed, and recombined; feverish commercial activity coexisted with deep spiritual hunger; and a worldly, ambitious people became fascinated—even obsessed—by issues of religious faith. Of Alexandria's million inhabitants, perhaps one-fourth were Jews whose forbears had begun settling there long before the disastrous rebellions of their Palestinian brethren against Rome. In the second century B.C.E., the Old Testament was translated into Greek for these Alexandrian Jews, for they had become Greek speakers like other educated citizens of the Eastern Empire. The translation then became available to the Christians, proponents of a new faith that used the synagogue as a springboard to reach out to believers in the old gods. By the end of the third century C.E., this offshoot of Judaism was sweeping up converts throughout the Mediterranean world.

Alexandrian Christianity had a special flavor. In this "turbulent and intellectually saturated melting pot,"[5] outstanding thinkers drew on the latest trends in Greek philosophy to explain biblical texts and expound Church doctrines. The results were frequently brilliant and almost always controversial, producing an intellectual history "marked by repeated innovations, by constant tensions, by innumerable disputes."[6] These disputes were no mere squabbles between intellectuals; they were Alexandria's favorite sport, an activity that ordinary laypeople found as passionately involving (and sometimes as bloody) as the gladiatorial contests that had fascinated their grandparents.

In the second century, Alexandrian Christians, inspired by anti-Semitic preaching, had launched one of the earliest riots against the city's Jewish community. Two hundred years later those who called Jesus "Lord" were battling each other in the streets . . . and lynching bishops. By the time George met his grisly death, religious riots had become commonplace throughout the region. Assassinations were less frequent, but militant believers employed a wide variety of violent tactics and imaginatively conceived dirty tricks to do each other harm. Bishop Athanasius, a future saint and uninhibited faction fighter, had his opponents excommunicated and anathematized, beaten and intimidated, kidnapped, imprisoned, and exiled to distant provinces. His adversaries, no less implacable, charged him with an assortment of crimes, including bribery, theft, extortion, sacrilege, treason, and murder. At their instigation, Athanasius was condemned by Church councils and exiled from Alexandria no less than five times, pursued on several occasions by troops dispatched by a Christian emperor to secure his arrest.

At times these hostile tactics were more laughable than lethal. In Antioch, the Syrian capital, a group of Arian priests disguised as laymen employed a prostitute to creep into an anti-Arian bishop's bedchamber while he slept so that he could be accused of fornication and discredited. But they did not consider that the lady in question might have a mind of her own.

The scheme backfired when, at the last minute, she declined to play her assigned role and exposed the plotters instead.

A FARCE? Surely—but such incidents reveal the peculiar intensity of religious struggles in the late Roman world. The almost obsessive quality of these disputes is nicely captured by a famous churchman, Gregory of Nyssa, writing twenty years after the lynching of Bishop George. In a sermon delivered at his church in Constantinople, Gregory deplored the contentiousness of his fellow Christians. "If in this city you ask a shopkeeper for change," he complained, "he will argue with you about whether the Son is begotten or unbegotten. If you inquire about the quality of bread, the baker will answer, 'The Father is greater, the Son is less.' And if you ask the bath attendant to draw your bath, he will tell you that the Son was created *ex nihilo* [out of nothing]."[7]

Gregory's wry comment is fascinating both for what it says and what it implies. It suggests that ordinary tradespeople and workers felt perfectly competent—perhaps even driven—to debate abstract theological issues and to arrive at their own conclusions. It reveals that disputes among Christians, specifically arguments about the relationship of Jesus Christ the Son to God the Father, had become as intense as the centuries-old conflict between Christians and pagans. And it implies that Arianism, which orthodox Christians now consider *the* archetypal heresy, was once at least as popular as the doctrine that Jesus is God.

Gregory's shopkeeper questions whether Jesus Christ is "begotten or unbegotten"—that is, whether he is a creation of God or the Creator Himself. The bath attendant says that he was created "from nothing," meaning that he was brought into existence like the rest of God's creatures. And the baker asserts that Christ is separate from and lesser than God. All these are Arian positions, so called because they were developed in sharpest form by an Alexandrian priest named Arius. The ill-fated George was also an Arian: one who believed that Jesus Christ was, indeed, the holiest person who ever lived, but not the Eternal God of Israel walking the earth in the form of a man.

How could one be a Christian and *not* believe that Christ was God incarnate? The Arians had an answer. To them, Jesus was a person of such sublime moral accomplishments that God adopted him as His Son, sacrificed him to redeem humanity from sin, raised him from the dead, and granted him divine status. Because of his excellence, he became a model of righteous behavior for us. And because his merit earned the prize of immortality, the same reward was made available to other human beings, provided that they model themselves after him.[8] From the Arian perspective, it was essential that Jesus *not* be God, since God, being perfect by nature, is inimitable. By contrast, Christ's transcendent virtue, achieved by repeated acts of will, is available (at least potentially) to the rest of us. Even though we may fall short of his impeccable standards, his triumph over egoism shows us how we also may become the Sons and Daughters of God.

Was Christ, then, to be considered human? In one sense, the answer was yes. Jesus of Nazareth was a real man, not some divine apparition or mask of God. But his moral genius and the importance of his mission raised him high above even the greatest prophets. The Savior was *sui generis*. Many Arians believed that the Eternal had somehow conceived him (or conceived of him) before time began, and used him as an instrument to create the rest of the universe.[9] Even so, they insisted, he could not possibly be God Himself. How could an all-powerful, all-knowing, all-good Creator experience temptation, learn wisdom, and grow in virtue? How could he suffer on the Cross and die the death of a human being? Surely, when Jesus cried out, "My God, my God, why hast Thou forsaken me?" he was not talking to himself![10] When he admitted that nobody knows the day and hour of Judgment, "not even the angels of heaven, nor the Son, but the Father only," he was not just being modest.[11] And when he told his disciples that "the Father is greater than I," he meant exactly what he said.[12]

To Athanasius of Alexandria, Arius's most formidable opponent, these arguments were worse than mistaken. In his view, they were enormously destructive, since they misused Scripture to obscure the central mystery of the Christian faith. Like the Arians, Athanasius took his monotheism seriously. He conceived of God as eternal and omnipotent, omniscient and perfect—an unchangeable Being infinitely superior to any mortal creature. For the Creator of the Universe to become human and submit to the power of other men must seem unimaginably humiliating. Yet, according to Athanasius, this was the only way to save mankind from moral and physical extinction. In order to free us from sin and death, God did the unthinkable: He descended into human flesh. Out of His infinite love for us, He became the man Jesus, who took the burden of our sins on his own frail shoulders, suffered, and died that we might gain eternal life.[13]

Without God, Athanasius contended, humans would inevitably abuse their God-given freedom of choice and suffer the terrible consequences: corruption of the soul and death of the body. Therefore, if Christ was any less than God, he could not save us. And if we did not believe that he was God, we would not be saved. Seen in this light, the Arians' apparent glorification of Jesus was sheer deception. Indeed, those who declared him inferior to God were worse than the Jews who denied him and the Romans who crucified him, since the Jews and Romans rejected him openly, while the Arians degraded him more subtly by turning him into some sort of demigod or human prophet.

If the heretics won, said Athanasius, Christianity would be shipwrecked. This was no mere academic matter; millions of souls would be lost eternally and Christ himself dealt a terrible defeat. So persuasive were the Arian misleaders, and so evil the consequences of their error, that Athanasius was convinced he saw in their reasoning the malicious cleverness of the Antichrist. The struggle against Arianism was therefore a fight against the devil . . . and, God knows, one did not compromise with the devil.

ATHANASIUS's language was more intemperate than that of most of his adversaries, but passions on each side of the controversy were explosive. Two factors, in particular, made the struggle over Christ's divinity particularly intense. In the first place, it was a contest to decide a genuinely undecided issue. Given the growing intolerance of dissent within the church, its outcome would decide which belief would be sanctified as truth and which vilified as heresy. Furthermore, it deeply involved the

Christian laity, including masses of urban workers and artisans with a strong propensity to express themselves by rioting. The lynching of Bishop George was neither the first attempt nor the last to decide theological issues in the streets.

Matters would have been a good deal simpler if one set of ideas or the other had come neatly labeled "orthodox" or "heterodox," but this was not the case. Today, many orthodox Christians consider Arianism obviously heretical, but during the first three centuries after Jesus' crucifixion, the idea that the Savior was separate from God and subordinate to Him was not particularly shocking. To patriarchal Romans, the very titles Father and Son implied a relationship of superiority and inferiority. Two of the most brilliant and influential of the Eastern Church Fathers, Origen and Dionysius of Alexandria, had taught that Jesus was inferior in some respects to God. And the idea of a hierarchy of power and glory in heaven matched what people saw on earth, as well as what they read in the Gospels.

"I can do nothing on my own authority," Jesus told his disciples. "As I hear, I judge; and my judgment is just, because I seek not my own will but the will of him who sent me."[14] The idea of representation was a familiar idea in the Roman Empire, where authority descended in carefully graded stages from higher to lower officials. An imperial officer was not the emperor's equal; on the contrary, without the ruler's superior power there would be no authority to represent. He was not a free agent either, in the sense of being free to do his own will. Nevertheless, the representative's subordinate role did not imply powerlessness; quite the contrary. Neither Jesus nor a great official could be considered a mere automoton or a theatrical mask through which some actor's voice spoke.[15]

In Rome's imperial hierarchy, a Caesar was considered inferior to an Augustus, but no one would deny that a Caesar was infinitely more powerful than an ordinary man and entirely deserving of obedience. Was Jesus, then, God's Caesar? No, the Arians replied, he was more than that. An ordinary official might act outside the scope of his authority. No one could know with certainty that it was his superior's will he represented and not his own. But Christ was a perfect representative. Just as a painting or statue "represents" its subject without being the subject itself, the Son was "the exact Image" of the Father.[16] Obviously, "exact Image" did not mean that Jesus looked like God or resembled Him in his human appearance; it meant that he was as closely attuned to God's wishes as anyone could be who was not himself God. As a completely obedient and reliable servant, the Son was always in agreement with the Father.

This reasoning did not persuade Athanasius and the other anti-Arians, who insisted upon a more complete and organic identification of Jesus with God. But many in the Greek-speaking lands where most Christians lived *were* persuaded, and, ultimately, it was the lay masses, not just the leaders of the Church, who would decide the issue. This may seem surprising, given the fact that the Roman Empire was a centralized, militarized state in which serious political dissent was punishable by death. Where religious issues were concerned, however, mass participation had long been encouraged by the very leaders who now complained about the prevalence of streetcorner theologians. Christian bishops and theologians would not have gained the enormous power they wielded in the fourth century had they not operated on the assumption that people of normal intelligence and little formal education had the ability to comprehend complex religious doctrines, the judgment to distinguish true gods from false, and the will (with God's help) to follow in Christ's path.

To a great extent, the active involvement of shopkeepers and bath attendants in thorny religious controversies was a result of the Church's centuries-long campaign to turn the empire's pagan subjects into Christians. Converting a pagan population was no mere matter of getting people to make an emotional "decision for Christ." It meant bringing them to an understanding of the basic theological and ethical concepts embodied in the Old and New Testaments. It was not just Christ the evangelists and theologians were teaching, but a worldview derived originally from Judaism—a passionate monotheism fundamentally at odds with the premises of pagan thought.

For example, the Church Fathers asserted that the natural world was not eternal, as most pagan philosophers had taught and common sense might suggest. Rather, an incomprehensibly powerful God had created the entire universe from nothing, and sustained it constantly against a tendency to collapse back into nonbeing. They taught, further, that this same Creator was not part of His creation or coequal with it, but that He existed outside time and space, separate even from the humans created in His image. Contrary to basic pagan beliefs, they insisted that God ruled the universe alone, not with the assistance of other gods or demigods. And—strangest of all—they taught that this invisible, unnameable, mysterious God was also a wise King, a just Judge, and a merciful Father who had sacrificed His own Son to save humanity from sin and death.[17]

That ordinary Christians were expected to understand ideas like this may not seem so strange when one considers their cultural environment. These Greek-speaking city folk were no country bumpkins, like those they called pagans—*pagani*—a term meaning "rustics" or "hicks."[18] They inhabited one of the liveliest, most urbane, and culturally diverse regions on earth. Many could read and write; the early Christians, like the Jews, considered themselves People of the Book and prized the ability to read Scripture. But even the formally uneducated tended to be knowledgeable and assertive, fond of hot debate, and inclined to form contentious groups. Imagine the working people of New York, Berlin, or Moscow early in the twentieth century putting themselves through school, debating politics and philosophy, organizing political clubs and street gangs, and you will get some of the flavor of life among the Christian commoners in the cities of the Eastern Empire.

In such a setting, bakers and bath attendants could consider themselves as competent as philosophers and bishops to discuss theological questions, especially when the learned men quarreled so bitterly among themselves. People in the street had great respect for spiritual heroes like the Egyptian monk, Antony, who had abandoned city life in order to face temptation alone in the desert. But ascetics like Antony spent their time talking to God and battling demons, not engaging in doctrinal combat with other Christians.[19] It sometimes seemed that leaders of the Church could not stop arguing with each other and contending for popular influence. And disputes as serious as the Arian controversy virtually compelled ordinary churchgoers to choose between rival theologies.

W̲HEN TWO BISHOPS, each representing a different approach to Christianity, laid claim to the same cathedral, congregants had to decide which leader—and which doctrine—to follow. In many great cities of the Eastern Empire, furthermore, the division of popular opinion between Arians and anti-Arians was quite even.[20] The unintended result, where religious issues were concerned, was to give large numbers of people without real social standing or political power a potent decision-making role. Given the passions aroused by doctrinal differences and the tendency of Eastern Romans to take their quarrels into the streets, eminent churchmen soon found themselves the heroes, and sometimes the victims, of volatile urban mobs.

Bishop Athanasius did not lead the mob that lynched George of Cappadocia, but if he condemned their acts, the record of that condemnation has been lost. We do know how he felt about the Arian bishop who had tried to replace him.[21] One can easily imagine him concluding that, distasteful as popular violence may be, the Alexandrian crowd on that occasion had done the Lord's work.

THE WORLD that incubated such violent struggles has often been described as an empire in crisis. Not long after the Arian controversy ended, the Visigoths would sack Rome and the Vandals would overrun North Africa. A few decades later the Western Empire would collapse, and by the year 700, Muslim warriors would conquer most of the East. The threat of foreign invasions, the enormous social and economic strains caused by the need for defense, and the anxieties generated by these interconnected problems clearly influenced people's thinking in the last centuries of Roman power. But widespread fear is only one side of the story. The other is an equally deep-seated and destabilizing hope. One cannot understand Christianity's revolutionary appeal, or the ferocious disputes that divided the Christian community into warring camps, without accounting for both sides of the equation: the hopes as well as the anxieties generated by a period of unprecedented change.

For fourth-century Romans, the feeling that the world was an utterly unpredictable place was no fantasy. For more than five hundred years, the empire's power had expanded steadily, culminating in the second century C.E., "the period in the history of the world," says the historian Edward Gibbon, "during which the condition of the human race was most happy and prosperous."22 A simplification, no doubt, but Rome's problems a generation or two later would make the previous age seem unalloyed gold.

Beginning in the 220s, Germanic tribes in the West and Persians in the East overran the empire's European and Asian frontiers, winning unprecedented victories over the Roman legions. Suddenly, the emperor's crown was a prize to be won by the strongest soldier, and a succession of thuggish generals (*seven-*

teen in seventy years) seized the throne once occupied by Augustus Caesar. To support the expanded military establishment taxes were doubled, redoubled, then doubled again. Scarce goods were diverted to military use, food prices soared, and inflation became uncontrollable. While a new breed of well-connected landowners and contractors became fabulously rich, the middling classes suffered and poor people were driven en masse into serfdom or slavery. Revolts and breakaway movements erupted in outlying provinces. Banditry became endemic. New building all but ceased. Plague struck the impoverished population, and sages wondered aloud if the prophesied end of the world were at hand.[23]

One generation later, miraculously, Roman power seemed more secure than ever. By the 290s the "barbarian" invasions had been fought off and internal rebellions suppressed. Commerce revived, new cities sprang up on the ruins of the old, and a measure of political stability returned, thanks to a Dalmatian general named Diocletian, the most capable emperor since Augustus Caesar. Art and literature flourished along with law and medicine; once again, the Roman peace made human progress seem possible. But even as expectations rose for a return to the days of prosperity and glory, the army and bureaucracy swelled to vast proportions. The empire's fiscal crisis persisted, class and ethnic divisions deepened, and migrating peoples put new pressure on the frontiers. Serious doubts about the future were unavoidable, but fear now mixed with hope to create a sense that almost anything might happen.

Where political and military issues were concerned, Rome's subjects were powerless to challenge their fate. The new breed of Roman rulers exercised an authority more absolute than anyone would have dreamed in the bygone era of the Republic. (Indeed, procedures at the Roman court increasingly resembled the absolutist rituals long practiced by the courtiers of the Persian Sun King.) At the same time, the very uncertainty of events seems to have generated a new sense of *personal* potency on the part of those fated to remain spectators or pawns on the chessboard of politics. On the political level radical unpredictability generated passivity and fear. But this same uncertainty, experienced internally as a sense of possibility, could give rise to the most extravagant and energizing expectations.

With powerful emperors like Diocletian reconquering lost territory, the Empire's revival might prove to be permanent. But even if Roman glory proved, in the end, to be transitory, it might not matter—not if the prize to be won by faithful Christians was life eternal. The Gospels said that it would not avail a man to gain the whole world if he lost his soul, but the converse also held true. The prospect of heaven would surely compensate believers for the loss of earthly security. This hope had a great deal to do with the remarkable success of the Christian movement in transforming itself in less than a century from a persecuted sect into a potential state church. The pagan gods, of course, had been considered immortal. The God of Israel was eternal by definition. Greek philosophers mused about the immortality of the human soul, and Jews talked hopefully but vaguely of inheriting "the world to come."[24] But neither paganism nor Judaism made the possibility of eternal life the centerpiece of its thinking. Christianity did, holding Jesus out not just as a model of right behavior, but an elder brother whose inheritance of immortality all God's children might share.

> When we cry, "Abba! Father!" it is the Spirit himself bearing witness with our spirit that we are children of God, and if children, then heirs, heirs of God and fellow heirs with Christ, provided we suffer with him in order that we may also be glorified with him.[25]

This was the other side of terrifying transformation. Amid general fears of a social collapse, one could nurture the radical hope that unpredicted change might be vastly for the better instead of for the worse. The rapid rise of the Church provided evidence that miraculous, beneficent transformations were possible. And on the individual level, it was clear, ordinary people could become new men and women in Christ. "I beseech you: be transformed," the great Origen of Alexandria pleaded.[26] Success in transforming oneself might be rewarded with the ultimate prize: godlike immortality. But just as God could save individuals from death, He could, if He chose, save the Roman world from extinction. Political "salvation," like the salvation of the soul, would depend both on the divine will and the faithfulness and righteousness of the people. Every Christian understood what had happened to the Kingdom of Israel when its people lapsed into idol worship and immorality. Either Rome would become a truly Christian empire, or the empire would cease to exist.

Either/Or. On one side, unprecedented dangers; on the other, dazzling hopes. Either believe rightly, act righteously, and be saved, or fall into error, sin, and be lost. With the stakes this high, the decision to choose Christianity or some other religion, or to side with one side or the other in a serious doctrinal conflict, seemed freighted with cosmic significance. Although such decisions were made individually, they could not be considered merely private; their consequences might well determine the fate of an entire civilization. Under these circumstances, it would be difficult to avoid hardening one's position and defending it against "diabolical" opponents. Indeed, to tolerate serious religious differences would seem grossly negligent. Rome had long permitted paganism to flourish . . . and look at the results! If Christians now abandoned their faith, or if they promoted heretical or idolatrous doctrines, the community, as well as the individual sinner, would surely feel the lash of God's wrath.

THE CHRISTIANS involved in the great controversy over Christ's divinity would soon find themselves gripped by the urge to persecute their adversaries. They were aware, of course, that a similar passion had afflicted Rome's pagan rulers and intellectuals when they and their followers sought to defend *their* worldview against the "vicious errors" of Christianity. To the Christians' credit, most of those involved in the Arian controversy avoided the worst excesses of the Roman emperors. But they could not avoid using their old enemies' tactics to some extent, since the same fear of disastrously erroneous beliefs drove both persecution campaigns. The intensely violent anti-Christian persecutions, furthermore, wounded the Church in ways that made later conflicts within the Christian community virtually inevitable.

In the first two centuries after Christ's death, the progress of the new faith (which most Romans at first considered an odd form of Judaism) was very slow.[27] The persecution of the Jesus movement by the Roman state was correspondingly static and inefficient. But during the great crises of the third century, the movement made significant gains, especially in the eastern half of the empire. By the year 250, the Christians were the most dynamic religious group in the Roman world, still not as large numerically as the Jewish community, but far surpassing it in its rate of expansion. Perhaps for this reason—the simultaneous decline of Roman fortunes and growth of Christianity—the same period also saw a murderous campaign of persecution mounted by the emperors Decius and Valerian, and strongly supported by many Roman subjects inclined to blame Christ-worshipping "atheists" for the misfortunes of the time.

Christians had been persecuted before, but this was the first systematic attempt by Rome to halt the spread of their religion. The strategy was simple: all subjects were ordered to sacrifice to the immortal gods or else risk the death penalty. It was also quite effective. The Christian movement had grown rapidly and now included large numbers of respectable citizens who had no taste for martyrdom or imprisonment. Far more of its members obeyed imperial orders or bribed their way out of trouble than risked the emperor's displeasure. In the first year of the persecution, says one historian, "Christians joined with their pagan neighbors in a rush to sacrifice," and "the Christian church practically collapsed."[28]

Nevertheless, when a decade of sporadic state terror ended, the Church emerged larger and stronger than ever, partially because the crisis itself and the discontents it engendered helped turn pagans into Christians. The empire *was* in deep trouble despite the fact that most Romans still sacrificed faithfully to the old gods. People might blame their ill fortune on the Christians, but how strongly could one believe in deities that failed to protect their own worshipers against foreign attacks and domestic abuses? Equally important, those who followed Jesus earned great respect because of their principled, self-sacrificing response to the crisis. While wealthy Romans abandoned the poor, bureaucrats enriched themselves at the expense of their subjects, and military chiefs overthrew their emperors, Christian bishops and their congregations fed the hungry, housed the homeless, cared for plague victims, and offered sufferers membership in a tight-knit, compassionate community.

Then, too, the persecution called further attention to the differences between Christian and pagan leadership. The list of those executed for refusing to offer the required sacrifices included a number of the Church's most famous bishops: Fabian and Sixtus II of Rome, Babylas of Antioch, Alexander of Jerusalem, Cyprian of Carthage, and others.[29] Although the great majority of laypeople and many churchmen played it safe, the heroism of a few was a more potent public influence than the compromises of the many. Particularly notable was the bravery of Christian women. Bishop Dionysius of Alexandria, who barely escaped martyrdom himself, describes how a local mob, worked up to a bloodthirsty pitch by the authorities,

> seized the wonderful old lady Apollonia, battered her till they knocked out all her teeth, built a pyre in front of the city, and threatened to burn her alive unless she repeated after them their heathen incantations. She asked for a breathing-space, and when they released her, jumped without hesitation into the fire and was burnt to ashes.[30]

Women, in fact, were the Christians' secret weapon in their struggle to win converts in all classes of Roman society, including the respectable upper classes. Overall, "It is highly likely that women were a clear majority in the churches of the third century."[31] There were several reasons for this. Christianity was *not* a feminist movement in the modern sense, but the community's yearning for sexual purity operated to the advantage of those long relegated to the status of sexual playthings or childbearing "vessels." Although the Church shared the strong patriarchal bias of Roman society, it protected widows (a large group because of girls' early marriages to older men), cherished virgins, considered adultery by either spouse a serious sin, opposed prostitution, and tried to prevent men from "putting off" their wives. It enabled women to play leading roles in the Christian community, and, perhaps most important, considered them no less capable than men of winning eternal life.

The prominence of upper-class women in the Christian ranks provoked the scorn of pagan spokesmen like the philosopher Porphyry,[32] but it was a sign that the growth of the Jesus movement might be unstoppable. From the 260s onward, in fact, the wave of Christian conversions swelled to tidal proportions, with the fastest growth occurring in the most prosperous and culturally advanced cities of the East. From the beginning, when the Synagogue was its main base of recruitment, the movement had appealed to educated and semieducated city dwellers. The Apostle Paul himself was a Greek-speaking urbanite, a sophisticated tradesman, traveler, and former government official.[33] Although Christianity opened its doors to women, slaves, and social outcasts, it was not a movement of the dispossessed but of a mass-based cultural vanguard.

This is precisely what made it so dangerous to guardians of the old order. An esoteric sect or protest group on the margins of society could be terrorized out of existence, but Christian thought had deeper social and psychological roots. It reflected a new consciousness, widely shared, of people's capacity for internal growth and change. The pagan world was a world of externalities, in which religious rites were a feature of one's public life as a member of a traditional civic collective. Christianity, by contrast, expressed a new sense of *interiority*: the perception of an inner space in which an individual could struggle with the devil, communicate with God, and discover his or her own spiritual identity. The Christian message had a profound appeal to the increasing number of Romans dissatisfied with frozen, public rituals and seeking "a God with whom one could be alone."[34]

By the closing years of the century, the question haunting Christians and old believers alike was whether the ancient communal deities were destined to be supplanted by the One God of the Christians and His Son, Jesus Christ. If the empire had continued to stagger from crisis to crisis, generating increasing discontent with the old order, the question would probably have answered itself fairly quickly. But one man was determined to put an end to both crises and Christianity. Force alone might not be effective against the new religion, he recognized, but a great revival of Roman power and glory would restore the health of society and undermine the Christians' popularity. Once weakened in this way, the worshipers of the executed Nazarene could be reduced to the status of an unimportant sect or else persecuted out of existence.

This ingenious strategist was the emperor Diocletian, the great reformer and restorer of Roman glory. As is well known, his plan to rid the Roman world of Christianity failed, with the result that the Church emerged poised to become the empire's dominant religious organization. But the legacy of Diocletian's Great Persecution was a century of bitter conflict between opposed groups of Christians. It is with this campaign of state terror that the story of the Arian controversy really begins.

Two

The Silence of Apollo

Eʟʀʟʏ ɪɴ ᴛʜᴇ ғᴀʟʟ of 299 the emperors Diocletian and
Galerius returned in triumph to Antioch. The arrogant, volatile
Galerius was the junior of the two men in rank and age, but it
was he who had engineered the Roman army's smashing victory
over the Persians after five years of bitter warfare. The great
cities of Nisibis and Ctesiphon had fallen. King Narseh's harem
and treasury were now in Roman hands. Armenia, where the
first battles had been fought, was again under imperial rule, and
the Persian king had been forced to acknowledge Roman sover-
eignty over some of his choicest territories.

In Antioch the sense of relief was tangible; freed of the threat
of a Persian invasion, her residents breathed easily for the first
time in years. There had been a time when such victories were
expected—when any Asian satrap or Germanic chieftain rash
enough to challenge Roman power would end his days (if he survived) as a trophy to be exhibited at the end of a triumphal pa-
rade. But sixty years of military reversals and civil instability had
deprived Roman citizens of their happy, almost unconscious,
sense of invulnerability.

Earlier in the century an assortment of Germanic tribes had
breached Rome's defenses on the Rhine and made incursions
deep into Gaul. The Goths, with their fearsome cavalry, attacked
the Danubian basin and overran large portions of Asia Minor.

Kabyle tribesmen in North Africa rebelled against Roman rule. Saxon pirates raided with impunity from the North Sea to the English Channel, and, for the first time, famous cities like Athens and Milan, Ephesus, and even Alexandria were besieged by invaders. But it was the Persians, above all, who sent tremors of fear throughout the rich cities of the eastern Mediterranean. These well-trained fighters were no barbaric nomads. As urbane and civilized as the Romans, they had been the Greek-speaking peoples' traditional enemies for more than eight centuries.

Recently, after a long period of subordination to Rome, the Persians had regained their fighting spirit under a new dynasty, the Sassanids. Antiochenes had particular cause to remember the Sassanid warrior-king, Shapur I, who in 260 captured the Roman emperor Valerian with his whole army, flayed him alive (or so the story said), and pinned his skin to the gates of his capital city, Ctesiphon.[35] Shapur and his troops entered Antioch in triumph, looted the city, and took thousands of slaves. Almost as painful as the defeat itself had been the humiliating recognition that "Peace Everywhere," the motto on Roman coins, was a lie. No one was safe anymore—not even the residents of Antioch the Beautiful.

Founded five centuries earlier by one of Alexander the Great's generals, the Syrian capital had long been a prize in the ceaseless contest between the Greek and Persian civilizations for supremacy in the Middle East.[36] Many people considered it the empire's loveliest city. From the sea one approached it by sailing up the River Orontes—a few hours' journey that ended in a blaze of light and color as a dazzling array of colonnaded temples, public buildings, and noble houses appeared dramatically on the river's banks. Famous for its multiplicity of temples and shrines, its schools of rhetoric, and its sharp business practices, Antioch was Rome's window on the East. From Mesopotamia, Arabia, and India came rare products and exotic beliefs to mingle with the staples of the West: Greek culture, Roman power, and Christian worship. Antioch was the first city outside Palestine to house a significant number of Christian converts. St. Peter was reputed to have been its first bishop. Because it was also the principal jumping-off point for military campaigns against the Persians, the city became an imperial residence early in the second century.

Now the emperors were once again in residence, waiting outside the palace for their triumphal procession to begin. Crowds jammed the sun-drenched streets shouting both men's names, but especially that of Galerius, who had made the city his principal headquarters. Their cheers were answered by a slow, rhythmic thumping, faint at first but deeper and more thunderous by the minute, announcing the approach of the victorious legions.

Troops of the local garrison herded the onlookers to the sides of the broad street. Heralds clad in white made an appealing but superfluous appearance. Then, to cries of delight and scattered applause, hundreds of fresh-faced young women materialized in the center of the avenue, strewing flowers along the baked brick pavement. Behind them a phalanx of local officials and priests paraded solemnly, incensing the route and blessing the crowds as they passed.

Fingers in the crowd pointed as several squads of noblemen appeared, mounted on prancing horses. Next came the emperors' household troops, marching in close order, their shields and breastplates gleaming. A pause in the procession . . . and then a great eruption of cheers as the two conquerors rode into view side by side, each man crowned with laurel and driving a chariot decked in royal purple. Captured Persian officers in chains trudged in their wake, followed by scores of mules pulling open wagons piled high with captured treasure. At last, standards fluttering in the sun, in seemingly endless waves of disciplined humanity came the army.

The crowd roared its approval. Galerius smiled and nodded proudly. Diocletian's face remained a remote, impassive mask, as if already sculpted in marble.

The emperor's cold demeanor was merely formal; it was the face the Ruler of the World presented to the public. In fact, he was not at all unhappy to see his younger colleague acclaimed. The need for talented commanders was what had led him to create the four-part College of Emperors in the first place, with two senior leaders (the Augusti) ruling the Eastern and Western halves of the empire, each assisted by a Caesar whom he had adopted as his son and heir. The Augustus of the East had no need to fear his own Caesar's popularity. The older man was recognized everywhere as Rome's supreme leader and savior: the ruler who, at long last, had turned back the barbarian invaders, reorganized the empire's finances and administration, restabilized central authority, and renewed the Roman world's faith in its future. He was already Diocletian the Great.

VIRTUALLY no one had expected the rough soldier from Dalmatia (Yugoslavia) to rise to such heights. Like virtually all the emperors of his time, Diocletian had seized the throne at swordpoint. In his case, this was no metaphor; his first act after being acclaimed Augustus by the army had been to haul a rebellious officer before his troops and run the hapless fellow through with his sword. Unlike his numerous short-lived predecessors, however, Diocletian recognized that the shaky Roman system could not be defended or revivified so long as any thug with a good army could lay claim to the crown. Stability at the top, he realized, was the key to a general revival. In his determination to end the chaotic succession of military rulers and assert his own legitimacy, this son of a freed slave re-created the position of emperor as a sacred office.

One did not approach the Augustus of the East as a Roman citizen of old might have approached Julius Caesar or even his nephew, the original Augustus. Surrounded by his household troops and legions of officials, the emperor inhabited a palace that was a small city in itself, with entry barred to all but a privileged few. The humble petitioner (whose admission to the imperial presence had probably been arranged by one of the powerful court eunuchs) was expected to prostrate himself at full length three times before daring to approach the throne—and, even then, to make eye contact with the Sacred Person seated thereon was considered a serious breach of etiquette. Swathed in purple brocade, crowned by a glittering diadem, the emperor moved as stiffly and deliberately as an icon. Here and there, a few discontented aristocrats might whisper that the trappings of Diocletian's court were more suited to those of a Persian than a Roman leader, but such grumbles were drowned out by the cheers of a relieved populace . . . like the Antiochenes who now shouted their approval of the stone-faced man in his chariot.

Many in the crowd remembered a different sort of procession down the same street less than two years earlier. Narseh, the formidable Persian warrior, had overrun Armenia, defeated Galerius's army in Mesopotamia, and smashed the Roman forts guarding eastern Syria. In desperation, Galerius was forced to call on his Augustus for support. Diocletian had come to the rescue with a Thracian legion, but before Narseh abandoned his invasion campaign, he inflicted severe damage on the joint army as well. Galerius was held responsible for these defeats. On the emperors' return to Antioch, he had been forced to walk in the street like any commoner, his face ashen and his purple robes dragging in the dust, while Diocletian rode behind him in his chariot.

Now victory had expiated disgrace. Their procession at an end, the two emperors rode together toward the large circular temple dedicated to Apollo, Antioch's tutelary god. There they dismounted and, surrounded by their retinues, entered the sacred precincts. The temple priests had scores of animals ready to sacrifice, for the purpose of this ceremony was not only to give thanks for victory over the Persians, but to foretell the future. Would the Persians and the German barbarians remain quiescent? Would the Roman world rid itself of the plagues that had begun to threaten it like the judgments of angry gods? Such questions could be answered by the haruspices: priests who had mastered the art of divining the future by examining the entrails of sacrificed animals.[37]

The huge crowd gathered outside the temple strained for a glimpse of the ceremonies through the colonnaded portico, glad at least to hear en masse what few could see. One can imagine the priests chanting in unison and the libations poured out on the thirsty ground, the knives flashing, the death moans of flawless bullocks and sheep, and the blood washed away by a gush of water through the conduits laid beneath the temple floor. Several minutes of silence followed within and without, while the exposed hearts, livers, and other organs were studied by the priests. Then, disquieting murmurs. Something was wrong. Incredulous voices were raised on the floor, out of the crowd's view. Finally, when all chatter had ceased, the ceremonies were repeated. Once more the priests could be heard chanting, while animals without blemish went complaining to their deaths.

The huge assemblage seemed almost to hold its breath while the blood was again washed away and the diviners went to work. This time, their dismay was unmistakable. The results of both sacrifices were, without exception, abnormal. Five-chambered hearts! Livers without lobes! Exploded intestines! Either some unimaginable disaster threatened Rome, or something had happened to corrupt the ceremonies.

Galerius, well known for his religious zeal, questioned the master of haruspices closely to determine the cause of the disastrous divination. The answer he received was infuriating but convincing. Alert priests had reported that each time the sacrifices were made, several of the emperor's household servants had made an occult sign in the air: the sign of the Cross. Clearly, this black magic had ruined the ceremonies. There was no other credible explanation.

Neither Diocletian nor Galerius doubted that the mysterious

sign had power; they differed with Christians only about whether it was power for good or evil. Nor did Christians question the universally accepted belief that unseen powers, among them angels and demons, were active for good and evil in the human world. Obviously, these supernatural beings affected people's health, moods, and relationships, as well as influencing divinations and other events.[38] The emperors' reaction to the corrupted ceremony was, in any case, immediate. All members of the imperial court, from household maids to the highest officials, were commanded to sacrifice to the immortal gods. Those who refused to do so would be dismissed without further notice. Furthermore, all members of the army were to do the same, or else resign their commissions.

The Great Persecution—Rome's final attempt to stamp out the Christian faith—had taken its first step.

THE ANTI-CHRISTIAN campaign began slowly. Soldiers and employees of the imperial service were required to demonstrate their loyalty to Rome and its civilization by participating in pagan ceremonies. They were not forced to abjure their Christian faith in any other way, and officials hoping to encourage their participation minimized the required ritual tasks. The point was not to humiliate the Christians, much less exterminate them, nor was it to assert the "superiority" of the old gods over Jehovah and Jesus. Diocletian's great cause was that of Roman unity in the face of barbarian invasions and internal divisions. His goals were to affirm the existence of a Roman community embracing many religions and to integrate the Jesus movement into it.

The Caesar Galerius despised the Christians, who dared deify a common criminal properly executed for disloyalty to Rome. He took real pleasure in punishing the seditious Jew's followers. What angered his senior colleague, however, was not so

much the Christians' particular beliefs as their *exclusivism*—
their apparent inability to respect other people's gods. Take
monotheism, for example. Diocletian could not fathom why the
belief in one God should separate the followers of Jesus from
other Romans. By this time many pagans had also come to believe in a supreme god, but they saw no reason to deny the existence and usefulness of less powerful deities, or to call them
demons as the Christians did. Didn't the emperor require assistance in ruling his earthly empire? Why, then, should the Christians assert as an inflexible dogma that the Creator ruled the
entire universe alone, or, more confusingly still, with His Son?

To question the existence of other gods, worse yet, to brand
them demonic spirits, was rude and divisive. A Roman who worshiped the Olympian gods would never call a devotee of Serapis
or Isis an atheist or demon worshiper. On the contrary, courtesy
and common sense dictated making a place for other people's
gods in one's own temple and paying them the respects all divine
beings were due. Why insult one's neighbors by denigrating their
deities? And, since all the gods *might* exist, why take the risk of
angering any of them? The Christians' attitude seemed fanatical,
like that of the Jews who made the suicidal mistake—twice!—of
rebelling against Rome's authority over Palestine. How could
one deal with such fanatics, except by force?

Then there was the issue of worship. Many Romans found
the Christians' refusal to take part in civic rituals unreason-
able—even, in time of war, unpatriotic—since there seemed no
reason *not* to participate other than sheer arrogance and fanaticism. For most believers in the old gods and goddesses, participation in sacrificial rites was little more than a time-honored
formality. It was a civic duty, something like the modern custom
of saluting the flag. For most people, pagan religion was not
really a religion at all in the sense of a systematic theology, a
transcendent ethic, or a quest for personal salvation. One's core
beliefs and the state of one's heart had little to do with it. For

centuries Roman citizens had paid their respects to assorted deities without compromising more intense personal commitments. Why violate the custom now, at a time when civic unity and divine favor were so vital to the health of the empire?

What most pagan leaders—even those as far-seeing as Diocletian—could not comprehend was the fact that the Christians had not merely added another god to the pantheon. They had redefined religion itself. Their God was an infinitely righteous but merciful parent, His Son an eternally loving and faithful friend. To call a Christian fanatical for refusing to sacrifice to other gods was like calling a monogamous lover fanatical for refusing to pay court to other men or women. "Just a little pinch of incense"? Why not just a little infidelity? In religion as in love, the only sacrifice that mattered was the gift of oneself voluntarily offered on the altar of fidelity.

Perhaps Diocletian understood that this highly charged personal and communal faith could not simply coexist with impersonal paganism. The logic of the First Commandment—"You shall have no gods before me"[39]—if taken to the extreme, is either isolationist, as much of Jewish history suggests, or expansionist. The Jews had always believed that when the Messiah came, the whole world would recognize the God of Israel and unite in His worship. "On that day," they prayed, "the Lord shall be One and His Name shall be One." In the hands of the Christians, who did not require that converts be circumcised or adhere to the Jews' peculiar dietary restrictions, these universalist aspirations did not seem far-fetched. Christianity might well aspire to be the empire's sole and last religion.

Forty years earlier, the emperors Decius and Valerian had attempted to terrorize the Christians into submission, but the end result of that sporadically brutal campaign had been another great surge of conversions. Still, those short-lived rulers lacked Diocletian's authority and subtlety, not to mention his staying power. Having restored the empire's financial and military health, he was determined to place it on a firm spiritual footing. Surely, the most innovative and effective Roman emperor since Augustus could contain a religious movement built on the worship of a dead rabbi.

THUS, the Great Persecution, Rome's final attempt to limit the expansion of Christianity. There is a tradition that Diocletian, a "good" emperor, was incited to use violence against the Christians by Galerius, who later earned a reputation for fanaticism and cruelty. But Diocletian had his own reasons for trying to weaken and marginalize the Christian movement. He and leading intellectuals of his regime believed that the old world could revive in all its glory, if only social and spiritual unity were restored. The problem was how to unify a society made ever more diverse by class divisions, regional differences, and ethnic migrations—a patchwork empire whose army was now made up largely of "barbarian" troops, and which had been invaded by a plethora of false religions.

Diocletian had already had occasion to deal with a competitive religion and had learned a lesson from the experience. The new movement, younger even than Christianity, was called Manicheism. The Mesopotamian visionary, Mani, had converted many people in Persia to his dualistic faith before being martyred there in the 270s. Now his followers were spreading his doctrines (which included recognition of Jesus as a divine prophet) throughout the Roman Empire, as well as eastward into India and China. Diocletian considered the religion not only corrupt but pro-Persian, and therefore subversive. In the spring of 302, enraged by their presumption, he ordered a number of Manichean priests to be wrapped in their books and burned to death. An undetermined number died, but their faith was not obliterated; Augustine of Hippo, the future saint, would later become a Manichean and remain one for most of his young manhood.

Where Christianity was concerned, the emperor had no desire to multiply martyrs. He recognized that heroic victims were, indeed, the "seeds of the Church." Nor did most Christian bishops, now more influential and well accepted than at any time since Jesus' death, wish to court bloody martyrdom. Still, as the purge of the army and civil service continued without curtailing the spread of the new faith, new voices were heard calling for harsher anti-Christian measures. In a fifteen-volume work entitled *Against the Christians,* the philosopher Porphyry branded the Jesus sect treasonous and immoral and called for the execution of its unrepentant members. Others, while not going quite so far, agreed that the dismissal of civil servants was insufficient—the leaders of the Church must be forced to abandon their campaign to convert the entire empire. Anti-Christian officials, no doubt including the Caesar Galerius, were particularly angered by the growing number of wealthy aristocrats who had embraced the Cross: traitors to Roman ideals and to their class.

For three years, violence gathered over the Christian community like a thundercloud. Finally, in 302, the storm broke. Diocletian was in Antioch preparing to conduct official business in the emperor's palace. Just as the usual sacrifice was about to be made (the equivalent of a modern invocation prior to the start of public business), a Christian deacon from Palestine burst into the room and horrified the assembled courtiers by denouncing corrupt pagan rituals. The talkative deacon, Romanus by name, was seized immediately and sentenced to death by burning, but Diocletian decreed that first his tongue should be cut out. Then he should be imprisoned for a year at hard labor . . . and *then* executed.

Shortly after this incident, Diocletian and Galerius visited the oracle of Apollo at the great temple of Didyma near Miletus on the coast of Asia Minor. Standing on the temple floor high above a vast subterranean cavern, they posed their questions. At Didyma, an oracle as famous as that of Delphi, a priestess of

Apollo responded to questioners by making indecipherable noises that were translated or interpreted by a learned priest, both figures standing out of sight in the recesses of the cavern. According to a later recollection of Constantine the Great, then a young officer attached to Diocletian's court, it was as if the god himself spoke from deep within the earth. Apollo could no longer prophesy through oracles, the voice moaned, because "the righteous on earth" were interfering with his communications with human beings.[40]

"The righteous on earth": the emperors had no doubt whom that phrase was intended to describe. On February 23, 303, during an ancient Roman festival significantly called Terminalia, they posted an edict banning Christian worship and ordering churches throughout the empire to be pulled down. Church officials were ordered to hand over their sacred books for burning. Ritual objects were to be confiscated by the imperial treasury. Christians who refused to abandon their faith were deprived of all privileges, in particular, the immunity of upper-class citizens from torture. Christian slaves could not be freed, or if already freed, must be returned to servitude. And, the decree provided, no one had a right to use the law courts unless he first sacrificed to the gods; so practicing Christians would be defenseless against personal assaults and seizures of their property.

These were harsh measures, but Diocletian did not at this point order mass arrests or executions of Christians. He wanted to impoverish the Church, divide it, and terrorize its most influential supporters. Nevertheless, as the campaign gathered momentum, violence was inevitable, especially when Christians actively resisted their persecutors. In the imperial capital of Nicomedia, officials battered down the doors of the church, burned copies of the Bible, and called on imperial troops to demolish the building. In response, a Christian of good family named Euetius tore down a copy of the imperial edict which had been posted on the city wall, commenting sarcastically, "More great victories over the Goths and Sarmatians!" He was promptly arrested for treason, tortured, and burned alive.[41]

Shortly after this, a mysterious fire broke out in the imperial palace. Although there was no indication of its origin, Galerius blamed the blaze on members of the emperor's household. Several of these, including two influential eunuchs, were, in fact, Christians. Diocletian's servants were ordered to sacrifice to the gods; those who refused were executed. Bishop Eusebius of Caesarea, the foremost historian of the age, describes one such punishment:

> In the city named above [Nicomedia] the rulers in question brought a certain man into a public place and commanded him to sacrifice. When he refused, he was ordered to be stripped, hoisted up naked, and his whole body torn with loaded whips till he gave in and carried out the command, however unwillingly. When in spite of these torments he remained as obstinate as ever, they next mixed vinegar with salt and poured it over the lacerated parts of his body, where the bones were already exposed. When he treated these agonies too with scorn, a lighted brazier was then brought forward, and as if it were edible meat for the table, what was left of his body was consumed by the fire, not all at once, for fear his release should come too soon, but a little at a time; and those who placed him on the pyre were not permitted to stop till after such treatment he should signify his readiness to obey. But he stuck immovably to his determination, and victorious in the midst of his tortures, breathed his last. Such was the martyrdom of one of the imperial servants, a martyrdom worthy of the name he bore—it was Peter.[42]

Most christian laypeople were not faced with Peter's choice, since the persecution was not yet aimed at them. The question of resistance was posed most painfully to the clergy, who faced the possibility of death if they refused to surrender sacred texts and ritual objects on command. As Eusebius's text suggests, there was no fixed penalty for disobedience. A contumacious Christian might be put to work in the mines of Palestine, or have an eye put out or the muscles of one leg severed. (Later, these marks of mutilation would become badges of distinction.) The forms of torture were gruesomely diverse. Even the forms of execution lay in the discretion of local officials. Martyrdom could take the form of hanging, beheading, crucifixion, burning, flaying alive, strangling, or any other measure the authorities considered an appropriate response to rebellious behavior and a salutory lesson to others.

These punishments were cruel, but not wantonly so. Their purpose was to take advantage of the Christian leaders' new state of mind, which was more future-oriented, political, and compromising than before. The clergy were no longer a handful of God-intoxicated souls anticipating the imminent end of the world and ready, even eager, to follow their Master to the Cross. Some, of course, fit this description; Bishop Anthimus of Nicomedia refused to cooperate with the authorities and was beheaded in 303, as were several churchmen in Egypt and North Africa. But the majority of church leaders, as well as their congregants, had become too successful, ambitious, and adaptive to play the role of otherworldly martyrs. They understood that if the Church could survive this persecution as it had previous terror campaigns, its position as the leading alternative to official paganism would be greatly strengthened.

A number of bishops and deacons therefore handed over Bibles and chalices to the authorities as ordered. Later, many of them would be called "traitors" after the Latin word for handers-over, *traditores,* and the Church would split bitterly over the question of their authority to perform their priestly functions. Other clergymen convinced ignorant or unconcerned officials to accept heretical works or even medical textbooks in place of holy books. In the same way, when Christian clergy and then laypeople were required to sacrifice to the gods, a few refused point-blank and were brutally punished, but many more went through the motions, persuaded someone else to sacrifice for them, or absented themselves altogether with the connivance of sympathetic officials.

The willingness of many Roman bureaucrats and soldiers to look the other way while imperial edicts were violated reminds us that, for all its violence, the Great Persecution was not an attempt to exterminate the Christians en masse. One reason for this was that repression in premodern times was as inefficient as any other form of administration. While some local officials carried out their orders to the letter, others interpreted them idiosyncratically, allowed themselves to be bribed, or simply ignored them. The ancients were bloody-minded, but not genocidal; they did not ordinarily pursue systematic policies of extermination. Killing tens of thousands of Christians, even if the emperors had had the taste for it, would simply have divided and weakened the empire further. Far better, Diocletian thought, to disrupt and disorganize the Church, demoralize it, and rob it of momentum by attacking it at the top.

The emperor's second edict (303) therefore commanded that Christian clergymen should be arrested and compelled to sacrifice to the gods of Rome. Most of those who refused to comply were imprisoned rather than executed, to the point that the prisons soon ran short of space in which to house ordinary criminals, and Christian prisoners were released on various pretexts. Contemporary witnesses report cases in which officials declared that a prisoner had recanted when he had not, or pretended that he had sacrificed voluntarily after forcing him physically to sprinkle incense on a pagan altar. At the same time, many powerful churchmen, including Bishop Peter of Alexandria, fled and went into hiding. From the point of view of most church leaders, this was an entirely rational and defensible response to persecution; in a war, the army's generals do not volunteer to be captured by the enemy. But others more attuned to earlier traditions of resistance and risk taking, or disapproving of the "political bishops" for other reasons, considered it an outrageous dereliction of duty.

Bishop Peter's flight from Alexandria, for example, greatly offended a small-town Egyptian bishop named Melitius of Lycopolis. Without a bishop in residence, who would care for the city's huge Christian community, not to mention the communities in southern Egypt and Libya under his supervision? By way of answer, Melitius came to the city, held church services in secret, and proceeded to perform the duties of a metropolitan bishop, which included baptizing converts, ordaining new priests, and disciplining the lesser clergy. (One priest he ordained may have been Arius, who will shortly play a major role in our story.) Meanwhile, from his self-imposed exile Peter denounced the "usurper," ordered him to cease performing the functions of bishop, and instructed the Egyptian and Libyan clergy not to obey him. Melitius, apparently unconcerned, ignored his decrees and continued to act as if he were the bishop—or, to use the title bestowed upon the metropolitans of the empire's greatest cities, the Pope of Alexandria.

Some time before Easter 306, Peter returned to the city. He rallied his supporters, convened a Church council, and had the disobedient bishop excommunicated for exceeding his authority. At around the same time, the Roman authorities arrested Melitius and imprisoned him in the mines of Palestine. There he performed the duties of a prison priest with bravery and distinction, returning to Egypt several years later. By this time (311), Peter had also been arrested. In the last burst of terror before the persecution ended, he was beheaded by the anti-Christian emperor, Galerius.

THE MARTYRDOM of Peter may have helped save Egypt from the kind of savage inter-Christian conflict that North Africa experienced following the persecution. In the provinces of Africa and Numidia (modern Tunisia and Morocco), the role of Melitius was played by a volatile, zealous priest named Donatus, who survived torture and imprisonment by the Romans and returned home to condemn the bishops who had handed over sacred objects, offered pagan sacrifices, or otherwise compromised themselves. With a network of supporters (later known as Donatists), he opposed the return of "traitorous" bishops and priests to their former positions and—a fateful step—denied that those who had returned could validly perform the functions of their offices.

According to the Donatists, the sacred powers of the priest, including the powers to grant absolution, offer the Eucharist, and ordain other priests, could not be exercised by corrupt clergymen. As instruments of God's grace, as well as legitimate leaders of the community, they could not be egregious sinners. Similarly, Christian laypeople who had lapsed to some extent during the persecution ought not to be readmitted to communion with the faithful until they had purified themselves by doing extraordinary penance. This rigorist position was rejected by most bishops and theologians, since a great many Christians, clergy and laity alike, had made compromises in order to save their skins (and, many would argue, to save the Church itself). Several Church councils later dealt with various aspects of the issue, but the general view of most churchmen is well represented by a letter issued by Bishop Peter in 306, shortly after his return to the city.[43]

The essential message of Peter's letter is "Forgive and forget." In his view, the Christians who, in effect, volunteered for punishment by provoking the authorities are not worthy of praise. Those who accepted unprovoked punishment rather than betray their faith are to be greatly honored, but such heroism is not expected of everyone. Believers who surrendered books to the authorities, bribed their way out of trouble, or (like Peter himself) fled to avoid arrest should be forgiven. Other lapses—for example, participating in pagan ceremonies or giving information to the authorities under duress—are sins for which penance must be made. But three or four years of penance will cure even the most egregious lapses, and, meanwhile, virtually no one is to be excluded from communion with other believers. The same standards, more or less, were later applied to govern the read-mission of "lapsed" clergy to their official positions. Except for the most outrageous cases of apostasy, priests, presbyters, and bishops were to be forgiven and restored to office after doing ap-propriate penance.

The principle Peter sought to establish was that the right and power to act as a priest did not depend upon the priest's personal holiness but upon the sanctity of his office. This approach viewed persecution as abnormal and looked forward to the time when the Church would be a stable, bureaucratically adminis-tered organization.[44] The problem was that a priest's personal morality could not be made entirely irrelevant to his competence to perform the duties of his office. To the Donatists, the corrup-tion of the *traditores* and apostates, which stank in the nostrils of God, had robbed them of all spiritual credibility and moral au-thority. By insisting that only *their* uncompromised bishops and priests had true authority, they effectively substituted their churches for the Catholic (i.e., universal) Church, and intro-duced a new and explosive cause of conflict into the Christian community: the issue of schism.

A century after the persecution ended, the Donatist and mainstream churches of North Africa were still locked in con-flict. St. Augustine himself advocated violent suppression of the Donatists, justifying massacres in the name of Christian unity. Armed groups formed to defend the "pure" churches, the so-called Circumcellions, perpetrated acts of terrorism in their name, and some committed mass suicide rather than yield to the forces they identified as the Antichrist. The virtual civil war among North African Christians would not end until the fifth century, when invading Vandals suppressed all the churches, Donatist and orthodox alike.

After Bishop Peter's martyrdom in Alexandria, the Egyptian church was able to avoid a similar schism and civil war. Though Peter's sacrifice played a role in moderating the split between compromisers and rigorists, Egyptian Christianity was probably too urbane and intellectual to begin with to produce violent mass support for a "fundamentalist" movement like the Donatists. Even so, conflict persisted in Egypt, although on a more moderate level than in North Africa. On his return, Melitius found himself surrounded by grateful admirers, including the priests and other Church officials he had ordained or appointed. Many of these "Melitians" were hostile to the wealthy and powerful leadership of the Alexandrian church and were determined to maintain an organized identity in the period following the persecution. While avoiding a Donatist-style schism and a frontal attack on the Church, they fought for decades to restore Melitius to his old post, validate the acts he had performed as Alexandria's "bishop," and undermine the authority of leaders they considered high-handed and corrupt. At the Council of Nicaea in 325, the bishops and the emperor would still be attempting to reconcile the Melitian movement to the official Egyptian church.

These clashes between Christians were traumatic, raising questions that would haunt the Church for generations to come. Did Jesus' life provide a realistic model for human behavior, or was it an ideal reachable only by a handful of saints and martyrs? Could an organized, unified Church embody Christian principles, or were worldly organization and religious zeal incompatible? What standards of belief and behavior ought to be required of the leaders of the Christian community? And, at what point would the acts of traitorous or immoral clergymen cause them to lose their priestly authority? The Church as a whole would soon adopt Bishop Peter's tolerant and realistic position that clergymen need not be saints, and that the office of priest was authoritative regardless of the holder's character. Applying these principles in particular cases, however, would prove more difficult and divisive than anyone expected.

In 303, satisfied with the way the anti-Christian campaign was proceeding, the emperor Diocletian traveled to Rome for the first time to celebrate the twentieth anniversary of his accession to office. He left the conduct of the persecution in the East to Galerius, who conducted it with real fervor, and in the West to the current Augustus, Maximian, another zealous anti-Christian. The following year, the persecution was made general; all Christians, not just the clergy, were ordered to sacrifice or suffer punishment. Maximian followed suit, and two years of real terror ensued, again undermined by administrative inefficiency and the ability of many Christians to steer a middle road between apostasy and martyrdom. The pace of persecution slowed for a while and then accelerated again in 310 and 311 before ending in a dramatic and unexpected way.

The weakest link in the imperial tetrarchy, from the pagan point of view, was the Caesar of the West, an army officer from the frontier town of Naissus on the Danube who had risen to be governor of Dalmatia before becoming Maximian's second in command. His name was Constantius, and the territory he governed comprised most of what is now France, Spain, and Britain, as well as Germany to the Rhine frontier. Constantius was a good administrator and an excellent military commander, but if the emperor's soothsayers had been able to foretell the future, he would never have been appointed Caesar, since his son was destined to become Rome's first Christian emperor.

Constantius had been married to a woman named Helena with whom he had a son, Constantine, but he divorced her in order to marry Maximian's daughter, Theodora. (Among the emperors it was customary for the Augustus to adopt his Caesar formally as a son, and for the Caesar to marry, when possible, into his "father's" family.) He and Theodora had six children, including one daughter named Anastasia. Although Constantius's religious views are not clearly recorded, Anastasia—Greek for resurrection—was a name commonly given to Christian girls. Whether or not he had Christian sympathies, it is clear that he was not interested in participating in the Great Persecution. In his far western domains the Christian clergy were, for the most part, left in peace. Even when Galerius and Maximian aimed their terror at Christian laypeople, Constantius demurred—an act of disloyalty, from Galerius's point of view, that earned him and his son the Caesar's enduring enmity.

Young Constantine had obviously been groomed for a position on the College of Emperors. While his father campaigned in western Europe, he spent the first years of the fourth century at Diocletian's court, traveling at the great man's right hand, watching him, and learning. Constantine was with the emperor when he left Rome after being coldly received by its haughty aristocrats, and he remained with him as he traveled first to Ravenna, then north and east to inspect the Danubian frontier. At a certain point he became aware that an illness contracted by the older man on the trip to Ravenna was not getting better; in fact, Diocletian was weakening and losing weight. His condition worsened as the court made its torturous way back to Nicomedia, and on his return to the capital everyone could see that he was seriously ill. In November 304, he collapsed after officiating at a public ceremony, and it was feared that his death was imminent. He did recover, but early in the spring of 305, weak, emaciated, and under great pressure from Galerius, he decided to abdicate the throne.

In May 306 Diocletian summoned a large assembly of generals, troops, and representatives of the Roman legions to the field outside Nicomedia where he had first accepted the emperor's crown. Tearfully, he announced that he was abdicating for reasons of health. Then he proclaimed his nominees (more accurately, those Galerius had insisted upon) for positions in the new College of Emperors. Naturally, Galerius would become Augustus of the East. Maximian, who had reluctantly agreed to abdicate as Augustus of the West, would be succeeded by Constantius. No surprises there. But instead of Constantine and Maximian's son, Maxentius, whom everyone expected to be named the two Caesars, Diocletian appointed two old cronies of Galerius's.

Visibly shocked, Constantine left the court immediately to join his father in Britain. Diocletian went into retirement in his Dalmatian homeland. With an aging Constantius on the Western throne, Galerius must have believed that he would soon be master of the entire Roman world. Constantius fulfilled one part of his plan by dying at York on July 25, 306. Galerius hoped to fill the vacant position with a loyal anti-Christian ally. But, to his dismay, Constantius's army (led, it was later said, by a barbarian chieftain) immediately acclaimed his son Constantine Augustus of the West. Galerius, whose fiscal policies had made him massively unpopular, was forced to accept the thirty-two-year-old man as an emperor, although he insisted upon demoting him to Caesar.

This unexpected change triggered a chaotic period of violent maneuvering and sporadic civil war between no less than seven contenders for the four positions in the College of Emperors. In the year 310, however, as Christian historians later reported, God intervened in the affairs of men. Galerius, the arch-persecutor, fell deathly ill with what was probably intestinal cancer. In April 311, as he felt his life ending, he issued a remarkable letter calling off the Great Persecution in the East. The letter explained that Galerius's only motive had been to persuade the Christians to return to the religion of their ancestors, but that the effort had failed. Thousands had been executed, gravely injured, or harassed to no avail; the majority of Christians were now entirely godless, having deserted both the traditional Roman faith and their own. Common sense and mercy dictated that the persecution stop, and that the followers of Jesus be allowed to assemble and worship peacefully. Finally—and perhaps most remarkably—the dying man asked the Christians to pray for his own health and that of the state.[45]

WE DO NOT know if Christians prayed for Galerius, who, in any case, expired soon after writing his letter. The following year, however, Christian prayers were answered in a startling way. In October 312, Constantine marched on Rome with his troops to confront Maxentius, his principal rival for power in the western half of the empire. Constantine was one of those "advanced" pagans who believed in a Supreme God: *Sol Invictus,* the Unconquered Sun. But he was also interested in Christianity and had acquired a Christian counselor, Bishop Hosius of Cordova, who seems also to have been a close friend. One day, it is told, while on the march toward Rome, Constantine and his soldiers saw a flaming cross in the sky, accompanied by the words *Touto nika*: By this, conquer. The following night he had a dream in which Jesus Christ appeared, showed him the sign of the Cross, and told him to inscribe it on his soldiers' standards. After Hosius of Cordova advised him that the dream was valid, Constantine commanded his army to replace their old pagan standards with the labarum: the Christian sign. Then he arrived at Rome and encamped outside the city.

Constantine expected a long siege, since the bridges across the Tiber River had been cut and the walls of Rome had never before been breached. Inside the city, however, mobs rioted against the unpopular Maxentius, who had a reputation as a brute and a sexual predator. Clearly, he could not control the city during a long siege. On October 28, Maxentius consulted an oracle who declared that "the enemy of the Romans" would die that very day. He then marched out of Rome with his forces, crossed the Tiber at the site of the Milvian Bridge over a temporary bridge built of boats, and attacked Constantine's army. The strategy proved suicidal. One counterattack scattered Maxentius's army, and the would-be emperor was last seen riding into the Tiber on horseback in a full suit of armor.

Constantine was now ruler of the West—and a convinced Christian. His principal ally in the East was Licinius, an experienced politician and general whom Constantine allowed to marry his sister, Constantia. Licinius was not a Christian, but *his* principal rival was a famous hater of Christians who renewed the persecution in the East, executing Bishop Peter of Alexandria and the famous scholar, Lucian of Antioch, among others. Together, Licinius and Constantine decided to play the Christian card. In 313 the two met in Milan and issued a joint document, since known as the Edict of Milan, in which they terminated the persecution of Christians, guaranteed their subjects freedom of worship, and decreed that all properties taken from the Christians or destroyed should be returned, or else that the victims of persecution should be indemnified for their losses.

Christians throughout the empire rejoiced—a bit prematurely as it turned out, since there would be one last burst of persecution to endure. In 316 the imperial brothers-in-law fell out under murky circumstances—each alleged a plot by the other to murder him and seize his throne—and began a war for control of a united Roman Empire. Constantine characterized the struggle as a holy war fought to ensure the survival and expansion of Christianity. Licinius now considered the Christians potential enemies and purged his administration of most of them. In the early 320s he began an on-again, off-again persecution of private citizens, which had little effect other than to enhance Constantine's reputation as Christ's general. Finally, in 324, Constantine defeated Licinius's forces in two key battles in Asia Minor, and both the persecutions and the war were over. The Roman Empire was united under the leadership of one man, and that ruler was a Christian.

In little more than one decade, Christianity had been transformed from a persecuted sect into the religion of the imperial family. Constantine was far too canny to attempt to outlaw his religious opponents, who still constituted a majority of Roman citizens. But there was nothing to prevent him from favoring the Church as his predecessors had favored the old religion. Among his first acts were decrees aimed at compensating Christians for the sufferings and depredations of prior years and granting Christian clergymen the special privileges formerly accorded only to pagan priests. His true goal, beyond favoring his co-religionists, was to unite the empire's diverse, quarreling peoples in one huge spiritual fellowship. Paganism was now clearly decadent, but once upon a time it had served this purpose. Why shouldn't the new religion play an equally vital and creative role?

Almost immediately, Constantine's advisors called his attention to a situation that appeared to jeopardize all these dreams. Its locale, not surprisingly, was that seedbed of religious controversy, Alexandria.

Several years earlier, it seems, an Alexandrian presbyter called Arius, possibly an ex-Melitian, had publicly criticized his bishop's Christian theology. The bishop in question, a distinguished churchman named Alexander, had convened a council of Egyptian bishops, condemned Arius's views, and expelled him from his church. But the stubborn priest, a man of some reputation among Eastern churchmen, had refused to accept this verdict and had appealed for support to powerful friends in Palestine, Syria, and Asia Minor. The local controversy had now gone regional and, according to theological experts, had the potential to spread throughout the Mediterranean world. Highly respected leaders of the Church had taken strongly opposed positions. Anathemas and decrees of excommunication were flying. Clearly, something should be done to investigate the case and formulate a sensible policy to resolve the conflict.

Constantine summoned his closest Christian advisor, Hosius of Cordova, who had been with him even before the victory at the Milvian Bridge. Would the bishop undertake a mission to Alexandria to determine the facts, evaluate them, and make recommendations? Hosius left Nicomedia for Alexandria two days later with his scribe in tow and Constantine's safe conduct in his traveling case.

Three

A Quarrel in God's House

Hosius of cordova was accustomed to controversy and understood the uses of power. His great skill was in negotiating agreements between the contentious princes of the Church. In Spain he had presided over councils of bishops convened to deal with the difficult doctrinal and organizational issues raised by the Great Persecution and the rapid growth of the faith. In Gaul, Italy, and the Balkans, he had served as Constantine's representative to diverse, often quarrelsome, Christian communities. A soft-spoken, thoughtful man, Hosius recognized that his own authority rested heavily on his role as the emperor's personal advisor and tutor in matters of faith. He had been at Constantine's side since his march from Gaul to Italy, and it was said that he was one of the few men in the empire who could prevail on the volatile ruler—sometimes—to restrain his famous temper.

The envoy had little doubt about the importance of his mission to Alexandria. His sovereign had a bright vision, which Hosius shared, of a Roman Empire as holy as it was powerful—an empire united across all lines of earthly division by indissoluble bonds of faith. The great revival that Diocletian had begun Constantine would bring to fruition, with the aid of Christ and his Church. Clearly, this unseemly doctrinal squabble between Eastern bishops and priests would have to end, and end quickly. Hosius carried a letter from the emperor outlining his vision, as well as reflecting his characteristic imperiousness when it came to dealing with obstacles to his plans. Constantine was a hot-blooded man. He had been wise to avoid being baptized while there were still so many sins of passion that he might commit.

The emperor's letter was addressed both to Alexander of Alexandria and to the rebellious priest, Arius. Hosius delivered it in person to the bishop at his palace. It is not known whether he met Arius as well during his visit to Alexandria, but this is unlikely, since if the priest had been in the city, he would have been lying low. Arius had returned several times in defiance of Alexander's orders to stay away. His followers were still holding unauthorized church services and fomenting trouble in the streets, and interviewing him, even if feasible, would clearly have been considered an insult to Alexander.

If he chose, Alexander might also have found Constantine's letter insulting. It was not diplomatic. "When I stopped recently in Nicomedia," he wrote,

> my plan was to press on to the East at once. But while I was hurrying towards you and was already past the greater part of the journey, the news of this business reversed my plan, so that I might not be forced to see with my eyes what I did not think possible ever to reach my hearing.[46]

The emperor made it plain that he considered the escalation of doctrinal conflict among high-ranking Christians not only disruptive of Church unity, but disreputable and almost certainly unnecessary. Christ's enemies rejoiced at this disorder. Pagans openly taunted Christians about their internal battles. Now that Christianity had finally emerged into the light—now that it might well be on the way to becoming *the* Roman religion—it seemed absurd that the unity of Christendom should be fractured by squabbling theologians.

Clearly, the emperor saw the quarrel jeopardizing his own dreams. His plan from the start, he wrote, had been "to bring the diverse judgments formed by all nations respecting the Deity to a condition . . . of settled uniformity," and "to restore a healthy tone to the system of the world, then suffering under the power of grievous disease."[47] Why put all this at risk by fighting about abstract, technical questions that nobody could answer with real certainty? One side said Christ was "begotten"; the other said "created." One declared him "divine by nature" and the other "divine by adoption." These differences were essentially trivial. Christian thinkers should imitate the Greek philosophers, who had tolerated disagreements far more profound than this without calling each other devils or organizing factions to suppress each other's opinions. The adversaries should reconcile and permit their emperor once again to enjoy "trouble-free days and nights of repose."[48]

The letter, which observed a strict neutrality in the controversy, must have dismayed the Alexandrian bishop. One can imagine Alexander talking about it to Hosius as one churchman to another. It pained him to think that he had given the emperor sleepless nights, but couldn't Constantine see how pernicious the Arian doctrine was? How insulting to Christ and the Church? Of course, the emperor, a busy, practical man, could not be expected to understand the importance of complex theological issues. And he was, after all, a Latin speaker unfamiliar with the subtleties of Greek thought. But surely he should recognize rebellion when he saw it! The priest's refusal to recant his heretical views, his plotting with other churchmen to overthrow the decision of his bishop, the arrogant tone of his letters, were proof of his utter disregard for right principles and good order. . . .

Hosius was inclined to agree. As a bishop himself, he understood the need to maintain discipline over the lesser clergy, especially in a jurisdiction as vast as that governed by Alexander. The metropolitan bishop's territory included all Egypt from the world's most populous city, Alexandria, to the rich farmlands that supplied most of Rome's grain, the towns and cities of the Nile valley, and the monasteries of the Theban and Nubian deserts. It also included Libya from the "Five Cities" of the urbanized north to the African desert. Alexander's authority as a religious leader extended to all the Christians in this vast region. In theory, the other bishops (more than one hundred in his domain!) were his equals, and important decisions were made by episcopal councils. In practice, the man his subjects called "Papa"—Pope—was far more than first among equals. There were only two or three churchmen in the world as powerful as the Alexandrian bishop. If a church council were needed, he would convene it, and its conclusions would almost always reflect his own views.

Then, too, Alexander was far more than a religious leader. Under Constantine's rule, great bishops were required to be as comfortable in the exercise of power as in the pulpit. Alexander supervised the city's only effective network of social services, arbitrated major disputes between Christians (and often between Gentiles), and was consulted by the civil authorities on a wide range of local issues. He managed the Church's burgeoning properties and finances, employed hordes of minor officials, builders, craftsmen, artists, and laborers, and supervised the affairs of several thousand priests, monks, and virgins dedicated to religious service. Perhaps most important, he played a vital mediating role between imperial authority and its subjects. Were people suffering because of food shortages? They looked to their "Papa" to bring greedy speculators to heel and make sure that the free grain provided by the emperor was distributed to the poor. Did the emperor require more soldiers and supplies for the army? He depended upon the bishop to help convince unwilling subjects to cooperate with the authorities.

Hosius admired Alexander, but he had been ordered to conduct an investigation, and he would do so before reaching any firm conclusions. What were the facts of the case? Who was this man Arius? And what of the brilliant young deacon who was supposed to be Alexander's right arm—a man called Athanasius?

Apparently, this matter was not going to be resolved quite as quickly and easily as Constantine had hoped. Hosius quickly got down to work.

THE FACTS of the case, as Hosius gathered them, were these: Arius, a priest of about sixty, had been born in Libya, in the area of the Five Cities. In 314, shortly after becoming bishop, Alexander had licensed him to preach at a church in the Baucalis district near the Great Harbor and to look after the district's residents. The tall, slender, gray-haired man was a famous speaker, or, perhaps, one should say singer, since he was in the habit of putting his theology into poetry and chanting it to his enraptured congregants. According to the bishop, this talent for vivid imagery and music had become part of the problem. Arius had recently written a long poem called *Thalia*—The Banquet—in a rhythmic meter ordinarily used for popular ballads. It was already chanted in port cities all around the eastern Mediterranean. Popular songs, like grain and news, traveled quickly by sea.

In his youth, Arius had studied Christian theology with the famous teacher and martyr, Lucian of Antioch. Before the Great Persecution, he had come to Alexandria to pursue a religious vocation, and he had reportedly behaved bravely during the terror, offering priestly services to parishioners and to Christians held in prison at considerable risk to himself. When Bishop Peter fled the city, he remained behind, but he did not, despite rumors to the contrary, join the group of priests loyal to the rigorist "usurper," Melitius. After his return, Peter ordained him deacon, which he would hardly have done if Arius had been a Melitian. Peter's short-lived successor, Bishop Achillas, made him a presbyter after the former's martyrdom in 311. There were unconfirmed reports that Arius had been a candidate for metropolitan bishop when Achillas died, but in any case, the Egyptian bishops elected Alexander to succeed Achillas. Shortly after his election, Alexander put Arius in charge of the Baucalis Church.[49]

Arius had been a successful minister. He was greatly admired for his personal purity as well as for his preaching and was a particular favorite of the sailors, dockworkers, and young women who flocked to his church. The church's sodality of virgins, in fact, had scandalized the neighborhood by protesting in public when he was ordered to leave the city by Bishop Alexander. And since his departure, the priest's partisans among the young men had clashed incessantly with Alexander's supporters.

The cause of this departure was a disagreement between the priest and Bishop Alexander over a matter of Church doctrine. It was this difference that Emperor Constantine had labeled trivial without knowing very much about it. As Hosius's investigation proceeded, it became clear to him that the dispute was far more momentous than the emperor realized, and that settling it would be no easy matter. Having condemned Arius's teachings and expelled him (or at least attempted to expel him) from the city, Alexander was most unlikely to reverse course and welcome him back. Nor, from all reports, did Arius show the slightest inclination to recant his beliefs and humble himself before the bishop. Was there some sort of compromise that both parties would accept? Hosius held that question in the back of his mind while focusing on the substance of the dispute.

In one sense, the controversy was an old one. Alexandria had long been a hotbed of theological innovation and debate—a place where outstanding Christian thinkers defended and explicated their faith using methods derived from Greek philosophy as well as from Jewish and Christian sources. A subject that much concerned its most creative and disputatious minds was the relationship of the Son, Jesus Christ, to God the Father—an issue still unsettled in the Christian community as a whole. A century earlier, Origen of Alexandria, the greatest theologian of his time, had caused an enormous stir by declaring that while the Son was eternal like the Father and united with Him, he was separate from and less than God.[50] One of Origen's dialogues read as follows:

Origen: Is the Father God?

Heraclides: Assuredly.

Origen: Is the Son distinct from the Father?

Heraclides: Of course. How can he be Son if he is also Father?

Origen: While being distinct from the Father is the Son also God?

Heraclides: He himself is also God.

Origen: And do two Gods become a unity?

Heraclides: Yes.

Origen: Do we confess two Gods?

Heraclides: Yes. The power is one.[51]

The "subordinationist" idea that Jesus was in some respects inferior to God was accepted by many Christians in the Eastern Empire, although Western churchmen generally rejected it. More recently, Alexandrian bishops like the martyred Bishop Peter had taken to attacking Origen vigorously, repudiating a number of his doctrines, including the idea that Christ was a second and lesser God.[52] Bishop Alexander followed in Peter's footsteps, while many other fourth-century bishops, including Arius's teacher, Lucian, and many of his friends in the Middle East, considered themselves "Origenists." Arius, however, had apparently taken that theologian's ideas a considerable distance further than Origen himself was willing to travel.

The tall priest had been preaching at his church for about three years when Alexander began receiving reports that he was advocating unusual ideas about the relationship of the Son to the Father. If the reports were accurate, Arius was questioning the divinity of Jesus Christ. Had he insulted Christ by writing that the Son was not eternal like the Father? Did he maintain that Jesus was created *ex nihilo*, out of nothing, like ordinary creatures, and that he was capable of sinning? Had he actually said that God could create other Sons if he wished, and asserted that "The Father knows the Son, but the Son knows not the Father"?

Further investigation proved most of the allegations true. Arius *did* preach that, "Before Christ, God was not yet a Father," and, "There was when he [Jesus] was not," meaning that he was not eternal, like God.[53] Rather than asserting that Jesus was divine by nature, Arius emphasized that he had earned his "adoption" as Son and his "promotion" to divine status through moral growth and obedience to God.[54] The priest did accept the idea, current throughout the East, that Christ was "preexistent"—that God had conceived him before time began and used him to create the universe.[55] But it was not clear whether Arius believed this literally, or whether he meant that God merely had foreseen Jesus' coming before his birth to Mary.[56]

The priest's new work, *The Banquet,* gave these ideas a provocative, poetic edge. Alexander had had reason to consider it a dangerous document.

> The Unbegun made the Son a beginning of things made and advanced him as His Son by adoption.
>
> Understand that the Monad was, but the Dyad was not, before it came to exist.
>
> Thus there is the Triad, but not in equal glories. Not intermingling with each other are their substances.
>
> One equal to the Son, the Superior is able to beget, but one more excellent or superior or greater, He is not able.
>
> At God's will the Son is what and whatsoever he is.
>
> God is incomprehensible to His Son. He is what He is to Himself: Unspeakable.
>
> The Father knows the Son, but the Son does not know himself.[57]

THESE WERE explosive ideas. Faced with the problem that had confronted all Christians since St. Paul—how to be a monotheist believing in only one God, yet still worship Jesus Christ—Arius advanced the view that Jesus was a creature intermediary between man and God. Origen had been a subordinationist, too, but he insisted (even at the risk of calling Christ a "second God") that the Son was with the Father eternally. Arius seemed to demote him even further, perhaps to the level of an angel ... or, Alexander worried, a man![58]

All Christians believed that Jesus' sacrifice redeemed humanity. What God did for the Son by resurrecting him and granting him immortality He could do for us as well, provided that we became new people in Christ. But if Jesus was not God by nature—if he earned his deification by growing in wisdom and virtue—why, so can we all. The Good News of the Gospels is that we also are God's potential Sons and Daughters. How, then, is Christ *essentially* different from or superior to us? And if he is not, what does it mean to call ourselves Christians?

Bishop Alexander decided that such questions could not go unanswered. In 318, he delivered a series of sermons maintaining strongly that Jesus Christ was Eternal God in the form of a man and that beliefs to the contrary were heretical. If the sermons were designed to provoke a public response, they succeeded. Arius published an open letter challenging the prelate's views; Alexander ordered him to appear before him to defend his own position; and the controversy escalated sharply.

Arius appeared at the bishop's palace on the day scheduled and stood like a gaunt shadow before Alexander. No record of this interview remains, but we can easily imagine the priest upholding his ideas with gentle but implacable determination. Bishop Alexander had asserted that the Son was uncreated and eternal. If so, did this mean that Christ was literally a second God? Clearly, for a Christian this result was impossible. But if he was not a second God, did the bishop believe that the Almighty had occupied a human body, suffered on the Cross, died, and then resurrected Himself? For a Christian this result was not only illogical but repellant. God was, by essence, bodiless, the source of all creation, but not in any respect a part of the material universe. His creative power was unfathomably intense. How could He enter into earthly matter without annihilating it?[59]

Did Arius deny Christ's divinity? He did not, since whether the Son was perfect by will or by nature, whether he was God's subordinate or his equal, God had raised him up to rule by His side in heaven and there was none like him. Surely, considering the difficulty of understanding such matters with certainty, there was room in the Church for differences of opinion about the Son's mysterious relationship to the Father! Alexander would have none of it. He ordered the priest on the spot to repudiate his errors and to agree to preach the correct doctrine that Jesus was no less than God on earth, the Creator become human to redeem our sins. When Arius refused to recant, the bishop terminated the meeting and called upon all Egypt's bishops to attend an important council in Alexandria.

The year was 318. Only a handful of church councils had been convened before this, most of them called to deal with issues arising out of the Great Persecution or technical matters having to do with liturgy and the calendar of holy days. Alexander's announcement therefore occasioned great excitement. More than one hundred bishops attended the council, and the proceedings were predictably stormy. A number of churchmen (Alexander did not say how many) supported Arius, although the majority accepted their bishop's position. The anti-Arians drew up a creed—a Confession of Orthodoxy—which was laid before Arius and his supporters with a demand that they sign it. When they refused, the council excommunicated them and banished them from Alexandria.

Even then, Alexander reported, the Arians resisted; they remained in the city for some time, stirring up trouble. The young women who passionately admired the poet-priest were particularly incensed by his dismissal and thronged the streets immodestly, demanding his reinstatement.[60] There was street fighting between Arius's supporters and groups favoring Alexander.[61] Finally, Arius dispatched a letter to a powerful friend, Bishop Eusebius of Nicomedia, the imperial capital. Its salutation was attention getting:

Arius, unjustly persecuted by bishop Alexander on account of that all-conquering truth which you also uphold, sends greetings in the Lord to his very dear lord, the man of God, the faithful and orthodox Eusebius.

The letter bitterly criticized Alexander's teaching that "as the Father is, so is the Son," and concluded,

We are persecuted because we say that the Son had a beginning, but that God was without beginning. That is really the cause of our persecution; and likewise, because we say that He is [created] from nothing. And this we say because He is neither part of God, nor of any subjacent matter. For this we are persecuted; the rest you know.

Farewell. As a fellow-disciple of Lucian and as a truly pious man, according to the import of your name, remember our afflictions.[62]

Arius must have had a quick reply to this letter, for a few weeks later he sailed from Alexandria with a group of sympathizers to rally support for his cause in Asia Minor and the East.

ARIUS AND EUSEBIUS of Nicomedia were contemporaries. They had both been "Lucianists"—students of the martyred teacher, Lucian of Antioch. And, it was clear, their theological views were similar, even if Eusebius did not accept all of Arius's formulations. (The priest had a habit of pushing his ideas to the limit, a tendency that the more politic Eusebius had learned to avoid.) When Arius left Alexandria in the winter of 318, he sailed directly to Nicomedia to seek refuge with his old schoolmate. Eusebius's endorsement would virtually guarantee the survival of his cause. A respected religious figure and superb politician, the Nicomedian bishop was, arguably, the premier leader of the Greek-speaking Church. In an era when personal attacks of the most scurrilous sort were typical of religious and political combat, not even his enemies could find anything to use against him.

Eusebius not only welcomed him but wrote other bishops on his behalf, with the result that an irate Bishop Alexander was soon receiving scores of letters asking him to readmit Arius to communion in Alexandria and restore him to his pulpit. The wily Eusebius then convened a church council of his own with the intention of minimizing the effect of the Egyptian council. In 319 or 320 the bishops of his province, Bythnia, met in Nicomedia to verify that Arius's views were "orthodox"—that is, within the range of ideas acceptable for Christians to hold.

Arius presented the council with a statement of belief stressing how close his own views were to Bishop Alexander's.[63] One detects Eusebius's fine hand in this creed, as well as in the conciliatory letter that Arius dispatched to Alexander at the same time. The priest now omitted several of his more extreme statements. For example, he did not state that Jesus was created "from nothing," nor did he continue to maintain that the Savior was changeable like human creatures. Better to avoid unduly inflammatory statements and stick to the major issues: the Father's superiority to all other beings, and the Son's indispensable roles as intermediary, Savior, and exemplar.

Guided by Eusebius, the Bythnian bishops had little difficulty declaring Arius's views acceptable. They admitted him to communion immediately and addressed a strong letter to Bishop Alexander demanding that he do the same. For the first time, one council of bishops had met specifically to reverse a decree of excommunication pronounced by another council. The odd result was that a priest denied communion with other Christians in one city was welcomed to church in another! There was no reason, of course, for the bishops of one diocese to accept the doctrines or decisions announced by those of another diocese. All bishops were equal, and while some (in particular, the prelates of Alexandria, Antioch, and Rome) ruled larger territories, no single bishop was authorized to serve as the ultimate validator of Christian doctrines. Clearly, if the process begun at Bythnia continued, each diocese would tend to become a "Church" unto itself, with its own standards of orthodoxy and right behavior.

The proof of this was provided by Arius's next move. Strengthened by the action of the Bythnian council, the controversial priest traveled south to Lebanon, where Bishop Paulinus of Tyre offered strong support, and then to Palestine, where the dominant figure was another Eusebius: Bishop Eusebius of Caesarea, the noted theologian, former advisor of the emperor, and the first great historian of the Christian Church.

Eusebius of Caesarea was far more accomplished as a scholar than his namesake of Nicomedia, but considerably less determined and skilled as a political organizer. He tended to fluctuate with the prevailing political tide. Knowing this, Eusebius of Nicomedia had written him immediately to urge him to support Arius against Alexander, and when the exiled priest arrived in the port of Caesarea—Palestine's leading city since the Romans' sack of Jerusalem—the bishop received him warmly.

To begin with, he threw the considerable weight of his scholarly reputation behind Arius's views. This Eusebius was a great admirer of Origen's theology, which he believed confirmed Arius's central principle: the inferiority of the created Son to the eternal Father. Then, following the Nicomedian bishop's example, he convened a council of bishops subject to his jurisdiction. Meeting in Caesarea in 321 or 322, the Council of Caesarea again vindicated Arius's orthodoxy and demanded that Bishop Alexander reinstate him.

At this point Arius returned to Alexandria. His return to the city without Alexander's permission was no crime, since the emperor and the civil authorities had not yet taken a position on the case, but it was clearly an act of defiance. The priest's request that the bishop meet publicly with him to discuss his readmission to communion was refused, and nightly disorders returned to the city's streets. But more serious, if less tangible, disorders were now dividing the Eastern Church. Arius could claim the support of almost all the Eastern bishops, including most of those with substantial reputations as theologians. To counter this, Alexander had circulated two letters to virtually every bishop outside Egypt. (His tendency, later accentuated by his successor, Athanasius, was to try to make up for organizational weakness in the East by developing support in the West.)

One letter, probably written by Alexander himself, warned churchmen everywhere against Arius and his colleagues, accusing them of "contending against Christ" in the manner of the Jews and Greeks, preaching that Jesus is equal to other men, and stirring up "seditions and persecutions" against the faithful.[64] The other, probably drafted by Alexander's deacon, Athanasius, criticized Eusebius of Nicomedia, instructed other clergymen to disregard his letters, and dramatically accused the Arians of "rending the robe of Christ."[65] Alexander and Athanasius secured two hundred signatures for it (most of them, it is true, Egyptian) in order to counteract the impression that their views represented those of only a small minority.

That is where matters stood in 325, when Hosius arrived in Alexandria with Constantine's letter. If, at this point, the matter were put to a vote of the Eastern bishops, the "Eusebian party" would probably have won. But the reaction of the defeated anti-Arians would surely have been violent. Already, Alexander was characterizing Arius's philosophy as a heretical attack on Jesus' divinity, and Athanasius had compared the Arians to the crucifiers of Christ. Language this inflammatory was an invitation to violence—and both sides were involved in increasingly violent street battles.

Furthermore, no matter how many bishops called for Arius's reinstatement, it was not at all clear that the emperor would accept an outcome that favored the Arian side. His natural tendency was to uphold authority against rebellion, and Bishop

Alexander, after all, was supposed to have full authority over all the priests of Egypt and Libya. Moreover, as a Latin-speaking westerner, Constantine had little patience for Greek theological niceties. So far as he was concerned, the Christ who had appeared to him in a dream, led him to victory, and given him an empire to govern was God. At the same time, though, Eusebius and his vast network of friends had already demonstrated that a "victory" by the anti-Arian party might well be the opening round of a conflict even more widespread and destructive of Christian unity. The gnawing question, then, was whether some sort of compromise might be possible.

SINCE BISHOP HOSIUS left no detailed record of his investigation of the Arian controversy, we do not know whether he interviewed Athanasius as well as Alexander. But it seems almost certain that he did, for although the fiery young deacon was only in his twenties, he was already a power in the Alexandrian church and a theologian of note. With a pronounced taste for the rough-and-tumble of urban administration and church politics, he was Bishop Alexander's good right arm and his choice to succeed him to the throne of St. Mark.

Athanasius's appearance belied his growing stature in the Church. He was a small redheaded man, almost childlike in size, but those who considered him insignificant or manipulable soon learned to regret their error. A popular story had it that the bishop had originally encountered him on the public beach, a boy of poor family with little education and no prospects, pretending to be a great preacher and declaiming to the waves. Impressed with the child's ability, boldness, and charm, he had brought him home, introduced him into his household, and raised him to fulfill his ambition: to become the most powerful bishop in Christendom. Formerly Alexander's secretary, now a deacon and the top member of his staff, Athanasius was reported to have written a number of the bishop's sermons and letters. He was equally at home in great houses and poor neighborhoods . . . and quite prepared to use the violent methods of the streets, when necessary, to accomplish worthwhile goals.

It is useful to imagine what the future leader of the anti-Arian forces throughout the empire might have told Hosius during his stay in Alexandria.[66] Surely, he would have argued the point that Hosius later accepted: compromise with Arius and his allies was out of the question. The differences between the Arians and true Christians were no mere matters of emphasis or alterable "opinion": they went to the heart of what it meant to be a Christian. Why did the Arians maintain so vehemently that God sent us a Savior who was less than God? Because, fundamentally, the idea of the Eternal becoming a man offended them, as it offended the Jews. They thought that identifying Jesus as God lowered the Almighty by embodying him in a physical creature. But God could, and did, take on fleshly form to fulfill His own plan of salvation without ceasing for a moment to be God.

The Arians, furthermore, had become prisoners of Greek logic. They thought in terms of either/or. That is why they accused Alexander and his allies of "Sabellianism": a heresy asserting that God and Jesus were simply aspects of (or names for) the same undivided reality. This merging of the Father and Son implied that the Son was not really human, or, perhaps, that only his body was human while his mind was divine. (Whether Jesus ate, drank, and eliminated like other human beings had been a hotly disputed topic among the Sabellians!) Arius was right to reject this thinking, Athanasius said, but in doing so he had fallen into the opposite trap. Either/or: either Jesus was really God or he was really human. The Arians could not really imagine that he might be *both,* and so the tendency of their thought (even though they denied it) was to turn him into a man—or into some sort of third creature, an angel or demigod.

Yet he *had* to be both fully human and fully divine, argued Athanasius. Could the death of a mere human being redeem our sins, grant us immortality, and, eventually, resurrect our physical bodies? Of course not! But could Omnipotent God, the Beginning and the End, suffer for our sake without becoming human? The answer was equally plain. Therefore, whether or not it seemed "reasonable" to people schooled in Greek philosophy, Jesus Christ was both true man *and* true God.

Hosius would surely have found this exposition convincing. *His* people—the people of western Europe—would not accept a Jesus who was too much like them. They knew they were feeble sinners, struggling to survive in a hostile environment. The Christ they wanted and needed was a High God who could save them by His grace and comfort them through the ministrations of His Church. In fact, Arian theology implicitly reduced the role of the institutional Church. If Jesus' life and character were supposed to serve ordinary Christians as a usable model of behavior, the principal mission of the clergy would be to help people transform themselves, not maintain theological and political unity throughout the empire. This was another reason Constantine would probably favor the doctrine of Alexander and Athanasius. The Church he needed was one that would help him keep order among ordinary folk: people who would never become immortal unless God decided for reasons of His own to save them.

Hosius made up his mind. He would write immediately to tell the emperor that compromise was impossible. The Arian heresy could neither be tolerated nor accommodated. It had to be suppressed. At the same time, he would recommend a strategy to end the division in the Christian community as quickly and decisively as possible.

T HE BISHOPS of the East had been talking for some time about the need for a great council to deal with a number of issues troubling the rapidly growing Church. Hosius would recommend that Constantine convene such a council in the spring, preferably in a city not far from his own headquarters—perhaps in Ancyra

(Ankara), whose bishop, Marcellus, was a passionate opponent of Arius and the two Eusebiuses. The emperor could use the council to persuade the assembled bishops to condemn Arianism. Not only was the cause just, but Hosius judged that few churchmen would dare oppose the wishes of the Rome's supreme ruler—the man Eusebius of Caesarea called "God's dearly beloved," and "the savior and chief bastion of the Church."[67]

More immediately, a council of bishops was scheduled to meet quite soon in Antioch to decide who should be that city's new prelate following the death of old Bishop Philogonius. Antioch was a key stronghold in any struggle for influence in the Eastern Church, since its metropolitan bishop had jurisdiction over the clergy of Syria, Lebanon, Palestine, Cappadocia, and Arabia, as well as lands to the east up to the Persian border. The beautiful city was currently in an uproar. The deceased bishop had been a strong ally of Alexander's, as was Eustathius, the candidate for the succession favored by Alexander. The Arians had apparently fielded a candidate of their own who was supported by Eusebius of Caesarea. As usual, each side was supported by gangs of street fighters, and the resulting riots had been considerably more destructive than those troubling Alexandria.

This was Hosius's chance not only to put an anti-Arian in the bishop's palace at Antioch, but to deliver a serious blow to Eusebius of Caesarea prior to the great council. The meeting in Antioch was certain to be dominated by the anti-Arian bishops ordained by Philogonius. Understanding this, several pro-Arian bishops, including Paulinus of Tyre, had sent excuses declining to attend. Eusebius of Caesarea, however, was coming in all his glory with a retinue of his allies. Perhaps the old man believed that he could sway the council with the power of his oratory. Or he may simply have felt that his reputation as an international spokesman for Christianity and his former relationship with the emperor rendered him invulnerable. If Hosius had his way, Eusebius would soon learn a lesson about vulnerability.

After conferring with his hosts in Alexandria (and, presumably, receiving Constantine's permission to intervene in Antioch), Hosius sailed for the River Orontes, arriving in Antioch early in 325 in time to participate in the final planning of the council. By the time the bishops assembled, the envoy had assumed the chair as presiding officer, and a draft Statement of Faith had been drawn up.

This statement, overwhelmingly approved by the sixty or so bishops assembled, might have been written by Alexander and Athanasius. The bishops were required to affirm, among other things, that they believed "in one Lord Jesus Christ, the only-begotten Son, begotten not from non-existence, but from the Father"; that the Son has always existed; that he is "immutable and unalterable"; and that he is "the image not of the will nor of anything else except the actual existence (*hypostasis*) of the Father."[68] As if this anti-Arian pronouncement were not clear enough, the council added anathemas to it—the first anathemas (literally, curses carrying a threat of excommunication) issued by any church council against errors of doctrine.[69] The views condemned were that Jesus is a creature rather than the Creator, that he is not eternal, and that he is not unchangeable by nature, as God is.

Everyone present declared his adherence to the statement and the anathemas except three bishops: Theodotus of Laodicea, Narcissus of Neronias, and . . . Eusebius of Caesarea. As presiding officer, Hosius called each man before him in the presence of the council and questioned him about his beliefs. Each expressed his views. The council then declared these opinions heretical and excommunicated all three bishops.

Eusebius of Caesarea, excommunicated! The shock rebounded, as Hosius knew it would, throughout the Christian world. Notice had been served prior to the forthcoming ecumenical council that the lofty stature of Arian leaders would not protect them from the judgment of "orthodox" Christians or the

emperor's wrath. But the council also softened the blow somewhat by declaring that the three excommunicants would be permitted to repent and to be restored to Communion at the "great
and holy council at Ancyra."[70]

Having supplied an incentive to repentance along with well-
merited punishment, Hosius returned to Nicomedia to report
the results to Constantine. The crucial struggle, of course,
would take place at the forthcoming Great Council. Perhaps the
emperor would decide to allow him to preside over that meeting
as well.

Four

The Great
and Holy Council

CONSTANTINE was pleased with his envoy's work. Hosius did not have to hint that he might like to be asked to preside over the Great Council. Impressed by his decisiveness at Antioch, Constantine suggested the appointment himself. There was one change of plan, however, that must have surprised the Spanish bishop, since invitations had already been dispatched to more than four hundred churchmen. Constantine had decided to move the meeting from Ancyra, two hundred miles inland on the Anatolian plateau, to his summer residence on the Lake of Nicaea near Nicomedia. Revised invitations had already been issued, with couriers dispatched to intercept the bishops already en route to Ancyra. The council was to begin its work, as originally planned, at the end of May 325.

Why this sudden change? The reasons publicly proffered included the goodness of the air at Nicaea, the beauty of the lake, the fine facilities at the imperial palace for a large meeting, and the difficulties of the trip inland for the older bishops. But more complex and interesting motives were almost certainly in play. Ancyra was Bishop Marcellus's city, and Marcellus—a brilliant but often reckless man—was such an extreme advocate of Christ's identity with God that even other anti-Arians found his views controversial. If Arianism were to be condemned in Ancyra, the site might suggest that Marcellus had played a leading role and that the council's outcome had been prearranged. Furthermore, Constantine now saw himself playing the role of host to the assembled bishops. But transferring the council to Nicomedia itself would not have been a good idea because of Bishop Eusebius's dominating presence in that city. And the imperial palace in New Rome, the new capital under construction that people insisted upon calling Constantine's City, was not yet ready for occupancy.

Thus . . . Nicaea.

Constantine's great hope was to convene a conference that would end the bishops' bitter wrangling and begin an era of harmony in the Church. Nicaea—an idyllic rural setting—must have seemed a perfect place to fulfill such a mission. Nicaea's own bishop was reputed to be a moderate Arian, but he was a person of no great influence who would virtually disappear if Constantine hosted the council on his own territory. The emperor, although unbaptized, liked to style himself a "bishop for the outsiders": a joke that was not entirely a joke. The large palace on the lake possessed facilities capable of housing his large personal staff. Extensive staff work would not be necessary, of course, if Constantine planned to function at the council merely as a ceremonial host and interested observer. The change of locale signaled his determination to play a role far more influential than that.

And there was something else, something more than egoism or anti-Arian strategy, that may have induced the emperor to offer personal hospitality to hundreds of Christian bishops. It was a matter no one dared discuss openly with Constantine: the strange fate of his brother-in-law, Licinius.

Constantine had given his sister, Constantia, in marriage to Licinius during the period when the two men were joint rulers of the empire. But then the civil war broke out. In 324, after losing the last battle of the war at Chrysopolis in Asia Minor, Licinius fled to Nicomedia. Hoping for mercy, he asked his wife and Bishop Eusebius, who had instructed her in Christianity, to go together to Constantine's camp to plead for his life. They did so and found the emperor magnanimous. How could Constantine refuse to spare his own sister's husband, especially when spoken for by a pious Christian cleric?

Licinius himself came into camp, humbled himself before his new ruler, and asked his pardon. Constantine responded graciously, giving his former enemy a safe conduct to Thessalonica and swearing a solemn oath not to harm him or his family. A few months later, however, after the first invitations to the Great Council had been dispatched, disturbing news arrived from Greece by special courier. Licinius had been killed—professionally strangled—at his villa, and his nine-year-old son, the former Caesar, had also been murdered. The assassins had disappeared without a trace and were nowhere to be found.

Officially, the murders remained unsolved, but there had been reports that Licinius's estate had become a meeting place for discontented noblemen and other enemies of the emperor. It was commonly believed that, because of Licinius's continued meddling in politics, he and his line had become a threat to Constantine's control over the West. If so, Constantine would be likely to deal with the challenge in traditional imperial fashion. Little wonder that he remained, technically speaking, a non-Christian throughout his reign and did not receive baptism until he lay on his deathbed. A good emperor—even a good Christian—would inevitably find himself compelled to choose between losing heaven and losing power. Having just assumed the throne, Constantine was by no means finished either with power or with committing the sins necessary to retain it. But presiding over the grandest council in Christian history might make up in the community's eyes (and, who knows, perhaps even in God's) for a certain number of moral lapses.

THE BISHOPS' mood, as they began to arrive in Nicaea, was certainly not censorious, nor, at first, did they seem overly concerned about the Arian controversy or any other matter on their agenda. As Eusebius of Caesarea wrote later, they felt that they were living a miracle.[71] A Christian emperor had invited them to his home!—and not only invited them, but promised to pay their travel and living expenses during the several months they would be away from their own cities. They arrived by the score, more than 250 strong, hardly daring to believe their good fortune.

Just a few years before, during Licinius's persecution, many Christians wondered if the age of persecutions would ever end. Now Constantine had favored and enriched them beyond their wildest dreams. In less than a year, the new emperor had returned or rebuilt virtually all their churches, given them back the jobs and honors taken from them, restored their civil rights, and made full compensation, out of the imperial treasury when necessary, for property destroyed or damaged. He had accorded Christian clergymen privileges formerly granted to pagan priests, including exemption from the taxes and levies that even prosperous citizens found crushing. He went on the offensive against paganism; though he stopped short of outlawing the old religion entirely, he banned the construction of new temples, the consulting of oracles, and animal sacrifices. That these decrees were enforced sporadically did not detract from their symbolic value. With the old faith in decline, new converts poured into the Christian churches.

As the author of these changes, Constantine was in a position strongly to influence—perhaps even to dictate—the course of events at Nicaea. The emperor, by nature an impatient and decisive man, had not given up hope for a quick resolution of the Arian controversy and other disputes troubling the expanding Church. But he understood that brutal intervention into a controversy whose roots and implications were more tangled than he had previously thought might have unexpected results. He agreed with Hosius that the dispute should be ended on terms favorable to Alexander and the anti-Arians. The question was how to accomplish this in such a way that the bishops did not leave Nicaea more seriously divided than they had been before they arrived.

Part of the answer was time. Considering the "Eusebians'" numerical strength and the depth of their feelings, it would take some time to bring all the participants to agreement. Constantine was prepared, if necessary, to spend most of the summer at Nicaea—the bishops traveling for weeks to get there would expect no less. More important than time itself, however, was the procedure to be followed at the council. Public discussion should not be avoided, of course, but acrimonious debate was as likely to harden positions as to change them. Working together on a proposed creed, however, might provide the bishops with the chance to listen more closely to each other, forge new connections, and, perhaps, discover language that they could agree on. Previous councils had promulgated statements of faith to bludgeon dissenters into submission. Perhaps creed-making at Nicaea could bring ecclesiastical harmony out of discord.

THE BISHOPS and their retinues began arriving in early May. Constantine welcomed them warmly and housed them, depending on their age and distinction, either in the palace or in one of the numerous outbuildings rimming the lake. A good many of them bore the scars of past persecutions: eye patches covering lost eyes, limps produced by severed hamstrings or Achilles tendons, backs deformed by hard labor in Phoenician mines. How satisfying to provide these sufferers with some of the worldly comforts they had so long deserved! Their gratitude was equally touching. Some bishops apparently believed they had already entered the Kingdom of Heaven, or at least a well-furnished anteroom.

At the same time, the new sense of power and possibility now infusing the Church could not help but produce conflict among the victors. While terror reigned, most Christian leaders had maintained a common front. Survival, not doctrinal purity, had been the order of the day. But victory raised questions that persecution had long suppressed: The victory of what? What should a Christian empire look like? Was the Christianity that emerged from the years of travail to be a religion for everyone, or only for those meeting certain standards of faith and virtue? Should the clergy's primary task be to help its members perfect themselves or to administer sacred rites and help maintain order, as the pagan priesthood had done? How much doctrinal unity was necessary and healthy to a growing Church? To what extent should ecclesiastical power be regularized and centralized? What sort of relations should the bishops maintain with monks and holy men? With emperors and state officials?

At the time, such issues were emerging only partially and incoherently. Yet it was impossible for Christianity to become a universal faith and a state religion without sooner or later confronting them. One reason for the passions aroused by the Arian controversy—and by intense religious disputes to this day—was that the main doctrinal issue acted like a magnifying glass, focusing the heat of many related disputes, not all of them strictly "religious," on one contested theological question.

The "Christological" dispute had its own integrity and urgency, of course. The old gods, false gods, had failed. The world had become a strange, confusing place, full of new threats and promises. People felt a deep need to make sense of their existence (and, if possible, to predict their own fate) by believing in a true God and accurately defining His relationship to humankind. But trying to define Jesus' relationship to God and humanity crystallized other concerns as well.

One underlying question was this: To what extent were the values and customs of the ancient world still valid guides to thinking and action in a Christian empire? Some Christians, among them Arius and Eusebius of Nicomedia, had a stronger sense of historical continuity than others. Those whose ideas and social relationships were still shaped to a large extent by the optimistic ideals and tolerant practices of pagan society, and for whom Christianity seemed a natural extension of and improvement on Judaism, tended to be Arians of one sort or another. By contrast, the strongest anti-Arians experienced their present as a sharp break with the past. It was they who demanded, in effect, that Christianity be "updated" by blurring or even obliterating the long-accepted distinction between the Father and the Son.

From the perspective of our own time, it may seem strange to think of Arian "heretics" as conservatives, but emphasizing Jesus' humanity and God's transcendent otherness had never seemed heretical in the East. On the contrary, subordinating the Son to the Father was a rational way of maintaining one's belief in a largely unknowable, utterly singular First Cause while picturing Christ as a usable model of human moral development. For young militants like Athanasius, however, ancient modes of thought and cultural values were increasingly irrelevant. Greek humanism and rationalism were shallow; Judaism was an offensive, anti-Christian faith; and while admirable figures like the hermit, Antony, could try to perfect themselves in the desert, most people's primary need was the need for security. Only a strong God, a strong Church, and a strong empire could provide helpless humans with the security they craved.

Not surprisingly, Constantine was drawn naturally to this perspective. The emperor believed in moral progress, but he was certain it could not be achieved without authority, uniformity, and regularity. He detested Judaism,[72] and his own experience convinced him that the world he had helped to create represented a "New Rome" very different from the old. Constantine saw the Great Council as an opportunity to strengthen the Church's position in this new world by unifying it doctrinally and helping it to reorganize it internally. Christianity had inspired his army, redefined his own destiny, and held out new possibilities for uniting his people. Now he would return the favor by teaching the Church the Roman virtues of law, order, and efficient administration.

THE GREAT COUNCIL began its deliberations early in June with more than 250 bishops in attendance, almost all of them from the Eastern Empire. It was the largest gathering of Christian leaders, up to that time, in the history of the Church. Only a handful of Western churchmen came to Nicaea, of whom the most important figures were Hosius, representing both the emperor and the church of Spain, Caecilianus of Carthage, Nicasius of Gaul, and two presbyters representing the Bishop of Rome. To some extent, this Eastern predominance can be attributed to the westerners' lack of interest in the Arian controversy, which still seemed to most of them an obscure "Greek" matter. But it also reflected the great size, strength, and vitality of Eastern Christianity—one reason that Constantine had decided to locate his new capital in Asia Minor.

The Council of Nicaea, then, was not universal. Nevertheless, it is everywhere considered the first ecumenical (or universal) council of the Catholic Church. Several later gatherings would be more representative of the entire Church; one of them, the joint council of Rimini-Seleucia (359), was attended by more than five hundred bishops from both the East and West. If any meeting deserves the title "ecumenical," that one seems to qualify, but its result—the adoption of an Arian creed—was later repudiated by the Church. Councils whose products were later deemed unorthodox not only lost the "ecumenical" label but virtually disappeared from official Church history.

That Nicaea did not disappear is largely the result of the council's adoption of the Nicene Creed, an amended version of which is recited today by Christians around the globe. Interestingly, though, for more than half a century the document had a precisely opposite effect. Not only did it fail to generate the consensus Constantine and Hosius hoped for, it split the Christian community even more violently along Arian/anti-Arian lines.

What is known about the Council of Nicaea is based on fragmentary comments by a few of the bishops who attended the meetings and on several documents that were copied and preserved, including, of course, the Nicene Creed. No minutes or other official records of the proceedings exist. Nevertheless, a number of dramatic occurrences are well attested,[73] and it is possible to reconstruct some of the most heated debates.

The bishops met in a large hall of the palace: Constantine's Judgment Hall.[74] They sat on benches arranged in rows running the length of the hall, with the most distinguished churchmen occupying front row seats. When all were seated, several of the emperor's Christian friends entered the room, and everyone rose. Constantine himself then appeared dressed in purple and wearing the imperial diadem: a gold circlet flashing diamonds. Recognizing that he was formally a guest at the meeting, he asked the bishops' permission to be seated and received a murmured assent. A small, elaborately worked stool was produced. Constantine seated himself at a slight distance from the bishops, but close enough to participate in their discussions. The bishops sat as well, and Eusebius of Caesarea arose to deliver the official welcome to the emperor.

Eusebius of Caesarea, excommunicated by the Council of Antioch, giving the opening panegyric! What he said, welcoming Constantine as a heaven-sent deliverer of the Christians, is not as interesting as the fact that he said it. Clearly, the excommunications delivered at Antioch were provisional, and not to be taken seriously—not, that is, if Eusebius and his fellow "subordinationists" were to reconcile themselves to their brother bishops at Nicaea. Eusebius of Caesarea had a long-standing relationship with Constantine, whom he had advised on religious matters during the emperor's campaign in the East. In allowing him to give the first speech, Constantine was exhibiting his desire for universal reconciliation and concord. Perhaps inadvertently, he was also demonstrating how little partisan excommunications meant in the heat of a passionate religious struggle.

The emperor made his own wishes clear in a brief welcoming speech in Latin, which was translated into Greek by his own translator. (Later, to the bishops' delight, he would converse with them in Greek, a language he could speak quite comfortably when not making a formal address.) The speech was well received. In it he compared the struggle in the Church to civil war, exhorting the bishops not to give the devil the victory that their persecutors had failed to win by force. He asked them to speak frankly and to air all their differences openly, for only by doing so could their conflict genuinely be resolved. Constantine took no public position on the issues in controversy; he simply pleaded for peace and harmony in the Church. Then, to general acclaim, he sat down. Several bishops who, following ancient custom, presented him with petitions asking him to intervene in particular disputes were treated to a sharp lecture on the need to keep their private complaints separate from the business of the council. A bit later these petitions would be symbolically burned.

The Arian controversy was the first order of business, and dealing with it consumed more than two weeks of the council's time. Arius himself was present, although, like Athanasius, his status as a priest rather than a bishop prevented him from addressing the group formally or participating in public discussions. Apparently he made an impression on the participants; one story, undoubtedly apocryphal, relates that a young Gallic bishop named Nicholas, afterwards the legendary saint of Christmas celebrations, was so incensed by Arius's heretical declarations that he slapped the old man's face! In any case, Arius's episcopal supporters, led by Eusebius of Nicomedia, were present in force, as were members of the anti-Arian group mobilized by Alexander of Alexandria.

THE ORDER of events following Constantine's speech cannot clearly be established, but fairly early in the discussion Eusebius of Caesarea made the case for his own orthodoxy. His nominal judges were the bishops, but the real audience for this appeal was the emperor. He presented a creed of his own that he said was based on the traditional baptismal creed used in his city, and asked, on that basis, to be readmitted to communion with his brother bishops.

The creed began with a statement of belief in "one God, the Father, almighty, maker of all things visible and invisible," and went on to proclaim the speaker's faith in

> one Lord Jesus Christ, the Logos [Word] of God, God from God, light from light, life from life, Son only begotten, first-begotten of all creation, begotten before all ages from the Father, through Whom all things came into being, Who because of our salvation was incarnate, and dwelt among men, and suffered, and rose again on the third day, and ascended to the Father, and will come again in glory to judge the living and the dead.[75]

The recital had the desired effect on Constantine. Before anyone else could respond, the emperor not only pronounced it acceptable, but stated that it reflected his own beliefs. There was only one amendment that he would suggest. Eusebius should add that the Son was *homoousios* with the Father: that is, that Jesus and God shared the same essence.

The emperor's "suggestion" was a response (very likely prepared in advance, after consultation with Hosius) to a tricky problem. On its face, Eusebius's creed seemed perfectly orthodox from the anti-Arian point of view, since it emphasized Jesus' divinity without appearing to subordinate him in any way to the Father.

The difficulty was that virtually every word of the document, as originally written, could be interpreted in an Arian fashion. The Arians believed that Jesus was divine, too, since God had adopted him as His Son and promoted him to godhood. "God from God, light from light, life from life"? These phrases did not necessarily mean that the Son was identical with the Father or equal to Him, only that he had at some point become divine. Arius himself had argued that Jesus was "God, but not true God."[76]

Similarly, to say that Christ was the *Logos* or Word of God (a reference to John, 1:1: "In the beginning was the Word, and the Word was with God, and the Word was God"), or that God created the world "through him," could be meant either literally or metaphorically. To say that Jesus was literally God's Word or creative power would mean that he was an aspect or activity of God. But this interpretation, in Arius's view, would deprive him of his separate existence and humanity; the human Son would disappear completely into the divine Father. For this reason Arius argued that Jesus was God's "Word" metaphorically, not literally, and that any supernatural powers bestowed upon him were powers granted by the Father to the Son, that is, by a superior to a subordinate.[77]

Not even the doctrine, popular in the East, that the Son was begotten before time began disturbed the Arians, since Jesus' "preexistence" proved that he was chosen to play a special role in cosmic history, not that he was God's equal. And one phrase in Eusebius's creed, "first-begotten of all creation," seemed to imply that, however unique Jesus may have been, he was part of the created order rather than part of the Creator.

For Hosius and the anti-Arians, therefore, the problem was how to devise a statement of faith that the "subordinationists" could not interpret in their own way and sign. The answer, so they thought, was to be found in one Greek word—perhaps the most important nonbiblical word in Christian history—*homoousios. Ousia* is usually translated as "essence" or "substance"; *homo* means "the same." If a creed were to declare that

Jesus Christ and God were *homo-ousios,* meaning that they were essentially the same, the hard-line Arians could not sign it in good conscience. And, it would have the additional advantage of being consistent with the idea that the Father and Son were different in some ways, even though they shared a basic identity.

Constantine may not have understood, however, that many bishops would consider the word a provocation. *Homoousios* had been kicking around Eastern theological circles for some time, but most churchmen did not like it, since it was a Greek philosophical term not found anywhere in Scripture. More important, it had been associated with the heresy of Sabellius: the idea that Jesus Christ was an aspect or activity of God lacking any real existence of his own. Shortly after the council began its discussion of Arius's ideas, a letter written by Eusebius of Nicomedia, leader of the Arian party, was read aloud to the bishops. It is not clear whether Eusebius delivered this statement himself or whether (which seems more likely) it contained some injudicious language, and was therefore "leaked" by the anti-Arians to embarrass him. If Eustathius of Antioch is to be believed, it was a bombshell that "produced among its audience a restless sensation of shock and earned indelible shame for its author."[78]

The letter itself has disappeared. Eustathius, a passionate anti-Arian, may well have exaggerated its effect. But other observers testify that the document was torn into pieces in the presence of all the bishops as an expression of their disapproval. According to Bishop Ambrose (later St. Ambrose) of Milan, one passage in the letter mentioned *homoousios* scoffingly, in order to show how ludicrous it was to equate the Son with the Father: Imagine! Some fools maintain that Jesus Christ, the Son of Man, and the omnipotent, unknowable Creator are made out of the same essential stuff. Did God somehow divide his own substance to make a Son? And, if so, how many more "Gods" might he produce by further division? No idea could be more absurd!

This rhetoric (or something like it) gave Alexander and Athanasius the weapon they were looking for. *Homoousios*—the "absurdity"—would become a test of faith and a method of smoking out those unable to accept Jesus' identity with God. Somehow, Constantine was brought to accept this strategy and to insist that Eusebius of Caesarea add it to his creed.[79] Very likely, the anti-Arians expected that he would refuse: an act of disobedience that would offend the emperor and, very likely, result in Eusebius's deposition and exile. To their consternation, the bishop willingly accepted the amendment and was accepted back into the fold.

WHY DID Eusebius agree to accept the *homoousios*? Certainly, the pressure exerted by Constantine had something to do with his decision. But another factor was in play: the key word was ambiguous. Though Hosius and Alexander went to great length to draft a document that would expose and isolate the Arians, their effort fell afoul of the fact that there are no truly unambiguous words. After Nicaea the term itself would become a cause of conflict, with some bishops of the anti-Arian party rejecting it and some Arian leaders accepting it. As one expert has remarked, "There were few words in Greek susceptible of so many and so confusing shades of meaning as *ousia*."[80]

Homoousios could mean "of the same essence," but it could also mean of the same "substance," "reality," "being," or even "type." The great Platonic philosopher, Porphyry, had written that the souls of humans and animals were *homoousios* (of the same general type).[81] If this was the meaning of the word as used at Nicaea, any Arian could accept it, since the Arians agreed that both God and Jesus were divine, although in different ways. An extreme Arian might even argue (although at this point none did) that human beings made in God's image are *homoousios* with Him. In any case, by accepting the amendment, Eusebius put his enemies temporarily in check. They suspected that he was interpreting the word in an unorthodox fashion, but they could hardly accuse him of heresy without questioning Constantine's judgment.[82]

When it came to drafting the final document that would become an agreed-upon test of faith, the anti-Arians tried to eliminate this ambiguity. The Nicene Creed[83] described Jesus Christ as

> the Son of God, begotten from the Father, only-begotten, that is, from the *ousia* of the Father, God from God, light from light, true God from true God, begotten not made, *homoousios* with the Father, through Whom all things came into being.[84]

The declaration that the Son is "true God from true God" was a response to Arius's assertion that Jesus was divine but not identical to the Creator. "Begotten not made" was intended to counter the view that Christ was created like other creatures of God. Finally, the Creed went on to condemn certain of Arius's specific teachings:

> But as for those who say, There was when He was not, and, Before being born He was not, and that He came into existence out of nothing, or who assert that the Son of God is of a different *hypostasis* or substance, or is subject to alteration or change—these the Catholic and apostolic Church anathematizes.[85]

The presentation of this document to the bishops caused them considerable discomfort. The hard-core Arians opposed it for obvious reasons, but even those less committed to subordinationism found the document's language novel and, in some ways, suspect. *Homoousios* still bothered them because it seemed to obliterate the distinction between Father and Son, so much so that for twenty years after the council disbanded, Athanasius himself did not consider it politic to use the term in his writing. And to say that Jesus and God were of the same "*hypostasis* [individual being] or substance" smacked of Sabellianism. When asked to sign the creed, Eusabius of Caesarea and other bishops therefore demanded further explanations of each of the phrases used in it. The anti-Arians attempted to respond in their own way, but Constantine muddied the water by offering several interpretations of his own, which were not particularly useful.

By mid-June it was obvious to Hosius that, whatever their differences of interpretation, the vast majority of bishops were willing to subscribe to the creed. He therefore read it aloud before the assemblage, declaring that it represented the position of the Holy and Apostolic Church. Constantine then sent court officials to each bishop's seat with copies of the document to be signed on the spot. Everyone signed with the exception of two of Arius's most devoted Libyan supporters, whom the emperor immediately sent into exile along with Arius and several priests. The signators included all the other Arians present, including the two Eusebiuses, Paulinus of Tyre, and Theognis of Nicaea. According to one ancient historian, the exiled Libyan bishops stopped at the bench of their erstwhile leader, Eusebius of Nicomedia, on their way out of the hall and criticized him bitterly for bowing to the emperor's will.

That there was pressure brought to bear by Constantine is undeniable. The sentences of exile passed on the hard-line Arians demonstrated the consequences of opposing him. Clearly, to the extent that the bishops felt they had signed the creed under duress, they felt justified later on in qualifying and "explaining" (some might say, explaining away) their signatures. Eusebius of Caesarea, for example, wrote a long letter to his congregants explaining that *homoousios* and "begotten, not made" did not mean that Jesus shared God's essence—that he *was* God—but only that he was a unique creation of God. Eusebius of Nicomedia went even further. He explained that while he affirmed the body of the Nicene Creed (interpreted in an Arian sense), he did not accept the anathemas, which were based on misconceptions of Arius's teachings. Whether because of this letter or because Eusebius offered hospitality in Nicomedia to some Arian priests,

Constantine sent him into exile along with Theognis of Nicaea three months after the council concluded its work.

With the Arian party decapitated, one might think that the controversy was effectively ended. On the contrary, within three years, over the vehement protests of the anti-Arians, Arius, Eusebius, and their fellow exiles would be forgiven by Constantine and welcomed back to the Church. Eusebius would become Constantine's closest advisor, and would insist that Athanasius, now bishop of Alexandria, readmit Arius to communion in that city as well. A decade after that, with Bishop Athanasius himself in exile, Arianism would be well on the way to becoming the dominant theology of the Eastern Empire.

THE COUNCIL of Nicaea remained in session for more than a month after Arius and his followers were expelled. Having established a basis for doctrinal unity in the Church (so they thought), Constantine and the leading bishops turned their attention to the problem of unifying it administratively. What they failed to understand was that efforts to make administration more uniform and efficient might inflame the religious struggle, especially if this meant further entanglement of the government in the affairs of the faithful. And to the extent that a consensus on basic theological issues had not been reached, continued religious conflict would play havoc with well-intentioned administrative reforms.

The need for reform seemed obvious. A Church emerging from decades of persecution was obviously ill suited to participate in the governance of the empire. From the emperor's perspective (which most bishops shared), the situation was dangerously chaotic. There was, of course, no single church official—no pope—with plenary authority over the Church, nor was one desired. Metropolitan bishops were generally assumed to have power over the clergy within their realms, but the extent

of their authority was unclear. Schismatic groups like the Melitians of Egypt thumbed their noses at the mainstream clergy.
Bishops, priests, and deacons moved virtually at will from
church to church and diocese to diocese. Each province func-
tioned in many ways like a separate Church, so that (as the Arian
conflict demonstrated) priests excommunicated in one province
might be asked to celebrate Mass in another.

Furthermore, the processes of ordaining or appointing clergymen were irregular and the qualifications for priestly or episcopal office vague and variable. The results were sometimes
scandalous, as when men known to be financially or sexually
corrupt were ordained priests and elected bishops. But even
when the clergy were well qualified and respected, each diocese
went its own way. In one jurisdiction, married priests were left in
peace; in another, they were compelled to separate from their
wives. Here, confessed adulterers were readmitted to communion after a short penance; there, the penances were long and
arduous. Not even the schedule of festivals was uniform. In
some places, Easter was celebrated on the Sunday after the Jewish Passover, while in others different calculations were used to
set the date of the holiday.

To Constantine this sort of diversity was intolerable. Compared with the Christian clergy, the pagan priesthood was a
model of good organization. Imagine setting Christian holidays
according to the Jewish calendar! The Church must break decisively with both paganism and Judaism and put its own house in
order.

Most bishops agreed. They adopted twenty canons or rules
of law governing the organization of the Church and the behavior of the clergy. They also attempted to deal with the Melitians
and other rigorist groups forged in the cauldron of persecution.
And they tried to set a uniform date for the celebration of Easter.
But without consensus—an underlying general agreement on
fundamental religious and political issues—legal rules tend to

become weapons in the hands of opposed groups. For this reason virtually every rule adopted at Nicaea, no matter how commonsensical and apparently neutral, became a cause of conflict rather than a method of resolving it.

Several of the Nicene canons grew directly out of the bishops' experiences in the Arian controversy. For example, the clergy were strictly forbidden to welcome into communion Christians excommunicated by the bishops of another province (as Eusebius of Nicomedia had done in the case of the Arians). The difficulty is that rules like this assumed a certain minimum agreement on the definitions of heresy and orthodoxy. What if "heretical" clergy seized control of a province and excommunicated "orthodox" bishops and priests there? Those in other provinces defining themselves as orthodox could hardly be expected to close their hearts and churches to their "persecuted" brethren. (This is exactly what happened several years later in the case of Bishop Athanasius, who was excommunicated by a pro-Arian synod. In this case, the bishop who welcomed Athanasius to communion was the pope of Rome, and his assertion of the right to overrule a council of bishops ignited a fatal conflict between the Eastern and Western churches.)

Other rules more loosely tied to the Arian conflict were no less productive of discord. Among other things, the council affirmed the authority of the "superbishops" of Alexandria, Rome, and Antioch over all other clergymen in their domains, prohibited ambitious churchmen from moving from church to church and see to see, and adopted a uniform procedure for the ordination of bishops. Considering that the position of bishop had now become enormously powerful—bishops were the highest-ranking Church officials and their councils the Church's chief rule-making bodies—the last regulation was particularly explosive. It provided that all the bishops of a province acting together should elect new bishops. If this proved impractical, however, three bishops could elect with the consent of their absent brethren and the metropolitan bishop.

Again, the rule seemed rational . . . so long as one assumed that responsible churchmen would not try to abuse it in the heat of conflict. But imagine a hotly disputed contest, say, to choose a successor to a deceased metropolitan bishop. What if a controversial candidate were to secure election in secret by three bishops, and then, with other bishops objecting, claim the consent of the rest? What if several candidates, bitterly opposed on questions of doctrine, were to claim to have been legitimately elected? Unfortunately for the peace of the Church, these questions did not long remain hypothetical.

Driven by its quest for order and unity, the Nicene council also took direct steps to deal with the Melitians, who continued to resist the authority of the bishop of Alexandria. The Coptic followers of the heroic Bishop Melitius thought of themselves as purer than the official clergy and continued to function, to some extent, as a separate church. Constantine considered such schisms intolerable, but in order to avoid driving the dissidents into open revolt, he took a more conciliatory line with them than he had with the North African Donatists. The council ruled that Melitius should remain a bishop, but without the power to ordain priests outside his city. The priests he had already ordained would remain priests, but they must not seek promotion or act independently without Bishop Alexander's permission. Not surprisingly, these measures of "soft repression" failed to bring the Melitians under control. A few years hence, they would ally themselves with the Arians in an all-out campaign to rid themselves of their Alexandrian oppressors.

A look into the future, then, shows us Nicaea as a watershed. While it looks forward to the ultimate resolution of the Arian controversy from the Catholic point of view—the identification of Jesus Christ as God—it also represents the last point at which Christians with strongly opposed theological views acted civilly towards each other. When the controversy began, Arius and his opponents were inclined to treat each other as fellow Christians with mistaken ideas. Constantine hoped that his Great and Holy

Council would bring the opposing sides together on the basis of a mutual recognition and correction of erroneous ideas. When these hopes were shattered and the conflict continued to spread, the adversaries were drawn to attack each other not as colleagues in error but as unrepentant sinners: corrupt, malicious, even satanic individuals.

From bad Christian to anti-Christian was a long step to take, since all men were considered sinners, even those baptized in Christ. The bishops at Nicaea did not go this far, although they considered Arius not only mistaken but obstinate. Still, others might. Alexander and Athanasius had already compared the Arians to those who had crucified Christ and divided his garments between them. From anti-Christian to agent of the devil would prove a shorter step, and one pregnant with violence.

Constantine had appeared at the council in the role of peacemaker. His decision to enforce what he took to be a theological consensus by exiling Arius, however, meant that the victors in religious disputes might now use the power of the Roman state against their enemies. This was a lesson that all parties to the conflict, including the Arians, were quick to learn.

Five

Sins of the Body,
Passions of the Mind

Before the bishops left Nicaea, Constantine provided an entertainment that none of them would soon forget. The occasion, celebrated on July 25, 325, was the emperor's twentieth year as Augustus: the traditional *vicennalia*. To celebrate both this anniversary and the conclusion of the Great Council, he invited all the participants to dine with him at the palace, an experience Eusebius of Caesarea ecstatically compared to the disciples meeting in heaven with Christ![86]

Constantine praised the bishops and honored them, told them about his conversion experiences, and gave them gifts. He removed all doubt about his commitment to advance the cause of Christianity throughout the empire and sent them home with advice to maintain the cooperative and peaceful spirit of Nicaea. The emperor clearly believed that the decisions of all the bishops meeting together in council were from God. As he wrote the Alexandrians soon afterward, "We have received from divine Providence the blessing of being freed from all error, and united in the acknowledgement of one and the same faith. The devil will no longer have any power over us." In the same letter, he described himself humbly as the Christians' "fellow servant," who at Nicaea "undertook the investigation of the truth."[87]

Oddly enough, however, it was Constantine's own need for peace and concord, almost certainly heightened by a shattering personal experience of his own, that helped undo the Nicaean settlement.

Constantine's eldest son was a muscular man in his mid-thirties named Crispus. His mother, Minervina, a woman of obscure background, was the emperor's first wife . . . or, perhaps, his consort, since it is not clear that he actually married her. In any case, the young prince, now governing the West as Constantine's Caesar from his headquarters at Trier, was clearly a prospect to succeed his father as emperor. To the qualifications of birth and administrative experience he added superior military skill. His decisive action in the Bosporus Straits during the recent civil war had destroyed Licinius's fleet and made possible Constantine's crucial victory at Byzantium.

Crispus's mother, however, was no longer Constantine's wife or companion. In 307, shortly after being acclaimed Augustus by his deceased father's troops, Constantine had divorced or abandoned Minervina in order to marry a young noblewoman named Fausta. This was a political marriage; Fausta was the sister of his temporary ally, Maxentius, whom he later defeated at the Battle of the Milvian Bridge. Whether she and Constantine came to love each other is unknown, but she remained with him at the imperial court and bore him three sons. Whatever the nature of the relationship, his conduct toward her was impeccable. The emperor believed strongly in the Roman ideal of the virtuous marriage—a belief that became tinged with fanaticism when he became a Christian.

Among Constantine's first decrees as ruler of a united empire were a series of draconian rules against rape, adultery, elopement, and female "impurity." Among other things, the new laws provided that guardians who seduced their wards should be deported and have their property confiscated, that a girl who eloped should be executed with her suitor, and that a servant who helped her elope should have molten lead poured down his or her throat. The rules treated women more harshly than men; one of their obvious purposes was to maintain the system of male domination. But male impurity was not spared, either. Men convicted of rape were to be burned alive without possibility of appeal. Adulterers were to be exiled. Married men were forbidden to keep concubines, and other forms of sexual misbehavior became punishable offenses, some meriting the death penalty.[88]

These laws were soon to strike home in a most unexpected fashion. When the Council of Nicaea ended, Constantine went to New Rome (Constantinople) to observe the progress of construction at his new capital. Then he traveled westward with other members of the court, including Fausta and Bishop Hosius. Early in the year 326, someone—it is not clear who—approached him with a series of devastating accusations against his eldest son. The specific charges were never revealed, but Crispus was accused of unpardonable sexual offenses. A tradition has it either that Fausta herself or someone acting at her instigation made the accusations. Their substance, the story goes, was that Crispus had fallen in love with his stepmother and had attempted to seduce her. Then, when she rejected his advances, he attempted to rape her.

Fausta had a motive to bring such charges, since eliminating Crispus would clear the road for her sons to succeed Constantine. The truth of the matter will probably never be discovered, but what is known is that Constantine sat in judgment on Crispus's case himself and found the evidence convincing. Unhesitatingly—maddened, perhaps, by this betrayal—he sentenced his son to death. Crispus was executed immediately after the trial at the royal estate at Pola, Italy. At around the same time, the emperor tried the apparently related case of a young Roman aristocrat, Ceionius Rufius Albinus, who was accused of adultery and black magic, convicted him, and sent him into permanent exile.

Still, Constantine's agony was not ended. In July he arrived in Rome, only to be confronted by his mother, the devout Helena, who had become a symbol of Christian piety throughout the empire. Dressed in mourning, she accused him of executing her grandson hastily on false evidence. Evidently, she offered evidence that Fausta had masterminded the plot in order to rid her sons of their leading rival for the succession. One can only imagine the scene that must have then ensued between Constantine and his wife, but the outcome is well attested. Fausta visited the steam room of the baths at the imperial palace and asphyxiated in the overheated air. She is generally believed to have suicided to avoid the executioner, but some have pictured her being hurled into the scalding steam by Constantine's agents, the doors held fast against her escape.

Not long after this, Bishop Hosius requested permission to leave Constantine's court in order to return to his see in Spain. The departure may have been prearranged, but one suspects that it was a response to the horrors the bishop had witnessed. Constantine granted the request, although it deprived him (and the anti-Arian cause) of a skilled advisor. Then he acceded to his mother's petition that she be allowed to make a pilgrimage to the Holy Land.

Whether or not Helena's pilgrimage was meant as a voyage of repentance or a method of distracting attention from the disaster and emphasizing the imperial family's piety, it had a salutary effect among Christians.[89] On her trip to Palestine the eighty-year-old matriarch made innumerable benefactions, founded churches in Bethlehem and Jerusalem (the churches of the Nativity and the Holy Sepulchre), released prisoners from the jails and mines, and sent exiles home. Legends about her good works began to sprout almost immediately; it was said, for example, that she had discovered pieces of the True Cross in Jerusalem and healed the sick. Not long after arriving back at the imperial court in Nicomedia, she died peacefully in her son's presence, ending the most difficult months of his reign.

Sex and politics have always made a potent combination, but the mixture was particularly explosive in the fourth century, when the empire became Christian and politics were saturated with the fumes of religious passion. Roman subjects were accustomed to hear of sexual hijinks and tragedies among members of the imperial elite; at court, matters of state were often family matters. But the ruling class now included bishops and other zealous Christians dedicated to—or obsessed with—ideals of sexual purity. Almost inevitably, disputes over religious issues took on a sexual cast. It was not enough to call one's opponent a bad Christian or a heretic; he must also be a seducer, a rapist, or a frequenter of prostitutes. This tendency to sexualize conflicts added an intensity (and potential for violence) that made them even more difficult to resolve.

The followers of Jesus were not the only people interested in a new sexual morality. Even among the pagans adultery and concubinage had fallen into disfavor, and female virginity was highly prized.[90] Christians, however, were particularly attracted to the heroic ideal of sexual renunciation suggested by Jesus' blessing of those "who have made themselves eunuchs for the sake of the kingdom of heaven."[91] Some zealots took this injunction literally, so much so that the bishops at Nicaea felt compelled to declare that men who had had themselves castrated should be disqualified from becoming priests. Voluntary castration was not acceptable (even though the great Origen had reportedly undergone the operation), but celibacy as practiced by ascetics like the Egyptian monk, Antony, was greatly admired. Wrote Eusebius of Caesarea:

> Two ways of life were thus given by the Lord to His Church. The one is above nature, and beyond common human living; it admits not marriage, child-bearing, property nor the possession of wealth. . . . Like some celestial beings, these [celibates] gaze down upon human life, performing the duty of a priesthood to Almighty God for the whole race.[92]

Similarly, a practice had grown up of dedicating female virgins to the Church. Widows were expected to remain continent, and lifelong virginity was considered a holy state. "Christian marriage"—marriage without sexual intercourse—was also valued. Yet clergymen were not expected to remain celibate. Priests usually married; it was commonly said that a priest's son should follow in his father's footsteps and train for the clergy. The Council of Nicaea ruled that, to avoid scandal, unmarried clergymen should not keep women other than close blood relatives in their houses, but a story dramatizes how that council stopped short of requiring that priests practice "Christian marriage." The Egyptian ascetic, Paphnutius, who had lost one eye in the Great Persecution, is said to have appeared before the bishops at a critical point in the discussion, "roaring at the top of his voice" that celibacy was impossible for most men and women, and that the council should not impose unnatural burdens on the clergy.[93]

Celibacy *was* recommended for bishops, but many bishops were also married. In one celebrated case, a Libyan priest nominated to be bishop of Ptolemaïs told the bishop of Alexandria that he would not accept unless he could continue to have intercourse with his wife. "I shall not be separated from her," he wrote, "nor shall I associate with her surreptitiously like an adulterer . . . I desire and pray to have virtuous children."[94] (Evidently, his request was granted.) This uncertainty about the sexual code applicable to the clergy reflected a more general ambiguity that troubled ordinary Christians as well. What did it mean to live as a righteous Christian in postpagan society? Was the desire of older men for beautiful boys, for example, which had long been recognized as natural and acceptable, now to be considered a sin? And, if so, how could one purify oneself of such desires?

The origins of this craving for sexual purity remain, in part, mysterious. One writer has written persuasively about the efforts of the Desert Fathers to develop "singleness of heart," to open themselves completely to possession by God by subjugating their desires to the point of ridding themselves even of sexual fantasies.[95] This all-out asceticism was an extreme example of a more general drive among Christians to transform and improve themselves in imitation of Jesus Christ. The second-century bishop, Clement of Alexandria, expressed this ideal in extreme terms:

> The human ideal of continence, I mean that which is set forth by the Greek philosophers, teaches one to resist passion, so as not to be made subservient to it, and to train the instincts to pursue rational goals.

But, he continued, "Our [Christian] ideal is not to experience desire at all."[96]

What is striking about this statement is not so much its "puritanism" as its astounding optimism about the human capacity for self-perfection. Like later revolutionary movements, early Christianity saw itself bringing into existence a new type of human being. And the fact that many people experienced this possibility as real, not utopian, suggests that they had begun thinking of their bodies and their moral character as plastic, malleable material to be worked on and shaped, almost as a craftsman or artisan might shape the raw material of his art. There was, in other words, a new sense of the power of the human will to master ancient physical and emotional "necessities"—a feeling that throws into sharp relief the Arian doctrine that Jesus perfected himself by the power of his will rather than because he was God by nature.

This radical optimism is one aspect of the quest for self-transformation. But the focus on mastering sexual desire also suggests that many people in the fourth century felt unclean and in need of purification. One source of this feeling may have been their continued attraction to the temptations offered by a society still imbued with pagan values. Another, less obvious source of shame was their (quite accurate) perception that, as subjects of a tyrannical and endangered empire, they were helpless in the face of overpowering external forces.

We know that the victims of crime, accident, war, and oppression often feel dirtied by the experience of powerlessness.
This is one reason that revolutionary movements in power so
often begin by attempting to purge their societies of "unclean"
practices and thoughts. This sense of shame may be heightened,
furthermore, by the appreciation that one's own passions are far
more unruly than one had thought. Classical civilization and Judaism had long taught that most sexual pleasures were harmless
or good, provided that they were pursued in moderation, under
the regime of reason. With the old order visibly crumbling, however, reason seemed a feeble guide. New attention and concern
focused on the impassioned will, which sometimes seemed as
uncontrollable and destructive as Fate.

Thus, the contradiction: men and women had a new sense of
the power to perfect themselves, but most were unable to exercise it. "The mind," wrote Augustine of Hippo, "orders itself to
will. It would not give the order unless it willed it, yet it does not
obey the order."[97] While Arians tended to emphasize people's
potential to follow the moral example of Jesus, anti-Arians like
St. Augustine focused on their continued self-enslavement,
which implied the need for a Christ who was God. Only God
could liberate His people from the crushing forces of habit and
concupiscence. Only a Christ who was God could forgive them
even if they remained helpless sinners. For both sides in the controversy, sex had become the dominant symbol of the power and
weakness of the human will.

WHILE CONSTANTINE and his court traveled west toward
their appointment with family tragedy, Arius was in exile in Illyria, near the Dalmatian coast, with several of his followers. Euzoius, an Antiochene priest, had gone with him and was
functioning as his chief assistant. Eusebius of Nicomedia, banished from the East, was in Gaul, very likely with Theognis of

Nicaea and a small retinue. There is no record of the exiles' activities during the period immediately following the council, but it is virtually certain that they communicated with each other and with cothinkers throughout the empire, since a coherent campaign to regain Constantine's favor and to undermine the position of the leading anti-Arians began to take shape almost immediately.

The Arian strategy was brilliantly simple, bearing all the hallmarks of Eusebius of Nicomedia's canny political judgment. Constantine wanted harmony in the Church above all else. He was convinced that the Council of Nicaea had been divinely inspired and that its creed could provide the basis for that harmony. Very well, if it was consensus the emperor was looking for, Eusebius and Arius would show him that there was a consensus, but not one based on the idea of Jesus' identity with God. They could demonstrate that their own interpretation of the Nicene Creed, *homoousios* and all, was shared by most of the bishops in the Eastern Empire. And they would offer to live in peace with those churchmen who disagreed with them. Then, if the anti-Arians insisted on excluding them from communion and attacking their colleagues, it would be they who would bear the onus of letting ideological fanaticism and personal animosity stand in the way of Christian unity.

Constantine expected Nicaea to produce peace and unity. If it did not—if the conflict between Arian and anti-Arian parties actually intensified—he would be faced with a difficult choice. Either he could outlaw a much larger number of bishops on one side or the other (most likely the Arians, but one could not be sure), or he could pressure both parties to live together despite their differences. Eusebius was betting that the emperor would choose the more conciliatory path . . . and Constantine might have done so even if he had not been chastened by grief. But the catastrophe of Crispus and Fausta left him longing for peace both in the Church and in his personal life.

By 327 the Arians were ready to mount their campaign for reinstatement in the Church. They were unwittingly assisted by the anti-Arians, who sought to consolidate their apparent victory at Nicaea by denouncing those whose interpretations of the Nicene Creed were, in their view, unorthodox. Eusebius of Caesarea was an obvious target for these hard-liners, since even before leaving Nicaea, he had written his congregation explaining that *homoousios* did not mean that Christ and God were the same or equal, only that their divinity raised them above the created order. Eustathius of Antioch, the anti-Arian bishop whom Hosius had helped install in power at the Council of Antioch, took violent exception to this commentary. In a series of letters and sermons, he angrily denounced the Arians for pretending to adhere to the Nicene Creed when they really intended to subvert its true meaning.

The attack was clearly a tactical error. Not only was Constantine longing for an end to the controversy, but with the departure of Bishop Hosius for Spain, his old friend Eusebius of Caesarea was now the senior Christian leader closest to him. Even so, Eustathius's tirades did not present much opportunity for counterattack until the aggressive bishop made two serious mistakes. First, he presented his own theology, which he insisted was a model of orthodoxy, as an antidote to Arian subordinationism. Second, although the matter remains somewhat murky, he may have made himself vulnerable to charges of sexual impropriety.

Of the two errors, the theological was the more serious. The problem that neither side in the controversy had yet grasped was this: whoever presented a detailed explanation of the relationship of the Father to the Son could fairly easily be accused of heresy. This is because it was difficult, perhaps impossibly so, to describe Jesus' relationship to God in a way that did not seem either to deny his humanity (the Sabellian heresy) or to question his divinity (extreme Arianism). The real root of the difficulty was that Judeo-Christian monotheism posited an infinitely powerful, mysterious, single God who had created not only the world of people and things, but time and space itself.[98] If Christ was actually this God, the human element in him seemed to dwindle into insignificance. But if he was other than God, then, unless one conceived of him as some sort of angel, he would be seen primarily as a man.

For the parties in the Arian controversy, the result was to privilege negative statements and punish affirmative ones. While it was safe to criticize an opponent's ideas, presenting one's own theology in any detail was dangerous. Arius had paid the price of speaking too clearly in *The Banquet,* in which he seemed to imply that Jesus was essentially a creature like other creatures. Eustathius of Antioch exemplified the opposite danger, for he insisted that *homoousios* meant Christ and God were one and the same "individual reality" or "person" (*hypostasis*).[99] One of the anathemas of the Nicene Creed said virtually the same thing, but this still made it seem that Jesus was merely an attribute or activity of God. On this point most of the Eastern bishops were inclined to accept the Arian view, which was that while the Father and the Son were "in agreement" on everything, they were two distinct realities that could not and should not be merged.[100]

Eustathius tried to defend himself against the charge of Sabellianism by arguing that Christ had a human nature, too, but he insisted passionately (and confusingly) that the two natures were entirely separate and different. God Himself, he argued, could not have suffered on the Cross. Therefore, when Jesus declared, "the Father is greater than I," when he maintained that "the Father only" and "not the Son" knows the date of the Last Judgment, and when he said, "Why do you call me good? No one is good but God alone" (all Arian "proof texts"), it was Jesus the man talking, not Jesus the Son of God.[101] This was a brave attempt to formulate a doctrine of Christ's dual nature, but the result was to turn Jesus into a kind of schizoid creature: a fallible, vulnerable human personality attached (but how?) to an omniscient, omnipotent, timeless God personality. This doctrine would not provide much protection against a determined Arian assault.

Fewer than two years after the Council of Nicaea completed its work, the Arians began their counterattack. In 327 Eusebius of Caesarea managed to convene a council of bishops to investigate charges of heresy and misbehavior in office brought against Eustathius by dissidents in Antioch, his own see. Constantine very likely compelled Eustathius to attend the council; otherwise, he should have had the power to prevent it from meeting. In any case, under Eusebius's leadership, the assembled churchmen had little trouble convicting Eustathius of Sabellianism and immoral conduct, excommunicating him, and deposing him from office. Six other bishops in the region with similar views suffered the same fate. Constantine reviewed their cases and examined Eustathius in person before sending him into exile in Illyria. The bishops then appointed Paulinus of Tyre, a known Arian sympathizer, to be the next bishop of Antioch.

While his interpretation of Jesus' true nature was of primary importance, the charges of immoral behavior against Eustathius were not insignificant. One commentator, while conceding that the charges may have been "exaggerated or partly invented," considers them more important than the accusation of heresy.[102] Apparently, they included allegations that Eustathius had an illicit sexual relationship with a woman not his wife, and that he had insulted the emperor's mother while she was on pilgrimage in the East.[103] This was the first appearance of such accusations in the Arian controversy, but hardly the last. Charges of corruption would now become a regular feature of the conflict, further escalating the struggle by giving it the character of a series of personal feuds.

Were these charges exaggerated? Very likely. Invented or faked? Not necessarily. Often there was some basis for charging bishops with corruption. This is not because fourth-century church leaders were particularly corrupt or venal men, but because standards of ethical behavior themselves were in flux . . . and riddled with contradictions. As I noted earlier, the issue of priestly celibacy was unsettled. If Eustathius kept a mistress, as was alleged, that would clearly be misconduct, but many priests and bishops were married. Presumably, some had courted their wives before marrying them. Any priest involved with a woman, however chastely, might therefore run the risk of being charged with apparent sexual misconduct. This is why the Council of Nicaea had ordered clergymen to get women other than their mothers and sisters out of their houses, but it is unlikely that this canon was much heeded or enforced.

Equally important, Christian bishops, while expected to be pure and peaceful men, were now among the most powerful political figures in the empire. The contradictions between the ideals of behavior represented by Jesus Christ's life and the requirements for holding office in the fourth-century Church were agonizing. The bishops' worldly duties and ambitions often involved them in political intrigue, financial chicanery, abuse of legal processes, and sheer thuggery against their opponents—all of which might generate charges to be used against them by political or doctrinal enemies. Moreover, since they were now servants of the emperor, churchmen like Eustathius could be accused of *lèse majesté* (insulting the sovereign, in this case, Constantine's mother), or worse. Soon, bishops on both sides of the Arian controversy would be defending themselves against charges of outright treason.

Constantine, however, wanted peace—and he was in a forgiving, paternal mood. As soon as the Council of Antioch had completed its work, Arius and the priest Euzoius wrote to Nicomedia asking for an audience. They expressed their desire to be readmitted to communion with other Christians and assured the emperor that he and the bishops would find their theological views acceptable. Constantine wrote back reminding them gently that they might have ended their exile earlier by being less stubborn. He ordered them to come to Nicomedia and received them in court in November 327.

With a man like Constantine, the personal was most certainly the political. On the one hand, he was the most powerful ruler in the world. On the other, he governed largely through force of personality, and the society of elite activists through which he ruled was relatively small and familiar. Travel by sea was fairly easy, and the important civil officials, army officers, businessmen, and church leaders knew each other well enough to have contracted strong friendships and enmities. A formal audience with the emperor might be framed by ritual, but at its heart was an emotional exchange. Constantine, who considered himself an acute judge of character, was often swayed by the apparent sincerity, intelligence, and depth of feeling of someone seeking his favor. If Arius, for example, seemed sincerely repentant and desirous of living at peace with his brother priests, Constantine might not worry that his views were somewhat at variance with the Nicene Creed.

Arius must have been a persuasive man. Notwithstanding the scurrilous labels bestowed upon him by his enemies ("heretic" was among the mildest of them), his devotion to Christ and the Church was genuine, as was his desire to live at peace with other Christians, even if he and they differed in matters of doctrine. When he and Euzoius came to court, Constantine heard them out and expressed his willingness to help them return to their posts in Alexandria, provided that they produce a written creed demonstrating their orthodoxy. The two men presented a document reminiscent of Eusebius of Caesarea's original creed; it affirmed their belief in Christ's divinity without using the word *homoousios*. Constantine found it acceptable, but only a Church council could overturn the decisions of another council. He therefore summoned a large group of bishops to Nicomedia to rule on the matter.

The Council of Nicomedia met early in 328.[104] The bishops studied Arius's creed, questioned him and Euzoius personally, and pronounced their views orthodox. They then solemnly readmitted the two men to communion. Arius, ecstatic, pledged to help the emperor bring peace to the Church. Constantine immediately wrote Bishop Alexander requesting that he be allowed to return to his city and his church. Meanwhile, as soon as the council's decision was made public, Eusebius of Nicomedia and Theognis of Nicaea filed petitions of their own for reinstatement. They agreed to accept the Nicene Creed in toto, including the *homoousios* (which, of course, they interpreted in a restrictive Arian fashion). Again, the council ruled their views orthodox, and again, Constantine ordered them restored to their positions. The anti-Arian bishops of Nicomedia and Nicaea were quickly dismissed and replaced by the exiles.

Little more than two years after the Council of Nicaea ended, its most significant practical decisions were thus overturned. The Arian movement not only recovered the crucial sees of Antioch and Nicomedia, but, in the person of Eusebius of Nicomedia, soon to become bishop of Constantinople, it regained its principal political leader. A few years later, Arius's most vehement opponent, Bishop Marcellus of Ancyra, would be excommunicated and deposed on charges of heresy similar to those brought against Eustathius of Antioch. Constantine's desire for peace in the Church had a great deal to do with the success of this counterattack, but so did the theological instincts of the Eastern bishops.

In the East, most churchmen were inclined to put some distance between the Father and the Son and to shy away from the *homoousios*. While glorifying Christ, they would rather affirm God's incomprehensible majesty and Jesus' usefulness as a model for humanity than identify Jesus as God. The return of the Arians was not just a product of clever maneuvering by Eusebius and Arius; it was an indication that the apparent consensus reached at the Council of Nicaea was, in large part, an illusion produced by the bishops' desire to please the emperor and to restore the unity of the Church. There were lessons to be drawn from this experience, but few had learned them. Consensus cannot be created by verbal formulas. Serious disputes are seldom resolved without a genuine change in the parties' thinking. And a false consensus may be more productive of conflict than an honest disagreement.

THE ARIAN MOVEMENT was riding high. For Arius himself, however, things were not going so well. Despite Constantine's blandishments, Bishop Alexander refused to permit him to return to Alexandria, arguing that there could be no place in the Church for unrepentant heretics. In 328, Constantine dispatched another letter to Alexander, insisting that Arius's views were now acceptable to the great majority of bishops and demanding that the Alexandrian church adhere to the decisions of the Council of Nicomedia. At this point, Alexander sent Athanasius to the capital to plead his case, but in April, while his protégé was in Nicomedia, the old man died, and the bishops of Egypt hastened to Alexandria to elect a new metropolitan bishop. Athanasius, whom Alexander had reportedly named as his successor, cut his trip short and rushed back to campaign for the position.

Only in hindsight can one recognize the pivotal significance of this moment. With the return of Athanasius to Alexandria, the history of the Arian controversy, and, with it, the history of the Catholic Church, takes a new turn. For if Constantine thought that Alexander was a stubborn "servant," he can never have met Athanasius. The redheaded deacon was one of the fourth century's "new men": a person who came of age after the Great Persecution had ended; whose parents were very likely pagans, but whose education was Christian, not classical; whose ambition was boundless; and who was very much at home in the "real" world of power relations and political skulduggery. For a similar combination of theoretical acumen, dogged adherence to principle, and political ruthlessness, one would have to await the advent of Martin Luther, John Calvin, and Vladimir Lenin.

Athanasius would soon be recognized as the anti-Arians' champion. But first, he had to become bishop of Alexandria—not an easy task for a man of about thirty. His age, in fact, was a source of dispute almost from the moment he was elected, since the rule that bishops should be at least thirty years old was one of the Church's few clearly established norms. Birth records were not well kept in those days, especially if the subject was of obscure parentage. Writers sympathetic to Athanasius generally date his birth to the years 295 or 296, which would have made him thirty-two or thirty-three when Alexander died. But he may well have been born as late as 299, in which case he would have been not quite thirty when the position for which he had been groomed suddenly became vacant.

Qualified by age or not, Athanasius sailed by fast ship to Alexandria, where more than fifty bishops were conferring day and night in an effort to elect a new metropolitan bishop. What happened after his return remains obscure, but more than one month elapsed while the debate continued. There is some evidence that the group meeting in Alexandria included both Melitians and bishops ordained by Alexander, and that they were seeking a candidate of whom both groups could approve.[105] The purist Melitians, formed when Bishop Peter fled Alexandria during the Great Persecution, were still a large and active faction in the Egyptian church. They may have objected to Athanasius because of his close identification with Alexander and his reputation for political roughness. Even some of the bishops loyal to Alexander may have disapproved of his youth and brashness.

Brashness, however, would carry the day. A widely accepted story has it that, losing patience with the assembled bishops, Athanasius convinced a few of them to go with him to the

Church of Dionysius and consecrate him bishop behind closed doors. (The Council of Nicaea had designated three bishops as the minimum number who could consecrate, provided that the candidate also received the written consent of the other bishops.) Using his considerable political influence, he then procured a decree of the Alexandria City Council characterizing his election as the people's choice, and sent it to Constantine with a letter alleging that he had received the consent of the Alexandrian bishops.

Constantine wished to avoid the kind of instability that was now plaguing several cities because of contests for vacant bishoprics. He may also have recognized Athanasius as a man of unusual talent and as Alexander's legitimate heir. In any case, he accepted Athanasius's claim without further investigation and wrote the city officially approving his appointment. But the emperor was mistaken if he thought that this would bring peace to the city. While the new bishop embarked on a tour of his domains, reorganizing the Egyptian clergy so as to put his own supporters in key positions, his opponents proceeded to elect a new metropolitan bishop of their own.

After a brief period of quiet, the Melitian bishops returned to their old habits, which seem to have included holding unauthorized church services and ordaining clergymen without Athanasius's consent. His response was to send gangs of thuggish supporters into the (mainly Coptic speaking) Melitian districts, where they beat and wounded supporters of the Melitian leader, John Arcaph, and, according to Arcaph, burned churches, destroyed church property, imprisoned and even murdered dissident priests.[106] These acts, and others like them, would haunt Athanasius's career for years to come. One writer sums up his style of governing as follows:

> In Alexandria itself, he maintained the popular support which he enjoyed from the outset and buttressed his position by organizing an ecclesiastical mafia. In later years, if he so desired,

he could instigate a riot or prevent the orderly administration of the city. Athanasius possessed a power independent of the emperor which he built up and perpetuated by violence. That was both the strength and the weakness of his position. Like a modern gangster, he evoked widespread mistrust, proclaimed total innocence—and usually succeeded in evading conviction on specific charges.[107]

On his return to Alexandria, Athanasius found himself confronted by a dual challenge. Not only did the Melitians refuse to accept his authority, but there was a letter from Eusebius of Nicomedia, newly installed as bishop in the imperial capital, requesting that he allow Arius, Euzoius, and their colleagues to return to their churches, as required by the Council of Nicomedia. The messenger who brought the letter may also have informed Athanasius that if he refused the "request," action would be taken by the emperor to depose him. The fledgling bishop, undoubtedly viewing this as a test of his determination, sent the messenger back with a reply refusing the request on the ground that those declared heretics by the Great Council of Nicaea could not be restored by any lesser body.

Eusebius must have then referred the matter to Constantine, for the next letter Athanasius received was from the emperor himself. No cause was more important than the peace of the Church, said Constantine. If Athanasius would not accept Arius and his supporters as fellow Christians, he would send an official to Alexandria to expel the bishop from his see. Athanasius waited a short time. Then he sent back a message declaring that, much as he would have liked to please the emperor, he could not comply. There was no place in the Church, he said, for the enemies of Jesus Christ.

Athanasius, the Arians' bitterest adversary, would soon become their chief target. Now the battle lines were drawn, and the struggle began in earnest.

Six

The Broken Chalice

In 330 Constantine dedicated his new capital on the site of ancient Byzantium at the intersection of Europe and Asia. With his eldest son, Constantius, at his side, he solemnly marked out its boundaries before entering the great basilica adjoining the imperial palace for the service of dedication. The emperor named the city New Rome, signifying that it was to be the Christian capital of the empire. He did not object, however, when he overheard people in the street calling it Constantinople: Constantine's City.

The pace of the new construction pleased him, as well it should. To build an appropriately magnificent capital, his master architects had employed thousands of artisans and laborers and tens of thousands of slaves. The city's obelisks, columns, and statuary—even the building blocks used to erect its monumental churches and palaces—had been requisitioned (looted, to be rude) from other cities around the Mediterranean. Whole regions, it is said, were depopulated as citizens migrated to the rising metropolis in search of opportunities for work and social life. The court itself, by now swollen to Oriental proportions, could have populated a small city on its own.

The capital's dominant structure, not quite ready yet for use, was the huge imperial palace overlooking the Bosporus—really, an interconnected series of palaces, courtyards, and office build-

ings designed to house the emperor's family and personal retinue, his household troops, and a horde of administrative officials. The basilica, called the Church of the Holy Apostles, stood
adjacent to the palace. Close by was the Hippodrome, whose
chariot races would soon delight (and often overexcite) the contentious, sports-loving populace.[108] There was some contradiction between the city's expansive inner space and its external
character, which was that of a fortress. The threat of barbarian
invasion, still omnipresent even in these relatively confident
years, dictated its location at a point roughly equidistant from
the Danubian and Persian frontiers. On the sea side lay the
Bosporus Straits, well guarded by the imperial fleet. On the land
side stood a double wall embodying the latest advances in
Roman military architecture—a defensive structure so strong
that a millennium would elapse before it was breached.

Constantinople's true originality, however, lay in the fact that
it was the first great metropolis founded by Christians and dedicated to Christian worship. It announced to the world that the
religion named for a condemned Palestinian rabbi would now
become the state church of Rome. In Constantine's city there
were no altars to Victory, no statues or paintings of gods and
goddesses, indeed, no representations of Jesus, Mary, or the disciples either, since many Christians still adhered to the Jewish
rule forbidding graven images of the holy. Eusebius of Caesarea's
sharp response to a request by the emperor's sister for a picture
of Jesus was already famous. "I do not know what has impelled
you to command that an image of our Savior be drawn," he told
Constantia. The request was senseless, the bishop said, since a
picture of Jesus' divinity would be impossible, and a picture of
him as an ordinary man, irrelevant! [109]

Even in constructing the Christian capital, it seemed, the
controversy over Jesus' nature was inescapable. Further conflict
was on the horizon. With the Arians and their sympathizers now
in control of Antioch, Caesarea, Tyre, and Nicomedia, attention

turned to Alexandria, where Bishop Athanasius was reported to be maintaining power by intimidating and terrorizing his opponents.

In the same year that Constantine dedicated New Rome, Eusebius of Nicomedia, again firmly ensconced in his see, received a delegation of Melitian clergymen from Egypt. Four bishops complained that Bishop Athanasius had sent violent gangs to beat and harass their followers, and that he was refusing to let them worship in their churches notwithstanding that the Council of Nicaea had confirmed their authority to act as Christian priests. Their letters to Constantine had gone unanswered. Therefore, they asked Eusebius, who was known to be in the emperor's favor, to present their petition to him and, if possible, to procure an audience for them at the palace in Nicomedia.

For more than one year, as rumors about Athanasius's violent behavior circulated in the East, Eusebius had waited for such an opportunity. He agreed to help the Melitians on the condition that they recognize Arius as a fellow Christian, even if they did not accept all his ideas. The bishops consented, and Eusebius prepared to put their case before the emperor. At some point in their conversation, one of the Melitians made another complaint that piqued Eusebius's interest. Athanasius, he said, had engaged in financial extortion by compelling the Egyptians to supply linen tunics to the church of Alexandria, and harassing them for money payments when the garments were not supplied.[110] Eusebius advised the Melitians to add the charge to their other allegations against Athanasius. The emperor would probably not be inclined to defend Egyptian "schismatics" against tough measures designed to force them to accept the metropolitan bishop's authority, but he might be less tolerant of corrupt administrative practices.

When informed of these charges, Athanasius sent two senior priests to plead his case before Constantine and left Alexandria, probably traveling to the Theban desert to stay with the monks there. Leaving the city was a judicious precaution when one might be arrested at any time by the emperor's troops. More-over, although many monks were Arians, Athanasius had already begun to develop his own base of support among them. His greatest "catch" was the famous hermit, Antony, who was some-thing close to an Egyptian national hero.[111] Meanwhile, Con-stantine investigated the charges against him. Based on the priests' testimony, he dismissed the accusation of extortion, al-though he ordered Athanasius to stop preventing the Melitians from holding church services.

Several months later, however, an incident occurred that was to cause the embattled bishop far more trouble than any charge of financial misconduct.

Athanasius was traveling in the Mareotis region outside Alexandria with a retinue that included the priest Macarius, one of the men who had defended him in Nicomedia, a trusted fol-lower with a taste for violent action. In that same region of Egypt lived a Coptic-speaking presbyter called Ischyras, a man whose credentials to serve as a priest were somewhat questionable. Is-chyras had been ordained years earlier by Colluthus, a sectarian troublemaker whose authority to act as a bishop was denied by the Alexandrian Church. Apparently in violation of Athanasius's command to stop performing priestly duties, Ischyras was minis-tering to the congregation of a small church. Athanasius dis-patched his henchman, Macarius, to enforce his order. Macarius visited Ischyras and beat him severely. He overturned the altar of his church, broke up the furniture, including a bishop's chair, and smashed a chalice used to celebrate the Eucharist.

Ischyras immediately sent word of his mistreatment to the Melitian bishops in Nicomedia. During the spring and summer of 331, charges against Athanasius continued to multiply. In ad-dition to committing acts of violence and sacrilege (breaking a sacred chalice), someone now swore that he had given a casket of gold to a high court official who was suspected of plotting against the emperor. This was a serious charge, since it would

have implicated him in possibly treasonous activity. The Melitians also renewed their accusation of extortion and added that
Athanasius had been illegally consecrated bishop when he was
not yet thirty years old. Summoned to court by Constantine, he
arrived in Nicomedia in the winter of 331 and met the sovereign
at an imperial palace in a suburb of that city.

Again, Constantine heard each side's case personally. Impressed by the Alexandrian bishop's apparent sincerity, obvious
intelligence, and strength of character, and not inclined to give
the Melitians' testimony much credit, he found the charges un-
proven and sent the Egyptian Church a strong letter criticizing
the Melitians for making trouble. Athanasius, he said, was "truly
a man of God."[112] There is no record showing how Athanasius
defended himself against the accusations of violence and sacrilege, but in writing about the matter later, he did not deny that
Ischyras was beaten or that the chalice was broken with his
knowledge. His defense was that since Ischyras was not a properly ordained priest, the chalice was not a sacred vessel! As one
commentator puts it, "In short, his opponents cry 'Violence and
sacrilege' and Athanasius replies 'No: only violence.'"[113]

Athanasius remained in Nicomedia for several months, suffering from an undisclosed illness. He may have taken the
opportunity to discuss the issue of Christ's divinity with Constantine, for the emperor would shortly write Arius a bitterly
critical letter reflecting his ideas. In any case, when Athanasius
returned to Alexandria in the summer of 332, his position
seemed stronger than ever. The emperor had endorsed his character! In the fall he traveled to Libya, Arius's home territory, to
pressure the clergy in the Five Cities region to reject several pro-
Arian priests who were seeking bishops' positions there. Arius
was also in the area at the time, probably seeking to mobilize
support for his own allies. Athanasius's activities so outraged
him that he wrote a letter to Constantine he would soon have
cause to regret.

Arius had reason to be angry. Four years after Constantine promised to return him to Alexandria and told Athanasius to readmit him—four years after the recalcitrant bishop had declined to obey the Council of Nicomedia's decision and his emperor's direct order—Arius was still exiled, in effect, from his own city, and Athanasius was still oppressing (and sometimes brutalizing) his followers. Intolerable! Arius sent a message to Constantine that has not been preserved, but that apparently reiterated his beliefs, criticized the anti-Arians, and demanded that the emperor enforce the decision of the Council of Nicomedia. If he did not, Arius wrote, he might be forced to order his large following to refuse to recognize the authority of the Alexandrian Church.

The peremptory tone of Arius's letter and its threat of schism sent Constantine into one of his famed paroxysms of rage. He wrote two letters that arrived in Alexandria early in 333, one addressed to Christians everywhere, the second to Arius and his followers. The first branded the priest an enemy of Christianity, ordered his writings burned, and threatened to execute those who disobeyed the order. This recalled the decrees outlawing heretical sects that Constantine had issued when he first became emperor—but, unlike the Arians, the sects originally suppressed, Gnostics, Manicheans, and the like, were almost universally recognized as heterodox. Fortunately for the Arians, Constantine never carried out the threats made in this missive.

The second, more revealing letter is a long, almost hysterical screed, read publicly at the Governor's Palace in Alexandria, which accuses Arius of being an "evil interpreter" and a "replica of the devil": a snake who writes venomous, threatening letters to his sovereign in which he asserts beliefs condemned by the Council of Nicaea. The level of personal attack is so low as to be shocking—until one remembers that Constantine (like many of his contemporaries) turned every heated dispute into a personal feud. Name calling is not at all beneath him. He calls Arius a "dishonest fool," an "impious ninny," and an "empty-headed chatterbox," and goes on to criticize his personal appearance:

> But God exacts vengeance on the criminal who inflicts wounds and scars on his Church. Look at Arius! His wasting and emaciated flesh, his careworn countenance, his thinning hair, the pallor of his visage, his half-dead appearance—all these attest his vapidity and madness. Constantine, "the man of God," has seen through Arius, who has cast himself into utter darkness.[114]

Very likely reflecting Athanasius's influence, Constantine's letter goes on to denounce Arius's "heretical" views, in particular, his insistence that the Son has a different *hypostasis* (individual being or personhood) than the Father. This is evidence, says the emperor, that he must be considered outside the Church, since the Council of Nicaea specifically condemned that belief. He also ridicules Arius's suggestion that to equate Jesus with God lessens God. ("No! I do not wish God to be involved with the suffering of insults," Arius had written. "Whatever you take away from him, in that respect you make him less.")[115] Finally, he threatens to fine Arius's followers and impose onerous public duties on clergymen in communion with him, and concludes by summoning him to court.

Arius did go to Nicomedia, although it is not certain when he made the trip or what, precisely, transpired at his interview with Constantine. We can be fairly sure that he apologized for his intemperate letter, spoke movingly of his own beliefs, and probably called attention to Athanasius's unpriestlike behavior. For by the time he reached the court, new charges had been made against Athanasius—this time involving an alleged murder—and the Eastern bishops, organized by Eusebius of Nicomedia, were moving against him in a more systematic way. Whether because the tide of clerical opinion was turning so strongly against Athanasius or because Arius impressed Constantine with his sincerity and reasonableness, the emperor again forgave him and promised him complete rehabilitation. By 335, he was ready to organize a triumphant reception for the ex-heretic in Constantinople.

To watch Constantine alternate between approval of the two enemies, Arius and Athanasius, gives one the impression of an unstable, vacillating man. The impression is not entirely accurate. True, the emperor was easily moved to anger or affection. He had the freedom of the very powerful to express himself spontaneously, and his emotional attachments could shift quickly depending upon his estimate of an interlocutor's fidelity and sincerity. But the matter goes beyond this. The dispute itself also caused shifts of opinion, because each side seemed to have seized on an indispensable portion of the truth. Many people less volatile than Constantine found themselves drawn first to one side, then the other—or, to end this troubling uncertainty, found themselves violently affirming that one side was in sole possession of sincerity, fidelity, and the truth.

Prior to Athanasius's visit to the capital, the emperor had taken the position that the Arians should be readmitted to the Church because, theological niceties aside, they were Christians at heart. Their subordinationist views were traditional in the East and shared by a great many devout Christians, including a large number of bishops. And they did affirm the divinity of Jesus Christ, the Son of God, begotten before time began, ruling at the Father's right hand in heaven, and destined to come again at the inauguration of His Kingdom. These certainly sounded like Christian beliefs! Why divide the Church so bitterly over a difference of opinion about the relationship between divine Father and divine Son?

Athanasius's answer, later expressed at length in his "Four Discourses Against the Arians,"[116] is that Arianism is fundamentally anti-Christian, since it leads logically either to the conclusion that Christ was a man, which is the Jewish position, or that he is a second God or demigod, which is pure paganism. If Jesus was a creature rather than the Creator, if he was perfect, as the Arians said, by force of will rather than by nature, if he owed his Sonship to "adoption" and his immortality to "promotion" by God, that might make him the holiest man in history, but it would not distinguish him in any essential way from other human beings. He would be a prophet, but still a man. Even if one thought that Jesus was the Messiah, as a few "Jewish Christians" did, he would still be no more than human. Clearly, it would be idolatry to worship a mere man, nor could there be any reason to worship him, seeing that no human being has the power to conquer sin and death.

But suppose one takes the Arians at their word. They claim to believe that Christ is a creature utterly unlike any other—that he is not a mere man but a divinity. This produces two possibilities. One, the Son is a second God equal to the Father. There are many ex-pagans who, in their ignorance, probably believe this. Obviously, the idea is as repulsive to Christians as to Jews. Two Gods? Why just two? If Jesus is a second God, why not declare the Holy Spirit a third? And why stop there? Open the floodgates, and there may be as many Gods as peoples' imaginations can create. Not even the Arians can tolerate this blatant polytheism; that is why they insist that the Father is greater than the Son.

But this subordinationism suggests a second possibility: Jesus is neither God nor man but something in between. The Arians suggest this when they say that Christ is God, but not true God. But what can this mean? If the Savior is some sort of creature intermediary between humanity and God, he must be either a demigod or an angel. Some pagans, misreading the story of the Virgin birth, consider him the child of a god and a human, like Hercules. To Christians, the idea of God fathering Jesus on Mary like Zeus impregnating some human maiden is too disgusting even to contemplate, much less believe. To avoid this im-

plication, the Arians talk about Jesus' creation in entirely abstract terms. But they cannot avoid the fact that the idea of God
producing a demigod offspring is pagan, no matter how the creature was conceived.

The alternative notion that Jesus is an angelic being is not
necessarily pagan, but it produces the same lapse back into Judaism that the "Jewish Christian" position does. Why should an
angel be any more worthy of worship than a man? The Jews orig-
inated the belief in angels, but they would not think of worship-
ping them! In fact, Athanasius concludes, this is why the Arian
doctrine is so unstable: without a solid center, it fluctuates back
and forth between the Jewish and pagan positions. True Christianity, on the other hand, insists that Christ is man and God, simultaneously and eternally. The Arians hate the idea that God
could have suffered on the Cross. But God can obviously do
anything He wants to do. The essentially Christian idea—the
idea that the Arians deny—is that He chose to become a human
being and to suffer for our sake. He *was* a human being. But he
was also God—and if this is hard to understand, it's hard to understand! Who ever said that it was easy to understand God?

O NE CAN IMAGINE Constantine, powerfully swayed by these
arguments, furiously dictating his angry response to Arius's rude
letter. When the "heretic" came to court a few months later,
however, he would have found ready answers to Athanasius's arguments. Athanasius argues that God the Father is also God the
Son. He says God actually *became* Jesus despite the fact that,
throughout the Gospels, the Son describes himself as being
other than the Father and less than Him. He ransacks the New
Testament for evidence to support his position, but the only
texts that he can find are two lines from the Book of John: "I
and the Father are one,"[117] and "He who has seen me has seen
the Father."[118] But it is perfectly clear from the context of these

statements that Christ is talking about *representing* God, not about *being* him.

Could Jesus have been God and not known it? Perhaps, if one wants to imagine a Being with two natures, each of which pulls in an opposite direction: an omnipotent, omniscient God harnessed to a weak and ignorant human being. Athanasius does not want to create such a monster, so, although he claims to believe that the New Testament is the word of God, he simply ignores the words that are inconsistent with his theory! In fact, since he cannot find any basis in Scripture for his conception, he and his friends borrow a word from Greek philosophy—*homoousios*—to express it.

What does this unscriptural word mean? Athanasius says that God can do anything he chooses to do, and that he chose to turn Himself into a man for the sake of our salvation. Jesus Christ is not one of God's creatures, he insists, but God Himself, incarnated in human form. These sound like clear statements, but, actually, they are hopelessly confused.

Can God do anything He chooses to do? Of course—*except* those things that are inconsistent with being God. Can He choose to be evil or ignorant? Could He be the devil—or nothing at all? No, the Christian God is the Eternal God of Israel, Creator of the Universe. Athanasius maintains that this utterly transcendent God transformed Himself into a man, suffered, died, and then resurrected Himself! Doesn't *this* mixture of Creator and creature sound pagan? The bishop recognizes this, and tries to avoid its implications. For example, he insists that God did not create Jesus, as the Arians believe, or adopt him as His Son, but that he "begot" him out of his own nature. As he says, the idea of God fathering offspring with human beings by natural means is too disgusting for any Christian to contemplate. He therefore hastens to add that the Father's method of generating the Son is beyond human understanding.

Indeed! Everything about this theory is beyond human understanding. The bishop ridicules the Arians for saying that Jesus, being a creature of God, had the power to grow or decline in virtue, and that he *chose* to be virtuous through the exercise of his uniquely powerful will. No, Athanasius says, Christ, being God, was perfect by nature and could not change as humans do. But how can Jesus be called virtuous if he had not the power to choose? How can he be a model for human behavior if he was incapable of change? The answer: this is a matter that is beyond human understanding!

The problem is not only that Athanasius's theory mixes God with His creation, but that it removes Jesus entirely from human society, from the universe of moral turmoil, and places him in the unchangeable heavens. If Christ is not a changeable, choosing creature at least *something* like us, how can we hope to imitate him? And if he is God Himself, not our representative and intermediary, how can he intervene on our behalf? Athanasius apparently thinks that Christlike behavior is to be limited to a few desert saints like Antony, while the rest of us sinners wait in hope of unmerited salvation. It substitutes the sacraments of the Church for sacrificial action in the world. What, one wonders, would Jesus have made of that?

W E DO NOT know whether or not Constantine found Arius's reasoning persuasive . . . but it is true that after interviewing him, Constantine ceased calling Arius a heretic and began to press actively for his readmission to the Church. At the same time, when the Melitians brought a new charge against Athanasius, the emperor took the matter very seriously, indeed.

The accusation was of murder. At Athanasius's orders, the Melitians said, one of his principal supporters, a bishop in upper Egypt, had burned down the house of Arsenius, the Arian bishop of Hypsele, and murdered its occupant. Not only that, he had taken a hand from Arsenius's corpse so that it could be used for purposes of sorcery and witchcraft! As evidence, the Melitians produced a severed hand. They also presented further documentation of their earlier accusation that Athanasius had beaten the priest Ischyras and destroyed the property of his church.

Constantine ordered his half-brother Dalmatius, the chief administrative officer in the East, to investigate the charge of murder. Then, very likely acting on Eusebius of Nicomedia's advice, he wrote to the bishops of Egypt and the East announcing that a Church council would be held in Caesarea early in 334 to deal with the matter.

Athanasius reacted quickly to these developments. He left Alexandria for an undisclosed location outside the city: a monastery, no doubt. There he dispatched his agents on two missions. The first was to obtain a statement from Ischyras admitting that the charges he had made against Athanasius were false and were the result of intimidation by the Melitians. The second mission, far more important, was to find Arsenius.

It took virtually no time to obtain Ischyras's "confession." The priest probably signed it under duress, since he later recanted his recantation, but for the time being it had the desired effect. Constantine removed the charges based on the mistreatment of Ischyras from the council's agenda. Locating Arsenius was a more difficult matter. Athanasius was fairly sure that he was alive, since he knew that after Arsenius's house had been burned to the ground, the bishop had been beaten and imprisoned in a hut, but had escaped from his captor and had gone into hiding.[119] While Athanasius's agents scoured the countryside for the alleged murder victim, the churchmen summoned by the emperor to Caesarea gathered in that city. The Censor Dalmatius wrote Athanasius demanding his presence. His bold response was to decline the "invitation" while the search for Arsenius proceeded.

Relief came suddenly. Athanasius's agents received a reliable report that Arsenius had been seen at the monastery of Ptermenkurkis in the Theban desert. They raced to apprehend him, but found that the slippery bishop had again disappeared. Perhaps aided by an informant, the agents accused the prior of the monastery, one Pinnes, and a monk named Elias of arranging the escape. When they denied responsibility, the agents seized both men and brought them under guard to Alexandria. There, following the practice of the time, they were tortured for information by the emperor's chief military official, the Duke of Egypt. Under torture they revealed that they had given Arsenius a boat and told him to sail to Tyre and to seek sanctuary with Bishop Paulinus, a well-known Arian leader. Athanasius's agents soon discovered Arsenius in Tyre, where he was living under a false name. Bishop Paulinus himself convinced the terrified bishop to reveal his true identity and submit to the authorities.

Athanasius immediately dispatched a message to Constantine revealing the details of the discovery of the live, two-handed Arsenius, and asking the emperor to disband the Council of Caesarea. The emperor complied, sending Athanasius another letter of commendation and condemning the Melitians for bringing false charges against him. But if the volatile bishop thought his troubles were over, he was very much mistaken. Many Eastern bishops, including some who sympathized with Athanasius's theological views, strongly disapproved of his violent methods.[120] Furthermore, Eusebius of Nicomedia understood that when Constantine became impatient enough with the constant turmoil surrounding Athanasius, he would turn his case over to a Church council, as he had tried to do at Caesarea. The obvious strategy, then, was to increase the pressure on Athanasius—and, therefore, on Constantine.

Here the clever and thoughtful Melitian leader, John Arcaph of Memphis, played a crucial role. In 334 Bishop John made a formal submission to Athanasius's authority. Then he wrote Constantine reporting the reconciliation and asking for an opportunity to meet the great Christian emperor. Delighted by John's reasonableness, Constantine summoned him to court, but once in Eusebius's orbit, John and the Arian leader joined forces against their common enemy. Soon the Melitian-Arian alliance was ready to provide new evidence of Athanasius's reign of terror in Egypt.

UNEXPECTEDLY, after his triumph in the case of Arsenius, Athanasius found himself in greater jeopardy than ever. The document sent to Constantine by John and Eusebius presented a picture of a violent, vengeful man unfit to be a Christian bishop. It rehearsed the charges of assault against Ischyras and the breaking of the chalice, adding that Athanasius's agents had assaulted Ischyras several times before the attack on his church. Moreover, a Melitian bishop named Callinicus was prepared to testify that when he broke off contact with Athanasius after the attack on Ischyras, Athanasius had had him arrested by soldiers and tortured. Five other bishops accused the bishop of having ordered them imprisoned because they questioned the legality of his election. And they identified the Athanasian bishop who had burned Arsenius's house, tied him up, and brutalized him: Plusanius was the zealot's name.

As Eusebius had predicted, Constantine reacted angrily to these accusations. He ordered a council of bishops to meet in Tyre, Lebanon, to sit in judgment on the charges, and sent another important official, Count Dionysius, to represent him there. For the first time the emperor took military action in connection with the controversy; he had Athanasius's man, Macarius, arrested in Constantinople and sent to Tyre in chains to guarantee his appearance at the council. Then he wrote Athanasius and numerous other clergymen and witnesses ordering them to attend or risk severe punishment.

There is good evidence (in the form of two papyrus letters discovered in 1914)[121] that, confronted with this demand,

Athanasius reacted with desperation. Unable to decide whether or not to attend the council himself, he had his agents terrorize the Egyptians who might have provided evidence against him and prevent them from leaving the country. In May 335, one Melitian monk wrote privately to another:

> For [Athanasius] arrested the bishop of the lower country and shut him up in the meat market and he shut up a presbyter of those parts also in the lockup and a deacon in the great prison, and [Bishop] Herascius has been imprisoned since the 28th in the camp. I thank the Lord God that the beatings which he was receiving have ceased. And on the 27th [Athanasius] forced seven bishops to leave the area.[122]

Clearly, the bishop recognized his peril. One of his supporters attempted to break Macarius out of jail, but the local authorities got wind of the plot and arrested the "kidnapper." Finally, Athanasius made up his mind to come to Tyre. He did not have much choice; this time the emperor was prepared to back up his commands with force.

Well over one hundred bishops attended the Council of Tyre.[123] While a number of the participants had Arian sympathies, anti-Arian leaders like Alexander of Thessalonica, Paul of Constantinople, and Marcellus of Ancyra were also present, and the non-Melitian bishops from Egypt made up a solid pro-Athanasian bloc. They did not do his cause much good, though, since they behaved so disruptively at the council meetings that the council later cited their activities as proof of Athanasius's unfitness for office. The Alexandrian bishop had good reason to believe that the Arians were out to destroy him, but, as one commentator puts it,

> the alliance of the Melitians with the Eusebians did not alter the fact that Athanasius' offence had nothing to do with doctrine. The charge against him at Tyre was the unscrupulous use of strong-arm methods against his opponents, and that

charge as a general accusation, whatever may have been said about individual incidents, was abundantly justified.[124]

The debate at the council was stormy, with many witnesses contradicting each other's stories, and much name calling. Ischyras now confirmed that Macarius *had* assaulted him and broken his chalice, a charge Macarius denied under oath. The Melitians repeated their stories of violence, and the Athanasians claimed that it was they who had been attacked. After weeks of squabbling, the bishops decided to send a commission to the Mareotis region to interview witnesses there and decide the truth of various accusations, including the matter of the broken chalice. The question of who should form the commission triggered further contention. Count Dionysius advised that the decision should be made unanimously, but that proved impossible, given the divisions among the bishops. Athanasius presented a list of known Arians whom he insisted should be disqualified, but all the commissioners chosen by the council were on Athanasius's list. They left for Egypt in August, accompanied by Ischyras and a company of imperial troops.

For the next two months Egypt was in an uproar. The commissioners' attempts to collect evidence were assisted by Ischyras and his relatives, the Melitian and Arian clergy, and Constantine's chief representative, Philagrius, the Prefect of Egypt. They were obstructed at every turn by clergymen loyal to Athanasius, who protested that Ischyras had never been properly ordained and that the proceedings were biased and unfair. The Athanasians charged that the commission was obtaining evidence by means of threats and torture. The commissioners charged that Athanasius's supporters were intimidating and kidnapping witnesses. By the end of September it was clear that their report would indict Athanasius. Before they could return to Tyre, however, the bishop fled the city by night in a small boat and made for Constantinople.

The bishops, meanwhile, had taken two weeks off to go to Jerusalem, at Constantine's request, for the dedication of the Church of the Holy Sepulchre. When they came back to Tyre, they quickly moved to condemn Athanasius for specific acts of violence and disobedience: ordering Macarius to beat Ischyras and to break the chalice, intimidating and obstructing witnesses, refusing to appear at the Council of Caesarea, attempting with his followers to disrupt the Council of Tyre, and fleeing the council to avoid its judgment. They excommunicated the bishop, removed him from office, and ordered him not to return to Alexandria. The council's acts were approved by virtually all present, including most of the anti-Arians. Riots against the decision broke out almost immediately in Alexandria. Athanasius was popular in the city, and his agents could always be counted on to mobilize a violent crowd.

Athanasius's flight, however, concerned the bishops more than riots in his old city. They knew how persuasive the Alexandrian leader could be, and how strongly he had impressed Constantine during his last stay at court. They also knew that if the emperor was moved to do so, he would not hesitate to act as a final decision maker, no matter what a Church council had decided. The bishops therefore commissioned six of their number, all identified with the Arian party, to go immediately to the new capital to present the council's case to Constantine. More than Athanasius's career hung in the balance. The outcome of the Arian controversy itself might well depend upon this final appeal.

Seven

Death in
Constantinople

On NOVEMBER 6, 335, Constantine returned to New Rome with a glittering entourage. In October he and his companions had visited Nicopolis on the Black Sea and had then made a stately progress home, greeting grateful townspeople and local officials in cities and villages all along the way. As the imperial procession entered the main square before the palace, the large crowd gathered there emitted a great roar of welcome. Constantine, still an impressive figure despite his years, rode erect on a massive charger, nodding to the cheering onlookers. All seemed in order, until a disheveled figure dressed in rags of mourning suddenly burst through the line of soldiers holding back the crowd, threw himself on his knees before the emperor, and began speaking in the sonorous tones of a tragic actor.

The man was Athanasius. With his dirty face and torn clothes, he was at first unrecognizable. Constantine had not seen him for more than three years, but when he finally recognized him, he was moved by his humiliated appearance and desperate words. [125] He may also have appreciated the bishop's sense of theater and the opportunity to play the role of all-wise, all-forgiving sovereign. Athanasius begged the emperor to save him once again from ravenous enemies. The Council of Tyre, which had condemned him, had been motivated purely by the Arians' hatred and self-interest. How could such a gathering be said to represent the will of God? He implored Constantine to summon the council members to Constantinople to explain their decision to excommunicate him.

Constantine hesitated. To comply with the request would be, in effect, to reopen the proceedings of the council. On the other hand, the decisions of Church councils were not self-enforcing; only the emperor could exile deposed churchmen. If the bishops at Tyre had *not* acted dispassionately, in the interests of the truth and Christian unity—if they were simply carrying out a personal vendetta against Athanasius—their decision would represent only the prideful will of petty men and should not be enforced. Constantine thought for a few moments, then granted Athanasius's request. The bishops still in Tyre were commanded to attend the emperor in Constantinople in order to demonstrate that they had not decided Athanasius's case unjustly, but on the basis of a fair and sober consideration of the evidence.

A few hours later the six bishops earlier sent by the council arrived at the palace and learned of Constantine's letter. When they asked to see the emperor, they were told by the master of admissions to return in two days. The emperor would be happy to grant them an audience, said the official, and he was certain that they would not object if several Egyptian bishops recently arrived from Tyre also took part in the discussion.

The Arian bishops gathered the following day to discuss the deteriorating situation. Very likely, John Arcaph and some of his Melitian followers participated as well. The victors of Tyre felt their achievement slipping from their grasp. Athanasius and his allies had had Constantine's ear for more than a week. What lies they must have told! Worse yet, although the council had turned up plentiful evidence of Athanasius's violent acts, the worst crimes that could be proved against him were the destruction of Ischyras's (arguably unsacred) chalice and other church property, the burning of Arsenius's house, and the brutalization of a few score Arian and Melitian priests. The Alexandrian bishop would continue to deny all these charges, but even if Constantine accepted them, he might consider the rough treatment of one's opponents part of the game of governance and let Athanasius off with a warning to mend his ways. After all, had not the most Christian emperor sometimes been compelled to treat his own enemies a bit roughly?

At some point in the discussion that master strategist, Eusebius of Nicomedia, may have asked his Egyptian informants whether they knew of any acts or statements by Athanasius that were directed against the emperor, not just against them. Or, Eusebius may have procured such evidence earlier but decided not to use it at Tyre, since it involved an offense against the state, not the Church. However he obtained the information, the Arian leader was ready to use it when he and his colleagues met the next day with the emperor, Athanasius, and the bishop's Egyptian supporters.

T HE AUDIENCE was predictably uproarious.[126] Athanasius and the Egyptians flatly denied the charges brought before the Council of Tyre, challenged the council's and the commission's procedures, and vilified their opponents as anti-Christian heretics and conspirators. The Arian bishops rehearsed the evidence presented to the council and described the Athanasians as unscrupulous gangsters and liars. But the intensity of these personal attacks and counterattacks played into Athanasius's hands. It seemed to Constantine that the council could not have acted dispassionately, but must have ruled in an atmosphere of tumult and vengefulness. He would *not* instruct the bishops elswhere to enforce the decisions of such a body. . . .

Then Eusebius of Nicodemia struck.

There was another matter of importance that required the emperor's attention, he said. When Constantine ordered Athanasius to attend the Council of Tyre on pain of criminal punishment, even then the bishop had considered disobeying his sovereign's order. Athanasius had boarded a ship bound for Tyre in the harbor of Alexandria and then disembarked in an agony of fear and rage, swearing that he would never attend the "enemy council." During this period, said Eusebius, the bishop told his confidants that if the emperor tried to force him to go to Tyre, he would know how to respond. He would use his control over the harbor of Alexandria to stop the Egyptian grain ships from sailing to other Mediterranean ports.[127]

Eusebius's statement struck even Constantine dumb. Athanasius was reputed to have considerable influence over the seamen and workers of the harbor district. His capacity for anger and for resistance to imperial authority was a matter of common knowledge. But such a threat . . . if it was made . . . was a sword pointed directly at the emperor's heart. Egypt and Libya, the richest agricultural lands of the Mediterranean, were the granary of the Roman world. Great cities like Constantinople and Antioch, Athens and Rome could not survive for a month without regular deliveries of Egyptian grain. To delay the grain ships meant to trigger riots throughout the empire, and, quite possibly, to unseat its emperor, Christian or not.

Constantine demanded that Athanasius answer the charge. According to eyewitnesses, the bishop denied everything. Weeping openly, he pleaded that he was only a citizen of Alexandria and a priest, not a man of great wealth and power. How could he stop the ships from leaving the harbor? How could the emperor believe that he would ever consider doing such a thing? Seeing his opening, Eusebius made the most of it. He would swear under oath, he said, that the bishop of Alexandria was very rich, very powerful, and utterly without scruples. He *could* delay the grain shipments. He *had* uttered the threat. And Eusebius could produce witnesses to verify it.

At this, Constantine began to berate Athanasius in typically violent style. Subjected to this unaccustomed abuse, the bishop also lost his temper. For a small man, his voice could be very large. "Be warned!" he is reported to have shouted. "God will judge between you and me!"[128]

Constantine, enraged, condemned Athanasius to indefinite exile in Gaul, in the frontier city of Trier. There he would remain for several years, while his Alexandrian supporters rioted periodically, and his anti-Arian allies, including the monk Antony, wrote Constantine letter after letter requesting that he be allowed to return to his see. In answer, Constantine called the bishop a violent troublemaker who could not be trusted to conduct the affairs of the Church. He criticized the Alexandrians for their riotous behavior and told Antony to stop interfering in matters that did not concern him.

Still, Athanasius's status remained anomalous. Constantine had made a point of *not* enforcing the decisions of the Council of Tyre. He would not, for example, approve any successor named by the Arians or Melitians to be bishop of Alexandria. The bishop-in-exile therefore remained in a sort of limbo, unable to return to power, but not condemned by any council recognized by the emperor. Of course, as a great Eastern churchman in the rough-hewn city of Trier, he was a giant among pygmies. Beginning a pattern of behavior that would prove of great significance both to his own career and to the Church, Athanasius used his intellectual power and the glamour of his "oppression" by the Arians to persuade Western bishops of the correctness of his views.

The embattled bishop was not yet forty. Alone but not alone among Latin speakers on the German frontier, he worked, planned, and waited for his opportunity to return.

As Athanasius's star fell in the East, Arius's rose. In 335, while the bishops conferred in Tyre, he was in Constantinople with his friend, Euzoius, and a group of followers. There he must have persuaded the emperor to take action to secure his readmission to the Church, for when Constantine invited all the Eastern bishops to travel to Jerusalem for the dedication of the Church of the Holy Sepulchre, he sent them an additional message. Arius and Euzoius had submitted a creed that he believed to be orthodox. He had interviewed them personally and found them sincerely committed to Christian principles and the welfare of the Church. The bishops should make up their own minds by examining the matter at a council in Jerusalem prior to the dedication ceremonies.

The letter was gracious and correct, but its message was clear. Athanasius and the anti-Arian forces had lost the battle. Constantine wanted to celebrate the thirtieth anniversary of his accession to the throne with a grand reunification of the warring branches of the Church. Gathered in Jerusalem in September, the Eastern bishops, most of whom were subordinationists of one sort or another anyway, read the emperor's letter, studied the creed, heard from Arius and Euzoius, and admitted them unconditionally to communion. Arius's doctrine was sound and apostolic, they said, and his acceptance by the Church would secure Christian unity and peace.

Only one bishop dissented. Marcellus of Ancyra, well known for his passionate animosity to Arianism, refused to communicate with the "heretics." The council gave him several months to change his views, but ordered that if he still refused to communicate with Arius at the end of that period, he should lose his position as bishop. The council members then proceeded to celebrate the dedication of the new church with a week of lavish festivities in which the Arian brethren were included.

Constantine immediately dispatched a circular letter to all bishops informing them that Arius's views had been found orthodox and requiring them to readmit him and his followers to communion. Arius must have felt that his long, arduous struggle had finally been crowned with success. Now it was time to reenter his own kingdom. At the conclusion of the ceremonies in Jerusalem, he traveled to Alexandria, where he was met by a large crowd of joyous friends. At this point Athanasius was in Constantinople, so the Arians sent messages to the leading Alexandrian bishops asking them to arrange ceremonies of readmission for Arius and his colleagues. But the bishops, ever loyal to Athanasius, would not hear of it. Meet with the "enemies of Christ"? Never! Not even Constantine's synodal letter could induce them to change their minds.

Some of Arius's followers may well have wanted to take the dispute to the streets, but either out of principle or because his forces were outnumbered, their leader judged it best to return to Constantinople and lay the matter before the emperor. When he reached the capital, however, he found Constantine gone, campaigning against the Sarmatians across the Danube, and the Christian community in turmoil. The old bishop, ninety-seven-year-old Alexander, was in poor health, and a struggle over control of this important see had already begun.[129] Paul, the anti-Arian candidate, had acted as Alexander's representative at the Council of Tyre. He had voted against Athanasius out of disapproval of his methods, but he was a passionate advocate of the Nicene Creed. The Arians were promoting the cause of their own candidate, a deacon named Macedonius, and street clashes between partisans of the two sides were everyday occurrences.

The situation in Ancyra was even stormier. Bishop Marcellus, perhaps Arius's bitterest enemy, had not only refused to communicate with the Arians as the Councils of Tyre and Jerusalem had demanded, he had sent Constantine a lengthy, bitter manifesto denouncing them as polytheists and heretics. Marcellus was brilliant but tactless. His own theology went so far toward identifying Jesus as God that he seemed to be denying the Son's existence as a separate entity. After the Second Coming, he said, Jesus's Kingdom would eventually end; the Son would be reabsorbed into the Father.[130] Clearly, statements like this made him vulnerable to charges of Sabellianism. And, since Marcellus had long been bishop of Ancyra, there were numerous abuses of power that could also be alleged.

Eusebius of Nicomedia therefore proposed another council of bishops, this one to meet in Constantinople on Constantine's return. The gathering could deal with Marcellus's heresy—and it could also take action to restore Arius to his rightful position in Alexandria. Late in the spring the emperor concluded his successful military campaign, returned to the palace, and immediately summoned the Eastern bishops once again to council.

More than a decade earlier, when he convened the Great Council of Nicaea, Constantine could not have imagined that the bishops would be meeting almost every year to rule on charges of criminal activity and heresy. Partisan control of these gatherings virtually guaranteed that condemned churchmen would attempt to rehabilitate themselves and punish their enemies by denying the authority of "illegitimate" councils and convening new ones. The emperor probably considered this a temporary problem. Surely, after blatant troublemakers and fanatics like Athanasius and Marcellus were removed from office, reasonable churchmen could learn to live together despite occasional differences of opinion! But this was to repeat the original mistake made at Nicaea. It was to assume that doctrinal differences among Christians were not *that* important, that they did not reflect serious divisions of class, culture, and moral values within the community, and that they could be resolved by discovering the correct form of words.

Quite reasonably, Constantine declined to make theological decisions or decisions relating to a bishop's fitness for office himself. Convening a Church council was one way to ensure that religious matters would be decided by religious authority. But the emperor would not relinquish the civil authority's right to punish (for example, by exiling condemned bishops), or the correlative right to pardon. If the divisions among Christians had not run so deep, it might not have mattered that he insisted on acting as an appellate judge in cases where condemned parties claimed to have been wronged. But they did run deep, and the result was that council decisions were never final. The losing side could always appeal to the emperor or, as a final resort, wait for him to die, since an emperor's death terminated the sentences he had personally meted out. Therefore, until one side or the other achieved hegemony, or a new consensus among the bishops developed, the war of the councils would continue.

In the summer of 336, the Eastern bishops met at Constantinople with the emperor in attendance. As at Tyre and Jerusalem, they were joined by several Western colleagues, including Valens of Mursa and Ursacius of Singidunum (Belgrade); Arianism was now making significant inroads into the Balkans. The members of the council studied Marcellus's long letter to Constantine and pronounced it heretical. Constantine exiled Marcellus to the West and the council replaced him with Basil, a moderate Arian destined to play a crucial role in the next phase of the controversy. Then they turned their attention to Arius and Euzoius. A creed submitted by Arius was read and discussed. Constantine himself interrogated the controversial priest. Declaring themselves satisfied with his creed and testimony, the assembled bishops again declared his views acceptable and ordered him readmitted to the Church.

This was the fourth council since Arius's return from exile to pronounce his theology orthodox. But considering his recent rejection by the Alexandrian Church, Eusebius of Nicodemia decided that this assemblage must go further. The council must make certain that Arius was readmitted to communion with due ceremony by a bishop whose authority would be recognized both by Arians and anti-Arians. The perfect candidate for this job was Alexander, the venerable bishop of Constantinople. Not only was he associated with the pro-Nicene side in the controversy, he was the metropolitan bishop of New Rome, capital of the Christian empire. After such a figure had presided over the ceremony of readmission, the Alexandrians would be hard put to reject him—and, if they did, Constantine would have every justification to crush them.

Athanasius's principal assistant, Macarius, was with Bishop Alexander when the order came from the council to receive Arius in the Church of the Holy Apostles. According to Macarius, whose story was later retold by Athanasius, the ancient man wept when he read the document, declaring that he would never communicate with "the inventor of heresy."[131] When Eusebius, Arius, and the bishops closest to Arius arrived at the basilica on Sunday, Alexander refused to admit them. Eusebius warned him that he was thwarting the emperor's will as well as that of the council, gave him the evening to think things over, and stated that when the group returned the next morning, they *must* be admitted to the church. According to Macarius, Alexander then went into his sacristy, where he wept, fasted, and prayed that he might be spared the ignominy of celebrating Mass with the arch-heretic.

WHILE the old bishop awaited God's answer (if one believes Macarius's story), Eusebius and the Arians met that night to prepare themselves for the following day's events. Very likely they discussed how to respond if Alexander continued to bar his door to them. Should they ask Constantine to send troops to force an entry? But, if he did, would that not defeat the whole purpose of the exercise? Suddenly, as Athanasius later described the scene, "a wonderful and extraordinary circumstance took place."[132]

Arius was speaking (talking "very wildly," according to Athanasius), when he was stricken by an agonizing stomachache and an urgent need to use the toilet. He went to the lavatory to relieve himself and sat down, but a wave of spasms shook him and the pain became unbearable. When his comrades went to find out what was delaying him, they discovered him sprawled on the floor beside the toilet. There was no need to call a physician to verify that their friend was dead.

Athanasius, retelling the story, cannot keep from gloating. He would never exult in a death, he says, but it was the Lord Himself who answered Alexander's prayers and "condemned the Arian heresy, showing it to be unworthy of communion with the Church." Most telling is the language he uses in describing the manner of the priest's death:

> Arius . . . urged by the necessities of nature withdrew, and suddenly, in the language of Scripture, "falling headlong he burst asunder in the midst," and immediately expired as he lay, and was deprived both of communion and of his life together.[133]

The biblical reference is to Acts 1:18: "Now this man bought a field with the reward of his wickednesss; and falling headlong he burst asunder in the midst and all his bowels gushed out." The man, of course, was Judas Iscariot. Athanasius obviously believes it fitting that Arius should meet the same end as Christ's betrayer. He goes on to say, interestingly, "Such was the end of Arius; and Eusebius and his fellows, overwhelmed with shame, buried their accomplice, while the blessed Alexander, amidst the rejoicings of the Church, celebrated the Communion with piety and orthodoxy. . . ."[134]

"Overwhelmed with shame" is probably hyperbole and may, of course, be a complete fiction. On the other hand, the late Roman age was somewhat more superstitious than ours. Many people believed that the manner of one's death was a resume of one's life, and death by diarrhea might seem ignominious even if the Arius/Judas parallel did not immediately come to mind. Furthermore, the coincidence of Arius dying the night before he was to receive communion could be portrayed (à la Athanasius) as no coincidence at all, but as a divine judgment on the heretic and his cause. Arius's comrades were probably not overwhelmed with shame, but they cannot have been happy with the form and timing of their friend's death.[135]

It would be surprising, in fact, if some of them did not agree that the coincidence *was* no chance occurrence, but the work of unjust humans rather than a just God. By this time, Arius was an old man, probably in his seventies; he would not have been the first person his age to die of an intestinal ailment, or, possibly, of a heart attack brought on by the combination of illness and the tension of awaiting one of the most important days in his life. Still, poison was the murder weapon of choice for many Roman intriguers, and from the point of view of Arius's enemies, one could hardly imagine a more urgent or convenient time for a murder than the eve of the arch-heretic's greatest triumph. A whisper of poison drifts about the event, captured by some of the literature on Arius's death,[136] although the only direct evidence for it is the timing and manner of his passing.

Except for the immediate propaganda advantage it furnished the Athanasians, Arius's death did not have a great impact on the subsequent course of the controversy. One commentator thinks that this is because "Arius had ceased to matter. He had long been discarded by both sides, and, as he himself painfully realized, he had become negligible."[137] But this seems an odd formulation; if Arius was "negligible," one wonders why the emperor and four church councils would have gone to such lengths to secure his recognition as a legitimate Christian theologian.[138]

What is clear is that Arius's role as a political leader was limited from the beginning by the fact that he was only a priest, not one of the lords of the Church. Particularly after his return from exile, the two Eusebiuses clearly dominated the movement, which was more often called "Eusebian" than Arian. And, however much they may have owed Arius ideologically or admired him personally, the bishops sympathetic to his views were far too proud to be considered the followers of any priest:

> We have neither been followers of Arius (because how should we who are bishops follow a presbyter?), nor have we accepted any other form of faith than that which was set out at the beginning, but we have rather approached him as investigators and judges of his belief than followed him.[139]

These are the words of the bishops at the so-called Dedication Council of Antioch (341), convened after the bishop of Rome had criticized the Eastern churchmen for following a heretical priest. They indicate how vast a distance in status separated bishops from lowly priests and presbyters. But they also demonstrate how conservative, relatively speaking, Arian views became after the Arians exiled at Nicaea began their campaign to regain Constantine's confidence and win readmission to the Church.

Arius did not become insignificant, but for a time his ideas, particularly as expressed by the bishops, lost their dangerous edge. The subordinationists moved towards the center in order to reassure both the emperor and the Church that while Christ might not be identical to God, he was far closer to God than we are. Perhaps at Eusebius's urging, Arius dropped or blurred those beliefs that implied Jesus' essential kinship with humanity: for example, the propositions that he was created "from nothing," that he did not "know" the Father, and that he was mutable and capable of sinning. Instead, beginning with the Council of Antioch in 328, Arian creeds focus on the Son's closeness and similarity to the Father. Repeatedly, almost ritually, they intone that Christ is God's Word, begotten before the ages; that he is a unique creation unlike any other; and that he is fully divine.

The Arian moderates' strategy, in short, was to emphasize the Son's *similarity* to the Father in order to solidify a consensus among churchmen that he was not *the same*. For two decades this approach predominated. By the 350s it had apparently succeeded in winning over a substantial majority of bishops and was close to becoming accepted Christian dogma. Yet the controversy was far from over. The movement to the center opened up unexpected possibilities of attack both from the left and from the right. While a new generation of Arian thinkers revived and developed the founder's more daring ideas, splitting the movement into radical and moderate wings, Athanasius would attempt to unite his allies with the moderates under the banner of a new pro-Nicene theology. For forty years after Arius's death the controversy that bears his name, inflamed by complex interconnections of Church and State, would continue to trouble the Roman world.

A SECOND DEATH in Constantinople was of greater consequence than Arius's. Among its other effects, it generated a wave of violence that found Arians and Athanasians battling with new ferocity in the streets and even in the churches of major Eastern cities.

The death in question was Constantine's. The emperor fell ill in April 337, just after Easter. He went first to recuperate at a spa and then visited the shrine of the martyr, Lucian of Antioch, in nearby Helenopolis, the city he had renamed in honor of his mother, but neither the healing waters nor prayers had the desired effect. In May he came back to Nicomedia, his old capital, a desperately sick man, and asked Bishop Eusebius to baptize him. Like many other powerful figures, Constantine had not wanted to become fully a Christian while faced with the necessity (as he saw it) to sin. Now, however, he knew that it was time to don the white robes of a catechumen.

Constantine lay on his deathbed. His purple robe was taken from him, signifying the end of his reign and his death to the material world. Eusebius came to him, heard his confession, and administered the last rites. His generals came to pay their respects; when they wished him a long life, he reminded them that God's call could not be ignored. He died on May 22, the Feast of Pentecost, after reigning for thirty-one years, the last seven as sole ruler of a united Roman Empire. A procession headed by his son, Constantius, brought the golden coffin containing his body to Constantinople, and he was entombed in a place of honor in the Church of the Holy Apostles.

Roman unity, however, could not survive the emperor's death. Constantine left three sons, each a Caesar controlling about one-third of the empire. Constantine II, the eldest, governed France,

Britain, and Spain from his capital at Trier. Constans, the youngest, resided in Milan and controlled Italy, while Constantius ruled the Eastern provinces from his headquarters at Antioch. There were other potential claimants to the throne as well, most related to Constantine through his father's second marriage. One of them (the son of the official who had heard the murder case against Athanasius) was a fourth Caesar ruling the Balkan lands. Virtually all would be dead in a matter of months.

As was not uncommon in this era, Constantine's demise was followed by a small bloodbath of royal relatives. Constantius, the Eastern ruler, may have ordered these murders, or the army, which proclaimed Constantine's sons Augusti in September, may have taken matters into its own hands. Whoever was responsible, the result was the massacre of some twenty nobles, including all potential claimants other than Constantius's young nephews, Gallus and Julian. (This was the same Julian who, as emperor, would later attempt to revive the worship of the old gods.) Soon afterward, the three brothers met in Pannonia and redivided the empire, with Constans and Constantius obtaining additional territory, but after a short time mistrust and violence infected their relations as well.

In 340, after invading Constans's territory, the impetuous Constantine II was defeated and killed in battle. This gave young Constans control of the entire West, but ten years later a Gallic general named Magnentius rose up against him, captured him as he attempted to flee, and executed him. Finally, in 353, having defeated Magnentius and destroyed his army, Constantius, the surviving brother, reunited the entire empire under his own rule.

These bloody events had a profound impact on the Arian controversy, for Constantius was close to Eusebius of Nicomedia, whom he soon made Bishop of Constantinople, and sympathized with the subordinationist views of most of the Eastern bishops. Furthermore, Athanasius, while exiled in the West, had had close contact with several of Constantius's rivals. The bishop and the emperor might have opposed each other for doctrinal reasons in any case, but the embroilment of the Church in the affairs of a violently divided State—and vice versa—gave the religious conflict a lethal dimension it had ealier managed to avoid.

This process of escalation began immediately following Constantine's death, when a decree issued by the three Augusti permitted all exiled bishops to return to their sees. The decree was in accordance with the custom allowing exiles to return following an emperor's death. Constantius signed it, but with weighty political and military matters on his mind, he probably did not consider the likely impact of permitting bishops condemned by Church councils to return to cities now under the control of their theological enemies. (Cities, I must add, whose excitable citizens were bitterly divided by these same theological issues.) Athanasius's host in the West, Constantine II, may have had a clearer perception of these consequences than his brothers.[140] In advance of Athanasius's return to Alexandria he sent the church there a letter that the bishop might well have written himself, exhorting the faithful to welcome the great man back.

Athanasius did not come directly back to Alexandria, however. He made what amounted to a political tour of the Danubian provinces, Asia Minor, Syria, Lebanon, and Palestine before returning to his own city. Everywhere he rallied the anti-Arian forces and helped return exiles to power, organized opposition to "heretical" bishops, and intervened actively in local disputes. Violence dogged his steps, since both sides had organized popular support and were quite ready to use angry mobs to expel churchmen they despised or defend friendly incumbents. The result in a number of key cities was something close to civil war.

In Constantinople, where old Bishop Alexander had recently died, Athanasius intervened on the side of Paul, the anti-Arian candidate, against the deacon Macedonius. Public opinion in the capital was deeply and bitterly divided. Paul was ordained bishop by a handful of colleagues (perhaps including Athanasius) in an atmosphere of tumultuous violence. When Constantius returned to the city a bit later, he nullified the results, sent Paul into exile, and replaced him with Eusebius of Nicomedia. Similar scenes were enacted in Ancyra, where Marcellus, backed by a mob, expelled Bishop Basil and took control of the see there, in Gaza, and elsewhere. Meanwhile, Athanasius returned to Alexandria where, according to his enemies, "he seized the churches . . . by force, by murder, by war."[141]

Several months later a large council of bishops met in Antioch to declare that, in addition to the older charges proved against Athanasius by the Council of Tyre, he had committed new atrocities. They found that on returning to Alexandria he had incited mobs to assault and murder, had handed over his opponents to be imprisoned and executed by the prefect of Egypt, Theodorus, and had financed his campaign of violence by misappropriating charitable funds. The council ordered him deposed, and Constantius wrote him immediately endorsing this decision. Athanasius's answer was to convene a council of eighty Egyptian bishops early in 338, which cleared him of all charges, accused his accusers of heresy, and characterized their activities as a conspiracy motivated by hatred of Christ. Then he induced the famous monk, Antony, to come in from the desert to testify that Athanasius was a man of God and Arianism a satanic heresy.

This did not help the bishop, however, when the leaders of the Eastern Church met again in Antioch in the winter of 338–339. With Constantius in attendance, they convicted Athanasius of violence and mayhem, renewed the verdict of the Council of Tyre, and again ordered him deposed. To replace him they selected Gregory, a presbyter of good reputation from Cappadocia. But this time their actions would be enforceable, since Constantius had granted a petition filed by Athanasius's Egyptian opponents to replace the pro-Athanasian prefect with Philagrius, an old enemy of the bishop's. Before adjourning, the same council deposed Marcellus of Ancyra once again, sent him into exile, and put Bishop Basil back on that episcopal throne.

On March 16, 339, Philagrius and a company of troops set out to arrest Athanasius at the Church of Theonas, where he had taken up residence. Warned by his agents, the bishop fled, and rioting and arson (which had also accompanied his return) erupted across the city. The violence intensified when Philagrius escorted the new bishop, Gregory, into the city on April 22. The Church of Dionysius was burned, a number of people on both sides were injured and killed, and fighting even broke out on Easter Sunday in the Church of Quirinius.[142] Several weeks later, the mobs supporting Athanasius had been suppressed, at least for the time being, and all Alexandria's churches were under Gregory's control. At this point, if Athanasius had been captured, Constantius might well have had him executed for capital crimes. So, on April 16 he escaped from the city and fled by boat to Rome.

What really happened in Alexandria during this stormy month? In a circular letter apparently written after he arrived in Rome, Athanasius describes the violence against his supporters as unilateral, unmerited, and "dreadful beyond endurance." He charges the "Arian madmen" and their tool, Philagrius, with inciting pagans, Jews, and "disorderly persons" to attack the faithful, set churches on fire, strip and rape holy virgins, murder monks, desecrate holy places, and plunder the churches' treasures.[143] He presents pictures designed to horrify and madden his readers: Jews, for example, are presented cavorting naked in the churches' baptismal waters. And, of course, he says nothing about any violence that his own supporters may have offered in his defense or in opposition to Gregory's installation as the new bishop.

The truth seems to be that in Alexandria and many other cities large groups of militant fighters could be mobilized by both sides, and that both sides made frequent use of them in the confused period following Constantine's death. It is highly unlikely that anyone incited the pagans or Jews to take violent action, or that they did so in an organized way, although sufficient chaos in a city always tempts people to settle old scores. But one can hardly imagine Athanasius, informed that Gregory had arrived in the city to replace him, *not* calling on his followers to defend the Holy Church against the "Arian madmen." As the bishop's circular letter makes clear, moreover, Gregory was not simply imposed on the populace by troops; he, too, was supported by violent mobs.

Athanasius had always had a following in Alexandria, but Arius was also an Alexandrian with his share of supporters, and the bishop was hated by substantial numbers of Melitians, Colluthians, and other opponents as well. Theology aside, the fact that the great bishops were high-ranking members of the imperial establishment made them lightning rods for popular dissatisfaction. And popular grievances, in this era, were intensifying.[144] The accusation that Athanasius diverted the proceeds of imperial charity to his own pockets may well have reflected dissatisfaction among the increasingly impoverished populace with the amount and reliability of these subsidies. It would not have been hard, therefore, for the bishop's enemies—Arian, Melitian, or simply poor—to have welcomed even a "foreign" bishop as a liberator.

The riots in Alexandria and elsewhere make it clear that the bishops did not necessarily speak for the people. Athanasius's backing by Egypt's bishops (many of them, of course, handpicked) at the Council of Alexandria did not necessarily translate into support in the streets, nor did the strength of the Arian clergy at the Council of Antioch prevent continual struggles for the control of that troubled city. What is most striking, in fact, is the closeness and bitterness of the conflict in important cities like Constantinople, Antioch, Ancyra, Caesarea, Tyre, and Gaza.

This more or less even split between Arians and Athanasians clearly contributed to the increase in violence, since it tempted each side to impose its will on the other, and made both victory and defeat provisional.

Bᴜᴛ ᴡʜᴀᴛ ᴄᴀᴜsᴇᴅ this deep division? Why could each side command widespread support but neither convert nor subdue its adversaries? Since so little is known about what ordinary people were thinking, there is a tendency to portray the conflict as a struggle between a small number of Church leaders who were willing to exploit the gullible, volatile, urban crowd. There is some truth to this, as there is in decrying the "vulgarisation of theology"[145] that the bishops promoted in order to attract the masses to their cause. But we are not told why vulgarized theology should matter so much to the people of Alexandria, Constantinople, and Antioch, or why the two-party battle that they waged continued so long on such relatively even terms.

Some elements of an answer have already been suggested. We know that these Greek-speaking city folk were a busy, impassioned, assertive lot, not unlike the urbanites of later eras. We know that they had virtually no voice in public policy and not much in the way of legal rights—security, for them, meant securing the protection of some powerful patron.[146] And we know that, where religious issues were concerned, the competition of the "great ones" placed them in a position both risky and rewarding. Participation in one party or the other could convey a sense of power as well as offer social and material rewards.

A missing piece, however, is their ideological motivation, or what "vulgarized" theology meant to them. Clearly, people in the street were not going to risk injury or death to defend Basil of Ancyra's interpretation of the preexistent *Logos* against that of Marcellus. But theology at a somewhat less abstract level involved them deeply, perhaps because it concerned a figure with whom they had developed an intense personal relationship: Jesus of Nazareth.

The historical Jesus, the rabbi who had once walked the earth, then died and returned, and who would soon come again to inaugurate his Kingdom, was fading into the background like a figure in an antique mosaic. His Crucifixion was more than three centuries old, and his Kingdom would come when it would come. The Church was triumphant, of course, but its triumph raised as many questions as it answered. For many Christians the great question now involved the *internalized* Jesus: that is, the image of Christ that people would keep in their minds and hearts. And the problem was that there seemed to be a multiplicity of images, not necessarily consistent, among which Christians could choose, depending upon their most pressing needs.

In the Second Creed of Antioch adopted at the Dedication Council of 341, for example, the following words are used to describe and glorify Jesus: God, King, Lord, Word, Wisdom, Light, Way, Truth, Resurrection, Shepherd, Door, Image of the Godhead, Mediator of God and men, Apostle of our faith, and Prince of life.[147] Intoning them with one's eyes closed, so to speak, might blur the differences between them or give them a mysterious unity. But if one focused intently on them, certain images seemed to negate each other, like the incompatible images of a profile and a glass used nowadays to demonstrate the mental organization of visual perception. Could Jesus be both God and mediator between God and men? King and shepherd? Judge and advocate? An all-powerful father and a faithful brother and friend?

Most believers wanted him to be all these things, but the split between Nicene and Arian Christians seems to reflect a rough division between those more in need of a powerful, just ruler and those more in need of a loving advocate and friend. Neither side in this controversy could afford to turn its back entirely on either image; the Arians therefore called Jesus "God from God,"[148] and the Athanasians called him "a paradigm and an example."[149] Each side put its primary emphasis on one image while paying lip service to the other, and each was prey to fears that the other side was aiming to obliterate "its" Jesus. While Athanasius denounced the Arians for lowering Christ to the point that his majesty and saving power would be lost, the Arians accused Athanasius and Marcellus of raising him to the point that his love (and God's majesty) would be lost. These fears may, indeed, have been one key to the violent mobilizations of the era, since each side perceived the other as a threat to fulfillment of its most deep-rooted and imperative needs.

The violence in the Eastern cities ended for the time being with the forcible eviction from their sees of Athanasius, Marcellus of Ancyra, Paul of Constantinople, and several other anti-Arian bishops, and their exile to the West. Many were now arriving in Rome, where Athanasius had already fled, to seek the protection of Bishop Julius and the emperor Constans. The Arians congratulated themselves on ridding the East of their most potent adversaries. But the uncalculated effects of these deportations would be to make the Roman pontiff a major participant in the controversy, to embroil the Western bishops, and, finally, to drive a great wedge between the Christian churches of the Greek East and Latin West.

Eight

East against West

WHEN ATHANASIUS reached Rome after his escape from Egypt, he went immediately to seek refuge with Bishop Julius. He spoke to Julius as one pontiff to another, aware that the Roman prelate was passionately committed to the principles of Nicaea, and determined to impress him with the atrocities perpetrated by the Arians on faithful Christians. He found Julius an apt and highly sympathetic listener. Perhaps the Roman bishop would consider playing a more active role in the controversy, for example, by calling a great council of his own to vindicate true Christian doctrine and help end the violence in the East. Julius considered the matter . . . and hesitated.

The pope had reason to hesitate; even for bishops in the relatively peaceful West the situation was dangerous. All three of Constantine's sons, of course, were Christians. Each was courted by Church leaders hoping for imperial favor. In the Christian empire the great bishops had become courtiers, and religious matters had become so entangled with imperial politics that taking one side or the other in a theological dispute might imply choosing one member of the royal family over another. Such choices were not made lightly. When emperors came to blows, blood flowed in rivers, and backing the wrong man (that is, the loser) could in retrospect be considered treason.

Who among the three emperors was the "right" man? Athanasius had been careful not to criticize Constantius directly, but it was clear that the Eastern ruler was primarily responsible for the exiles' plight. Constantius could be considered an "oppressor," but he was also Constantine the Great's favorite son: a clever, determined strategist who could be subtle or ruthless, depending on what the situation required, and who had the long memory characteristic of Roman rulers. He was not a person one would want to offend unnecessarily.

In contrast to Constantius, whose gravity belied his youth, Julius's own sovereign, Constans, seemed flighty and irritable. This may have been a result of his tender age and precocious experience; now sixteen, he had been named Caesar at the age of ten and was fourteen when his father died. His relations with his older brothers were strained; at the division of the empire, Constantius had insisted on adding European Thrace to his own domains, and Constantine II, at twenty-four the eldest son, was known to be discontented with his relegation to the backward Atlantic provinces.

As Julius well knew, Athanasius was already involved with both of Constans's brothers. Not only was he Constantius's *bête noire*, he had become a confidant of Constantine II during his first exile in Trier. Faced with these complexities, the Roman bishop waited. His caution was justified by the events of spring 340, when Constantine II launched his ill-advised invasion of Constans's territory. Although there is no evidence that Athanasius had prior knowledge of the attack or that he advised it, his previous relationship with the invader made him suspect, and Constans would not deign to meet him for several years hence.[150]

Even so, as the Eastern exiles began to arrive in Rome, each with his own story of Arian atrocities and official oppression, Julius gradually made up his mind to support them. His decision was strongly influenced by long-standing differences between the churchmen of the East and West. Among the Latin bishops there was great suspicion of the overly clever Greeks, with their tendency to produce novel combinations of Christian and Platonic ideas. Western churchmen had not been persecuted to the extent that their Eastern brethren had, but they toiled in a rougher physical and social environment, less urbanized, more exposed to barbarian threats and incursions, and less completely Christianized. These beleaguered clergymen had little taste for high-flown theory and no sympathy at all for Eastern attempts to qualify the divinity of Jesus. The Christ they preached to their ex-pagan congregants was God on earth, period—and if this produced difficulties for some Middle Eastern intellectuals, so be it.

As a result, Julius could easily rally the Western Church to support Athanasius (an intellectual *and* an upholder of Christ-as-God) and to oppose Arianism. But would Constans approve? With Constantine II out of the way, the young Augustus now ruled the entire West, as his father had before becoming sole emperor. Constantius, standing astride the East, played the role that Licinius had enacted before the civil war with Constantine. To the extent that the Arian controversy took the form of a religious struggle between East and West, Constans would be following the precedent set by his father, who had risen to absolute power by championing the True Faith against an Eastern persecutor. In fact, if the emperor thought about the matter in pure power terms, he might even see supporting the exiles as a way of keeping disorder alive in Eastern cities, thus weakening his brother's hold on his own base.

After Constantine II's defeat in 340, Marcellus of Ancyra arrived in Rome.[151] Together with other exiles, he and Athanasius renewed their request that Julius ask both Eastern and Western bishops to attend a great council under his presidency. There is no direct evidence that Julius discussed the matter with Constans, but it seems unlikely that he would have acted as he did without his master's enthusiastic consent. Using two priests as messengers, he dispatched a letter to the bishops in Antioch that was, in effect, a declaration of theological war. In the message,

Julius referred to the Eastern bishops as "Eusebians" and "Arians," criticized them for abandoning the principles of Nicaea, and held them responsible for the recent civil disorders. Then he invited them to a council for the purpose of reviewing the cases of Athanasius, Marcellus, and others unjustly deposed![152]

The council that Julius proposed was precedent-shattering in several respects. It would be convened by the Roman prelate, not an emperor. It would consist of both Eastern and Western churchmen, probably with a Western majority. (At the Council of Nicaea, only a handful of the 270 to 280 bishops present had been from the West.) And, most important, it would presume to review the decisions made by Eastern bishops at properly constituted Church councils. Julius must have understood how the East would react to these innovations. The Roman pontiff was the leading bishop in the West, with broad powers over the clergy under his supervision, but four "popes" in the East were accorded similar powers.[153] Because of Peter's and Paul's connection with the city, Rome had a special place in Christian history, but the pope's authority outside his own domain was not generally recognized and, up to this point, had not been asserted. The Latin bishops took care of their problems in the West, and the Greeks of their own in the East.

The Eastern bishops waited to respond until January 341, when ninety-seven of them met in Antioch to dedicate the golden, octagonal church that Constantine had originally begun there. The reply of this Dedication Council was predictably hostile. As earlier noted,[154] the bishops rejected the label "Arian" ("for how should we who are bishops follow a presbyter?"). They discussed and adopted several creeds that tried to steer a middle course between extreme Arianism and those doctrines of Athanasius and Marcellus that equated Jesus with God.[155] Then they fired back a letter putting Julius unmistakably in his place.

No, they would not come to Rome for a great council! The date was *most* inconvenient. Moreover, Julius's invitation violated the established practice whereby Eastern and Western bishops accepted each others' judgments in matters affecting their own clergy. What right had the bishop of Rome to sit in judgment on the decisions of Church councils outside his jurisdiction? Julius praised the Nicene Creed, but according to the canons of Nicaea, councils of bishops were not permitted to to reverse decisions made by prior councils, nor were bishops allowed to have communion with clergy excommunicated elsewhere. The decisions made at the councils of Tyre and Antioch were perfectly lawful. Therefore, if Julius continued to embrace excommunicated bishops, the East would cease communicating with him.[156]

Julius received this answer (one assumes, without great surprise) and immediately counterattacked with a long letter approved by a council of fifty Western bishops.[157] To begin with, he finds the tone of the Dedication Council's statement insulting.

> I have read your letter which was brought to me by my Presbyters . . . and I am surprised to find that, whereas I wrote to you in charity and with conscious sincerity, you have replied to me in an unbecoming and contentious temper; for the pride and arrogance of the writers is plainly exhibited in that letter.[158]

What gives the fractious easterners the right to lord it over their more peaceful Western colleagues? To the charge of overturning decisions of earlier councils he replies *tu quoque*—you, too!— since it was the Arians who had overturned Nicaea by pardoning heretics and readmitting them to communion. By contrast, indicates Julius, Athanasius and Marcellus are perfectly orthodox Christians. After examining both cases in detail, he finds their condemnation indefensible. It is not he but the Arians who have generated shameful disorders by evicting blameless bishops from their sees and replacing them with unqualified hacks.

As to his right to convene a great council, Julius answers in a few cryptic phrases still debated by scholars. He seems to assert a general right to judge cases involving the occupants of other important sees, but his phraseology is unclear.[159] What is quite clear, however, is that he puts the cases of Athanasius and Marcellus on the same theological and moral footing—probably a mistake, since the Eastern bishops had never accused Athanasius of heresy, only of violence, and Marcellus's theology *did* seem to make the Son disappear entirely into the Father. The significance of this exchange of letters, in any case, transcends the immediate issues they address. With this invitation and refusal, the Arian controversy becomes a major factor in the escalating conflict between East and West.

Early in 342 an incident occurred that awakened Constantius abruptly to the perils he faced. He was again fighting the Persians, who had risen under King Shapur against the Roman occupation of Mesopotamia, when his old friend Eusebius of Nicomedia died. The emperor had orchestrated Eusebius's appointment as bishop of Constantinople a few years earlier, after exiling the rabid anti-Arian, Paul, to the West. Now, in a moment, the situation had changed. The principal leader of the Arian movement was gone. Constantius and his army were more than one thousand miles away, separated from the capital by bad mountain roads and winter weather, and one of the empire's most important sees was vacant.

The anti-Arian exiles must have been wild with excitement. Paul's supporters in the city assured him that if he returned, he would be welcomed by enormous crowds. Perhaps emboldened by Athanasius, and almost certainly with the consent of Constans and the bishop of Trier, the exiled bishop made an unauthorized return to his city. He was greeted, as promised, by large crowds of militant supporters and installed as metropolitan bishop in the Church of the Holy Apostles. But his opponents were also active. They elected the moderate Arian, Macedonius, as bishop and mobilized their own substantial forces for street action.

Constantius heard the news in Antioch, where he was spending the winter with the army. Enraged by Paul's presumption, he dispatched Hermogenes, one of his top generals, to Constantinople by boat with a small company of troops on board. Hermogenes's orders were to evict Paul from the cathedral, arrest him, and hold him until the emperor returned from his spring campaign. When the general entered the city, however, he found it in chaos. Paul's supporters were battling the partisans of Macedonius; many people had already been killed, and portions of the city were in flames. Hermogenes decided to rest his troops for the night and consider the next day how best to arrest Paul . . . but at the height of the violence the mob found the house where he was staying and set it afire. Then they seized the general and his hosts, pulled them into the street, and beat them to death.

Constantius could scarcely contain his wrath. Braving the winter weather, he marched north and west at the head of a large body of troops, entered Constantinople, and arrested Paul. It is not clear how much resistance there was to this intervention, but there were undoubtedly more deaths and injuries. Constantius checked the impulse to have Paul executed; killing bishops was not a good idea unless one wanted to create martyrs and provoke further disorders. He also decided not to massacre Paul's supporters or imprison them en masse, but they were numerous enough to justify punishing the city for their misdeeds. The emperor reduced Constantinople's subsidy of free grain by one-half, hoping that the city's residents would blame the anti-Arians for their suffering. Then he had the bishops install Macedonius as metropolitan, and saw to it that Paul was put in chains aboard a westbound ship.

Paul came immediately to Constans in Trier. The Western emperor now asked Athanasius to attend him as well, and then wrote Constantius the first in a series of increasingly threatening letters. He insisted that his brother send a delegation of Eastern bishops to explain why Athanasius and Paul had been deposed and exiled, and to defend their own beliefs.

It would be a mistake to assume that Constans was making

cynical use of the religious controversy for his own political purposes. Of course, he was interested in weakening Constantius, and, if the opportunity presented itself, in displacing him. He knew that his brother was tied down on the Persian frontier and could not afford to challenge him directly, especially with a deeply divided populace at home. On the other hand, he probably took religious issues as seriously as did the other members of his family. His famous guests, Athanasius, Marcellus, and Paul, were charismatic leaders, clever theologians, and spectacular victims. Constans may well have believed that in defending them against Constantius and the Arians, he was taking the side of true Christianity against heresy and oppression, as his father had done in his contest with Licinius.

Constantius quickly acceded to his brother's request. As Constans had recognized, he was in no position to fight a war on two fronts, especially with disorders disrupting the orderly conduct of business in several of his major cities. Moreover, Constans had already begun talking about the need for a great council such as that proposed by Bishop Julius, and Constantius may have thought that a tactful visit by an Eastern delegation could head it off. Four bishops therefore arrived in Trier late in 342, bearing copies of a creed (the Fourth Creed of the Dedication Council) that struck a more conciliatory note. Though the statement did not use the Nicene *homoousios*, it did denounce the extreme Arians "who say that the Son is from nothing or is from another *hypostasis* and is not from God, and that there was a time when he was not."[160] It also contained one phrase clearly critical of Marcellus's theology. The document (and, very likely, the oral explanations that accompanied it) suggested the basis for a possible compromise: the East would condemn extreme Arianism if the West would give up its advocacy of Marcellus's "Sabellianism."

The proferred deal, if that is what it was, was unceremoniously refused. A few months after receiving the Eastern delegation,

Constans sent his brother another message insisting that a general council of Eastern and Western bishops meet at Serdica (modern Sofia), just on the western side of the East-West border. Constantius understood that the council would be controlled by Constans's people, but he did not feel that he was in a strong enough position to refuse the demand. He therefore sent a relatively small number of bishops (seventy-six is the number most frequently given) to the meeting place in the company of three of his top officials.

THE COUNCIL of Serdica was a disaster with strong overtones of farce—a spectacular failure that threatened to create a permanent breach between the Greek and Latin halves of the Church. In the spring of 343, more than ninety Western bishops came to the Balkan city. Their leader was old Hosius of Cordova, Constantine's advisor and the presiding bishop at the Council of Nicaea. Hosius arrived in the company of the Eastern exiles, although Paul of Constantinople, whose bloody attempt to reclaim his see had become a major embarassment to his allies, was absent. Bishop Julius attended but played a quiet role; with Hosius in the chair and Maximinus of Trier at his side, the council was clearly under Constans's control.

With one or two exceptions the westerners were united, and they were very confident on their home grounds. They stayed with friends in the city, whose population had been swollen by the arrival of a large "cheering section" composed of anti-Arian militants from Alexandria and several other Eastern cities. The Eastern bishops, by contrast, arrived looking like a group of Daniels on their way to the lion's den. They had caucused a few days earlier at Philippopolis, just inside Constantius's territory, and had discussed how to deal with the fact that they would almost certainly be outvoted (and, very likely, excommunicated) when major issues were decided by the full council. Feeling quite besieged, they sheltered in a wing of the imperial palace along with Constantius's representatives.

From these headquarters, the easterners played for time. They sent Hosius and the westerners a message refusing to meet in council with men like Athanasius and Marcellus, who had been cast out of the Church by properly constituted Church councils. Their opponents responded that they would not exclude bishops with whom they were in communion, and who they believed had been wrongly condemned and exiled. The Arians should leave their palace and let the council begin. The diplomatic duel continued for days. Hosius made an offer to mediate the issue, and the East rejected it. The easterners countered with an offer to send a joint commission to Egypt to reinvestigate Athanasius's misdeeds, and the West rejected that. Stalemate.

In the midst of this intense maneuvering, a letter suddenly arrived from Constantius announcing a dramatic victory over the Persians. Seizing on this as an excuse to leave Serdica (almost any excuse would have sufficed), the easterners breathed a sigh of relief and departed in haste, leaving a message explaining their conduct in care of a local priest. Once safely arrived in Philippopolis, they dispatched an encyclical letter to all priests and bishops that reiterated their condemnations of the exiles and excommunicated several Western bishops, including Hosius, Julius, and Maximinus of Trier. Briefly and angrily they charged their opponents at the council with heresy, crimes of violence, and immoral conduct. Finally, they subscribed to a creed identical to that earlier brought to Constans, except for the addition of additional anathemas aimed at the extreme Arians[161] and at the Athanasians.[162] Then they left for their home cities, promising to meet again later in the year at Antioch.

The Western bishops, meanwhile, remained at Serdica long enough to produce eight documents. Furious at their enemies' secretive departure, they addressed a letter to all Christian clergy that began:

The Arian heretics have often committed many rash acts against the servants of God who preserve the true catholic faith. Pushing their bastard doctrines, they have tried to persecute the orthodox. And now they have attacked the faith so violently that it does not escape the religious piety of the most clement emperors.[163]

The letter goes on to denounce the flight of the Eastern bishops. It names eleven Arian leaders to be excommunicated and deposed, and declares that nobody should communicate with them, since they are of the devil. The westerners defend the anti-Arian exiles and denounce the violence against orthodox Christians in the East. (They are careful not to criticize Constantius directly for this; all blame falls on those whose lies have misled the noble emperor.) Finally, they attach a long, rambling, and vituperative Profession of Faith that would later prove embarrassing to Athanasius, since its crude theological formulations virtually abolished the distinction between the Father and the Son.[164]

Thus ended the Council of Serdica—a noncouncil, really, since the opposing sides never met as a single body. At this point, both sides drew back in something like horror, shocked by how far they had allowed their differences and their anger to take them toward a complete split between East and West. Hindsight tells us that several centuries later the breach would become irreconcilable, dividing the Christian world permanently into separate Latin and Greek faiths. In the fourth century, however, such a schism seemed, if not unthinkable, then wildly inadvisable. The Church had triumphed only two decades earlier. How could it now be allowed to fragment? The emperors whose enmity had helped fuel the controversy must have wondered how either of them could hope to rule a united empire if the Church ceased to exist as a single entity. And for devout Christians, of course, the Church was more than an organization. It was Christ's own congregation, the fruit of the Holy Spirit, and to split it would be to desecrate the very body of the Savior himself.

A period of reconciliation was thus in the offing. But neither the clash of Greek and Latin cultures nor the central issues of the Arian controversy had been resolved. How could reconciliation begin while church and state remained embroiled in each other's affairs, and the competition between the emperors continued to escalate? These were the questions that haunted the parties to the conflict as they tried to stop it—to stop themselves—from plunging the Roman world into all-out civil war.

A FEW DAYS after the Eastern bishops left Serdica, the Westerners sent another message to Constantius, far more moderate in tone, asking him to order his magistrates to "refrain from surveillance of religion." The clement and gracious emperor should allow his subjects to choose their bishops and priests without interference. He should put an end to civil violence and the oppression of sincere Christians by envious, disingenuous opponents. The bishops implored Constantius to restore the exiles to their rightful positions and to turn his back on the "novel and terrible plague" of Arianism.[165]

This letter seems on its face to be a plea for separation of church and state, but, of course, it is not. Neither side in the controversy believed in this modern doctrine; Athanasius and his allies would have been delighted to have the emperor send his troops to expel all the Arians from their sees and replace them with good Athanasians! Nor did anyone seriously contemplate permitting the common people to choose their own religious leaders. Still, the letter reveals some of the complex and unexpected effects of mixing religion with politics.

Christianity had been forged in the cauldron of persecution; Christ himself was a victim of state terror. One of the religion's most dramatic narrative themes, therefore, was the conflict between persecuted Truth and oppressive Power. In a controversy that was not only a war of ideas between bishops and a power struggle between emperors, but also a fight for the allegiance of ordinary Christians, persecution (at least within limits) conferred certain advantages. To be oppressed by the state did not "prove" that one was in possession of the truth, but it evoked a set of powerful associations based on the imagery of the indifferent Pilate, the stiff-necked Jews, the brutal Roman soldiery, and the suffering Lord.

Athanasius and his allies knew how to make use of these images and did so at every opportunity. At present they portrayed Constantius as a sort of Pilate, basically well meaning, but weak, unprincipled, and easily swayed by evil, purposeful men. A bit later the imagery would shift, and Athanasius would compare him unfavorably to Judas and Nero! Constans also grasped the propaganda opportunity created by Constantius's "oppression." While the Eastern bishops arrived at Serdica with a political escort, the Western emperor kept his officials (and himself) out of sight, thus underlining the anti-Arian argument that Arian theology required state power to prop it up. If Constantius would cease persecution of the "orthodox," they insisted, the people would acclaim Athanasius and Marcellus as Christian heroes.

This was untrue, of course. At the popular as well as the episcopal level, the East was deeply and passionately divided over the issues posed by the Arian controversy. It was the closeness and intensity of this division, in fact, that tempted both sides to use imperial power whenever possible to tip the balance toward themselves. On his own territory Constans was less interventionist than his brother, in part because the West was not much interested in the controversy, and because state power in the West was not as efficiently organized as it was in the East.[166] Constantius was more apt to take sides in local religious disputes, but, although sympathetic to subordinationist ideas, his interest always lay more in maintaining civil order than in promoting Arianism. The real initiative for involving the Roman state in the affairs of the Christian Church, it seems clear, came from the Christians themselves.

Why should believers who understand the meaning of persecution involve the government in disputes over religious doctrines? For one thing, when a highly successful religious movement is on the verge of conquering society, government sponsorship may promise to make its beliefs universal. Constantine the Great played the role of "universalizer" for Christian believers by granting the Church the same privileges (plus a few additional rights) that Rome had previously granted the pagan priesthood. His attempt, through the bishops, to stamp out Arianism at the Council of Nicaea was really part of the same project: defining the doctrine of the universal Church. In both cases, the state was not thought of as imposing religious views on unbelievers so much as ratifying and organizing an existing religious consensus. For this reason, in addition to immediate advantage, most believers did not feel threatened by the Christian emperor's heavy involvement in Church affairs.

State intervention may seem even more necessary when people feel that their religious organization or vision is in serious danger of extinction. Then they turn to the state as Arius and Eusebius turned to Constantine, and as Athanasius and Marcellus turned to Constans, for defense against a powerful and aggressive competitor. In such cases the endangered party asks the government to play an openly partisan role, but partisanship is justified on the grounds that it is the only way to prevent the triumph of evil . . . and that the state is already involved in the dispute, but on the wrong side. When Athanasius asks Constans to put him back in the bishop's chair in Alexandria (we will see that this is his next move), he uses both justifications. Arianism, he argues, is fundamentally anti-Christian, and Constantius's oppressive power, which supports it, can only be nullified by Constans's liberating power.

To modern eyes this sort of argument may seem terribly benighted and old-fashioned. Why not simply separate church and state as liberal democracies have learned to do? In fact, this sort of separation seems to work best when most people do not care desperately about religious ideas, and when neither a universal-izing opportunity nor a danger of extinction exists for any major group. In the last days of Rome—and, according to some pas-sionate believers, in our own time—both scenarios seemed to exist simultaneously and to reinforce each other. The Roman masses cared deeply about religious ideas. Christian belief had swept paganism away and was now reaching even the lands oc-cupied by the barbarians. But "true" Christianity (differently de-fined, of course, by Arians and Athanasians) was in danger of extinction by an evil enemy with access to state power.

How could one *not* invoke the aid of the state under such circumstances? There seemed so very much to gain by doing so—and so very much to lose if one did not! And so Athanasius, who had subscribed to the Western bishops' statement demand-ing religious freedom in the East, had no hesitation in calling upon Constans to force his brother, if necessary, to readmit him to Alexandria and to restore the other exiles to their sees. Free-dom was not the real issue here. The issue was Truth, for on it hung salvation. To achieve this goal, it would be worth risking even the horrors of civil war.

A MOST UNLIKELY series of events—a comedy if one does not count the trouble it caused—aided Athanasius's campaign, and may even have helped avert an East-West war.

The site of the action was Antioch, Constantius's military headquarters and the center of Arian religious power. After the dangerous split at Serdica, the Western bishops sent a small del-egation to the city to deliver their message to Constantius, along with another mild letter from Constans requesting that he con-sider readmitting some of the exiles to their sees. Two bishops, Vincentius of Capua and Euphrates of Cologne, and one of Con-stans's generals, carried the letters to the palace, where they paid their respects to the emperor. Then they returned to their lodgings while Constantius considered the issues raised by these new communications.

The bishop of Antioch, Stephanus by name, was one of the Arian leaders who had been singled out for abuse and excommunication by the Western bishops. Still enraged by this treatment, and apparently determined to sabotage the westerners' mission, he sent two of his priests in disguise to a well-known brothel. Their instructions were to hire a prostitute to spend the night with the delegation's senior member, Euphrates of Cologne. In the morning the bishop would be "discovered" with a lady in his bed. He would leave Antioch in disgrace, his cause would be besmirched, and the insult to Stephanus would be avenged.

The priests did exactly as they were told, but they made one mistake. They did not tell the lady in question that her client was an aged Gallic bishop! When she found the old man sleeping peacefully in his bed with his bishop's regalia laid out on a nearby chair, the prostitute (what a shame we do not know her name) thought quickly. Pretending that she was being attacked, she began screaming for help. The bishop's bedroom was soon full of rescuers, and the clever woman was able to tell her story without fear of reprisals by Stephanus or his men.

The story spread quickly through the city, and by dawn an angry mob had gathered outside the doors of the cathedral, demanding that Stephanus explain himself or face deposition. Constantius was forced to send officials to placate the crowd. An immediate investigation was promised and quickly completed. The keeper of the brothel identified the priests who had sought his services; the priests confessed that Stephanus had put them up to the ugly prank, and in the summer of 344, the bishop of Antioch was excommunicated and deposed by the Council of Antioch.

Constantius, who had no patience for this sort of infantile meddling in affairs of state, let the council know that it was time to conciliate the westerners, not provoke them. Stephanus was quickly replaced by a moderate, and the council adopted the famous "Long-lined Creed," a lengthy document that "breathed the spirit of appeasement."[167] Four members of the council took it to the Western bishops at Milan. The creed affirmed the spiritual unity of Jesus and God more strongly than any previous Eastern statement had done:

> [The Father and Son] are united with each other without mediation or distance. . . . They exist inseparable, the whole of the Father embracing the Son, and the whole of the Son attached and adhering to the Father, and alone resting on the Father's bosom continually.[168]

At the same time, as a further sign of his desire for compromise, Constantius released a number of Athanasius's supporters from exile and ordered his officials to stop treating the pro-Athanasian clergy in Alexandria as plotters against his regime.

The West, too, made conciliatory gestures. The Council of Milan (345) condemned and deposed one of Marcellus of Ancyra's extreme disciples, Bishop Photinus of Sirmium. Moreover, without condemning Marcellus himself, both Athanasius and the Western bishops drew away from him; publicly, at least, he was on the way to becoming a "nonperson." Each side, in fact, was attempting to muzzle its extremists and alter its language in order to demonstrate its good faith, but without surrendering the beliefs it considered too vital to compromise. The question was whether these conciliatory gestures could produce a peaceful settlement without dealing with essential items of theological disagreement or the continuing power struggle between the emperors.

The areas of religious disagreement seemed to have narrowed, but the differences that remained were critical. Although they soft-pedaled their subordinationism, the easterners could not give up the idea that the Father, Son, and Holy Spirit were three separate and unequal entities. Nor could the Western bishops at Milan stop themselves from insisting that the Eastern delegates formally denounce Arius and his essential teachings—an act that they refused to perform and that resulted in their leaving the council in a huff.[169] Furthermore, the two emperors could not rest easily as joint rulers of the empire. Their chess game continued, with Constans sensing a strategic advantage and inclined to press it whenever possible.

Probably with Constans's connivance (although this is not known for certain), Paul returned to Constantinople in 344 and reoccupied its cathedral—a "dare," in effect, to Constantius, for if Paul were openly challenged as he had been two years earlier, or if he were injured or killed, his supporters would surely riot. The Eastern emperor would again be compelled to march westward, this time from far-off Mesopotamia, and by the time he arrived, his capital would be in flames.

Several days later, ensconced in the cathedral, Paul received a long-awaited invitation. The city's chief civil official, the Praetorian Prefect Phillipus, graciously asked him to visit him in the baths of Zeuxippus. Paul knew exactly what this meant; an invitation to bathe in the company of other well-bred men was one of the customary methods whereby one aristocrat honored another. The emperor could not recognize Paul himself without alienating his Arian allies, so he must have told the prefect to do so in his stead, discreetly, as a way of preparing the public for a change.

Paul went to the baths at the appointed hour. He found them empty, except for the prefect and an armed escort. Too late to escape: the doors were barred. Before he could even consider shouting for help, the unlucky bishop was bound, gagged, and put aboard a ship in the Bosporus Strait. When he was released from his bonds at sea, he learned that his destination was Thessalonica, in the territory of his protector, Constans.

WITH PAUL back in his court and the Council of Milan fruitlessly ended, Constans decided that he had had enough of polite diplomacy. In the summer of 345 he sent Constantius an ultimatum that left little to the imagination:

Athanasius and Paul are here with me. From questioning them I have discovered that they are being persecuted for the sake of piety. Accordingly, if you undertake to restore them to their episcopal thrones, expelling those who are vainly clinging to them, I shall send the men to you. But if you were to refuse to take this action, be assured that I will come in person and restore them to the thrones which are theirs, even against your will.[170]

This was an unmistakable threat of war. Constantius might well have yielded to it in any case, but in June 345, Gregory (who had replaced Athanasius as bishop of Alexandria when he was exiled) died suddenly, leaving the great see vacant. An election by the Egyptian bishops would have been uproarious, and Athanasius would probably have won it. He had maintained contact with his supporters during his exile, and tended to be more popular while out of the country, playing the role of persecuted hero, than when in power. In any case, Constantius knew when to lay down his king in a game of chess. From the Persian front he sent a message to Athanasius and Constans offering the bishop safe passage to Alexandria and full restoration to his episcopal office.

In Aquileia with Constans, Athanasius perused the letter, with its ornate diplomatic language and false sentiment. "Our unwearying piety has not abandoned you while you have been deprived of your ancestral hearth and stripped of your belongings and wander in savage wildernesses."[171] Athanasius may have been overjoyed to be returned to office, but he was not fool enough to rush back to claim his bishop's chair. He understood quite well that Constantius had restored him, in effect, with a sword at his throat, and that if relations between the two brothers were to deteriorate, the Eastern emperor would consider him an enemy. Therefore, as he had done before, he took a lengthy and circuitous route home, pausing in city after city to rally his supporters, collect testimonials, and solicit guarantees of protection from imperial officials. He apparently met Constantius in Antioch and received personal assurances that the enjoyment of his office would be undisturbed. Only then—in the summer of 346, about one year after receiving Constantius's letter—did he reenter Alexandria.

It was a triumphant return. Not only had Athanasius maintained a loyal base of supporters among the Egyptian clergy, his popularity among the common people had grown. In part this was a result of his travails and his exile, but it was also a result of potent feelings of local patriotism. It is much too early, of course, to speak of Egyptian nationalism. In any case, the locus of loyalty was not Egypt so much as Alexandria—a proud city with a long history of cultural achievement, independent thinking, and hostility toward imperial power. The people of Alexandria (once Cleopatra's city) had developed a strong sense of their vulnerability to oppression by powerful rulers housed in Rome, or, for that matter, in Antioch or Constantinople. Athanasius may have been an oppressive ruler in his own right, but he was no outsider—he was one of theirs.

Constantius, too, understood the special role played by Egypt in conflicts between imperial rivals. Common usage might divide the Roman world into East and West, but, with some justification, Alexandrians considered their part of the world *sui generis*: in language, Greek; in politics, part of the Eastern Empire; but with a unique character of its own, vital economic resources, and ties to the West antedating Julius Caesar. One could never be entirely sure of the Egyptians' loyalty, and because they had the capacity to play a makeweight role in East-West struggles, they were often courted by both sides. Constantius allowed Athanasius to return not only because Constans demanded it, but because it was better to have the Alexandrian hero under his watchful eye than conspiring with his brother in Europe.

Athanasius returned to Alexandria overland from Jerusalem, like an emperor marching home after a long, victorious war. His reception was even more impressive than an emperor's, for while it was customary for a monarch to be greeted ten miles from his city, great crowds of supporters met Athanasius at the hundredth milestone.[172] As he entered the city and moved toward the cathedral, flowers were strewn in his path. Masses of thanksgiving were celebrated in all the churches. Alexandria rejoiced, and if the stormy bishop still had enemies everywhere, they remained for a while invisible.

Paul returned to Constantinople at about the same time, and other pro-Nicene exiles were also allowed to return to their sees. But Constantius would not forget that these priests had been befriended by his brother—his enemy—and imposed upon him by force. He understood quite well that one can lose a game of chess without losing the entire match.

Nine

The Arian Empire

For three years Arian and Nicene Christians coexisted uneasily, fundamentally unreconciled but impotent to alter the balance of forces that prevented either side from securing a decisive victory. By appealing to the Roman state for support, bishops and theologians had tied their fortunes to the outcome of the struggle between Constans, emperor of the Nicene West, and Constantius, Arian ruler of the East. Athanasius and his allies had returned to their cities, but the vast majority of Eastern bishops remained hostile to their theology, and Constantius considered them both traitors to his regime. The West was predominantly anti-Arian, yet Constans was unprepared to carry the Nicene faith at sword point to the East. For the moment there was stalemate . . . but it would not last very long.

The first sign of change came from the Persian front. In 349 King Shapur lifted his siege of the city of Nisibis in Mesopotamia, relieving some of the immediate pressure on Constantius. Swarms of insects had attacked the Persian troops, forcing them to retreat—an event that Christians in that city attributed to divine intervention in response to the prayers of their popular bishop.[173] In fact, Shapur's withdrawal was temporary, as were all Roman victories at this point in history. There was no possibility of permanent relief from the inexorable pressure of migrating peoples on the empire's four-thousand-mile-long frontier.

But for the time being the East gave thanks, acclaiming Constantius as defender of the Faith against the infidel hordes.

The emperor's reputation as a Christian champion was further enhanced by a series of missions that he personally sponsored to convert the barbarian tribes. He welcomed to court the remarkable Ulfila, a Goth from the trans-Danubian region who had been converted to Christianity and then ordained bishop by Eusebius of Nicomedia.[174] Ulfila, whose Greek grandmother had been carried into capitivity by the Visigoths, was now translating the Bible from Greek into Gothic. With Constantius's support, he promised, he would win his huge tribe to the Christian faith. The emperor provided the aid, and Ulfila kept his promise. Not only did the Visigoths remain Arian Christians for the next two centuries, they converted additional tribes to the Arian faith, including the Ostrogoths, Burgundians, and Vandals.

Subsequent missions went from the imperial court to Ethiopia, Arabia, and India, but it was not just in foreign affairs that Constantius showed himself to be a zealous promoter of Christianity. He continued his father's policies of granting special privileges to the Christian clergy and disadvantaging the pagans. A bit later he would attempt to close the old believers' temples and to prohibit animal sacrifices. He also legislated against the Jews, banning marriages between Jewish men and Christian women and forbidding Jews to circumcise their slaves[175]—measures suggesting that there was still competition between Christians and Jews for new converts. Meanwhile, Constantius exempted bishops, priests, and their children from paying taxes to the cities, freed them from making payments in kind for the support of the army, and so favored them, in general, that even those who considered him unorthodox found it hard to portray him as a conscious enemy of the Church.

The Eastern emperor's position was further strengthened by developments in the West. The haughty and unstable Constans had never inspired great affection among Gauls and Britons, but if the reports Constantius was receiving were accurate, his brother's position as Western ruler had become dangerously shaky. If popularity among the common people, although helpful to a Roman emperor, was not essential to the maintenance of his power, loyalty among his top administrators and generals certainly was. The glamour of being Constantine the Great's son had initially won the young man some breathing room, but Constans now had few defenders among his own people. They considered him violent and capricious, unreliable, a poor administrator, and—a serious problem for a Christian emperor—personally corrupt. The charges against him ranged from pederasty to soliciting bribes, but his principal problem was a lack of confidence among his general staff. With Frankish warriors challenging Roman defenses all up and down the Rhine, the troubled youth seemed incapable of decisive action. His own officers were rumored to be plotting against him.

Did Constantius, perhaps, encourage these plots? One would not be surprised to learn that he did, but there is no evidence to support the allegation. On the other hand, he did not hesitate to take advantage of Constans's weakness to rid himself of local enemies. Clergymen he admired and trusted reported that Paul and Athanasius still refused to communicate with those they insisted on calling heretics and agents of the devil. Moreover, to leave Alexandria, with her precious grain supplies, and his own capital, Constantinople, in the hands of disloyal prelates would be as foolish as his brother's erratic behavior. There was no longer any reason to delay moving against the anti-Arians, beginning with the most vulnerable target, Paul of Constantinople.

A long list of crimes could be attributed to Paul's account, including the devastating riots inspired by his earlier return to the city. Continued pressure by imperial agents had steadily weakened his organized support in the capital, and he could now be deposed without inspiring riots. Not long after King Shapur turned back from the gates of Nisibis, therefore, the bishops of Asia Minor met in council outside Constantinople, deposed Paul, and sent him to Constantius in chains. The emperor would no longer exile such men to Europe to plot with Constans against him. This time, instead of putting the bishop on another westbound ship, he dispatched him with a military guard to Cucusus, a remote village in the Taurus Mountains of eastern Cappadocia, where he would remain under close surveillance.[176]

Soon after this, another council meeting in Antioch condemned and deposed Athanasius. Again the councilors cited a long list of past offenses, focusing on the Alexandrian bishop's violent acts and political plotting rather than on doctrinal issues. They accused him of working to turn Constans against Constantius and noted that his return to Alexandria, accomplished through political pressure, contravened the prior decisions of at least four Church councils. Their choice to replace Athanasius was George of Cappadocia, a committed Arian who had spent time studying in Alexandria. Constantius had already commanded the praetorian prefect to accompany George to Alexandria, when stunning news arrived from the West. Constans had been overthrown and brutally murdered by a previously unknown usurper.

THE REBEL, it turned out, was Magnentius, a Gallic general of common birth and uncommon military talent. In January 350 at Autun in central Gaul he had himself acclaimed emperor by the army. The takeover was well prepared; there was virtually no resistance on the part of Constans's few remaining supporters. The young fugitive fled south to Narbonne on the Mediterranean coast, hoping to escape by sea, but Magnentius's men captured him just outside the city and executed him on the spot.

Magnentius (also a Christian) immediately asked Constantius to recognize him as Augustus of the West, but there was never any chance of that. While Constantius wound up his Persian campaign and prepared to move his army west, Magnentius seized the North African provinces and moved quickly into Italy, where he crushed an uprising by one of the emperor's nephews. In the Balkans, however, Constantius's half-sister, Constantina, saw to it that a general loyal to her brother was proclaimed emperor, thus keeping that strategically vital territory out of the usurper's hands. The compliant general, Vetranio by name, would resign in Constantius's favor as soon as his army crossed over into Europe.

Constantius's army entered the Balkan region early in 351. He added Vetranio's legions to his own, established his headquarters at Sirmium, the imperial capital just south of the Danube, and sent his army westward to do battle with Magnentius. The victory was not as easy as might have been expected. The war, which would last more than three years, was lengthened not only by Magnentius's military skill and the good quality of his army, but by the deepening separation of the Greek and Latin halves of the empire. Though Constantius could make a far stronger claim to legal legitimacy than the usurper—who desperately sought a royal connection by marrying one of Constantine the Great's granddaughters—his invasion of the West had the air of a foreign conquest and probably solidified support of the Gallic challenger by the locally recruited Western army.

Magnentius might have resisted Constantius's legions for a long time if he had been willing to fight guerrilla-style, but that was not the Roman (or, for that matter, the "barbarian") way. In September 351, after a number of smaller battles had been won and lost on both sides, the rebellious general was maneuvered into fighting an enormous drawn battle at Mursa in the northern Balkans. The casualties were terrible, but the victory went to Constantius's forces. The following year the emperor brought Italy under his control, and in the summer of 353 his army crossed the Alps into Gaul and defeated Magnentius's troops decisively. On August 10 the usurper committed suicide in Lyon, leaving Constantius sole ruler of the Roman world.

Not quite sole, perhaps. When the civil war began, Constantius recognized that he could not rule the entire empire single-handedly. Upon arriving in the Balkans, he called upon the two nephews whose lives he had spared in the familial massacre that accompanied his and his brothers' accession to power. The elder nephew, Gallus, he made Caesar of the East, giving him his sister in marriage. Gallus was to rule from Antioch and to guard the Persian frontier while Constantius was in the West. But the arrogant young man proved to be a wilder version of Constans: an incompetent ruler whose irresponsible abuse of power first triggered a revolt among the Palestinian Jews, and then brought the entire regime into disrepute. After defeating Magnentius, Constantius induced Gallus to come to court in Milan, stripped him of the imperial insignia, and had him tried for high treason. He was executed immediately afterward at the imperial estate at Pola, where Constantine's son, Crispus, had met his end almost half a century earlier.

Gallus's younger half-brother, Julian, was cut of different cloth. When Constantius took the field against Magnentius, Julian was studying philosophy with an assortment of Christian and pagan thinkers and disclaiming all interest in worldly power. Constantius ordered him to court at the same time that he summoned Gallus to his death and had him closely watched. After a while, satisfied of his loyalty, the emperor permitted him to study in Athens, where he came strongly under the influence of neo-Platonist philosophers and wonder-working pagan priests, and developed a passionate attachment (that he kept carefully hidden) to the ancient mystery religions.

In 355, knowing none of this but requiring help to combat the Germanic tribes, Constantius made Julian Caesar of the West, with his capital in Trier. The Frankish warriors had crossed the Rhine and sacked Cologne and Mainz, opening a serious breach in the Roman defenses. Constantius probably thought that he could not err by appointing the young scholar Caesar. Either Julian would help him defeat the barbarians—a victory for which Constantius would claim full credit—or, more likely, the Franks would kill him, thus ridding the emperor of another enigmatic relative. To everyone's surprise—perhaps even Julian's—the young man proved to be a resourceful and popular general. He and Constantius, each in command of an army, collaborated brilliantly in turning back the Franks and restoring security to Rome's Rhenish frontier for the first time in many years.

With the West at least temporarily pacified, Constantius left Julian in Trier and returned to Sirmium, confident that he had at last appointed a competent soldier and administrator to represent him in Europe. Julian ruled as a Christian, apparently favoring the Nicene cause advocated by most Western bishops, but scrupulously avoiding taking sides. Constantius was impressed by the young man's maturity and good judgment. There would come a time, however, when he would regret his apparently judicious choice of Caesar.

CONSTANTIUS HAD NOW achieved his father's exalted status: supreme ruler of an undivided Roman Empire. Within the Christian community—perhaps one should say the partially overlapping Greek and Latin, Arian and Nicene communities— the question on everyone's mind was how he would use this extraordinary power. Bishop Athanasius, not ordinarily a fearful person, waited in Alexandria like a defendant awaiting the announcement of his sentence. He had just learned the fate of Paul of Constantinople and wondered if it would be his destiny as well.

Poor Paul! Once exiled to far-off Cucusus, he must have thought that he would be immune as a bishop from further punishment. But he did not reckon with the effects of the civil war.

Near the start of the conflict, Magnentius had made serious efforts to gain the support of Constantius's enemies in the East. As soon as it became clear that the emperor would not recognize him as the Western Augustus, he had sent envoys eastward—clergymen accompanied by diplomats or soldiers—with messages of friendship for the leading anti-Arian bishops and promises to promote the Nicene cause if his own campaign proved victorious.

Athanasius had had the good sense to turn Magnentius's delegation away and to appear in public the next day, surrounded by high civil officials, to pray loudly for the success of "the most pious Augustus Constantius."[177] Paul had been less judicious. He received either the envoys or their message at his place of exile and evidently made some ambiguous or favorable response. Paul was indiscreet enough, in any case, to provide Constantius's agents with evidence that treasonable contact had been established. The emperor said a word to his chief "enforcer," the Praetorian Prefect Phillipus, and Phillipus passed a message to Paul's guards in Cucusus. The custom of granting Christian bishops immunity from physical punishment was abruptly abrogated. The guards threw Paul into a prison cell, starved him for six days, and then strangled him.

If Athanasius avoided a similar catastophe, this was not just because he had prayed publicly for Constantius, but because the emperor did not want to confront him while Magnentius was still a live threat to his regime. Athanasius was clearly the most powerful man in Egypt in the early 350s. Alarmed by the possibility that Magnentius might attempt to detach Egypt from the Eastern camp, Constantius postponed the attempt to replace the Alexandrian bishop with George of Cappadocia. Then he sent Athanasius a message asking him not to believe the rumors that he had had anything to do with Constans's death. ("Your wisdom will easily be able to judge with how great a sorrow I was afflicted, when I learned that he had been murdered by the vilest treachery.") The letter admonished Athanasius to fulfill his duties as bishop. It concluded, "For it is our resolve that, in accordance with our wishes, you be bishop in your own place for all time."[178]

Brandish the letter as he might, after the war began in earnest Athanasius could not avoid accusations that he had had treasonable communications with Magnentius. A council of Arian bishops meeting in 351 accused him on two counts: first, that he attempted to turn Constans against his brother; second, that he had become an active supporter of Magnentius. To document this accusation the bishops produced a letter to the usurper, allegedly in Athanasius's handwriting, in which he promised to assist him against his godless opponent.

Athanasius defended himself against these charges in a document entitled "Defense before Constantius." In the first place, he insisted, he had never met privately with Constans. All his meetings with the Western emperor were public, and high officials present would testify that he had never spoken ill of Constantius before his brother. Nor had he even considered corresponding with the traitor, Magnentius. "What reason was there to induce me to write to such a man?" he asked rhetorically.

> How could I have commenced my letter, had I written to him? Could I have said, "You have done well to murder the man who honored me, whose kindness I shall never forget?" Or, "I approve of your conduct in destroying our Christian friends and most faithful brethren?"[179]

As to the alleged letter to the usurper, it was nothing more than a clever forgery:

> [E]ven if [my accuser] can show writing resembling mine, the thing is not certain; for there are forgers who have often imitated the hand even of you who are Emperors. . . . I would then again ask my accusers, Who provided you with these copies? And whence were they obtained?[180]

Would Athanasius have been so foolish as to commit treasonous acts in writing? Was it credible that he had never met privately—not even once—with Constans? Whatever the truth of these matters, Constantius undoubtedly considered the charges superfluous. As the war turned in his favor, two things seemed quite clear. The first was that Athanasius was an incurable troublemaker and inveterate enemy who must be gotten rid of. The second was that an immediate frontal attack was unwise. Not only did the bishop's popularity make the cost of suppressing him high, but Constantius had also come to understand that the source of the problem was not Athanasius himself or even the Arian controversy per se. It was the overlap of that controversy with the East-West split in the Church.

THE DIVISION between Latin and Greek Christians had already proved a threat to Constantius's power as well as an offense against Christian unity. When the civil war ended, with God's help, he would be ruler of a legally undivided empire . . . but what good was legal unity if his people were divided in every other way? If the problem were not solved, the same cultural and religious split that had helped turn Constans against him would make further rebellions inevitable and would weaken Rome's ability to repel the barbarians. No, he would not give up his father's dream of using Christianity to unify all the Roman peoples. At the war's end he would isolate the religious fanatics, East and West, and bring the moderates of both camps together in harmonious union.

Of course, when Constantius spoke of moderation, what he meant was moderate Arianism. A story that made the rounds at the time attempted to link his victory in the civil war with his advocacy of the Arian cause. According to one fourth century historian, the emperor awaited news of the Battle of Mursa at a chapel near the battlefield, knowing that the outcome of the civil

war might well be decided by that single contest.[181] The bishop
of Mursa was Valens, a well-known Arian theologian. According
to the (anti-Arian) tale, the conniving bishop employed swift
messengers to determine the outcome of the battle before anyone else had news of it.[182] Then he came to the chapel and told
Constantius that an angelic host had appeared to him in a vision
and had proclaimed his victory. Constantius thereupon made
Valens one of his principal advisors.

We do not need the story, however, to explain the emperor's
strong inclination toward mainstream Arianism, or the importance of Western Arians like Valens of Mursa to his plans. Arian
Christianity was the religion of his region, with deep roots in
Eastern intellectual history. The idea of a hierarchically ordered
"Godhead," with Father, Son, and Holy Spirit ranked according
to their appropriate degrees of power and glory, had a strong appeal in the rank-minded East, and may have been particularly
attractive to a hereditary member of the imperial elite. Furthermore, there was a rationalist element in Arianism, an insistence
on clarity and logic, and on coherent readings of the Gospels,
that those schooled in Greek philosophy were particularly likely
to appreciate. Most of all, Constantius would have appreciated
the temperament of the moderate Arians: their relatively optimistic view of people's potential to make moral progress and to
assist in their own salvation; their capacity (again relative) to tolerate a variety of theological perspectives without declaring their
opponents agents of the devil; and their modest disinclination to
claim knowledge of matters beyond human understanding, like
the precise relationship between the Father and the Son.

Conversely, the Nicene doctrine, especially as expressed by
Latin zealots like Ambrose of Milan and the wild-eyed Sardin-
ian, Lucifer of Caralis, seemed presumptuous in its claim to
knowledge of divine relationships. Overly fond of paradoxes, in-
tolerant of other theologies, and inclined to pander to rural prej-
udices, it did not seem a reasonable faith at all. And Constantius

was keenly aware of the Nicene bishops' tendency to bemoan imperial "interference" in the affairs of the Church. Hypocrites! They had applauded when Constantine exiled Arius and his supporters, and they would have nothing but praise for him if he were to dispatch the rest of the Arians beyond the Pillars of Hercules.

Clearly, now that Constantius stood astride the Latin and Greek worlds, it was time to take on the problem of the dangerous split in the Church, which Nicene intransigence was inflaming. The emperor knew that many Latin churchmen had opposed him both in his rivalry with Constans and his war with Magnentius, and he was not inclined to be solicitous of their views. At the same time, he did not want to play a purely punitive role—the conqueror imposing his own views on an unwilling clergy and populace. His goal, to preside over the unification of Rome as a Christian community, was the same as Constantine's. But his intention was to surpass his father. Constantius would do what Constantine had attempted to do at the Council of Nicaea, but do it better.

His father, after all, had been a man of the rough West, not a cultured Greek speaker who understood the Eastern passions for ideological and political combat. Advised by the naive westerner, Hosius of Cordova, Constantine had not taken the Arian controversy seriously enough. Seeking a quick resolution, he had forced a narrow, divisive, ill-considered creed on the Eastern bishops. Then, to make matters worse, he had failed to back up his own decisions with sufficient consistency and determination. Constantius was determined to correct both parental errors. His efforts would be empirewide, not just regional. He would convene a series of smaller councils designed to culminate in a truly ecumenical meeting uniting the Eastern and Western bishops. The purpose of this process would be to establish the broadest possible basis for a doctrinal agreement—not the Nicene Creed, which had become a source of violent contention in the community, but some formula closer to the theological center. Then, having isolated the fanatical and disloyal elements, he would enforce the new consensus with all the power at his disposal.

History repeats itself, but "the first time as tragedy, the second as farce."[183] Achieving consensus was exactly what Constantine thought he had done at Nicaea, but the apparent unity manifested there proved illusory. The hastily designed creed with its controversial *homoousios* reflected the thinking of most Western bishops and an Eastern minority centered in Egypt, not the ideas and sensibilities of most Greek-speaking churchmen. This reality forced Constantine to abandon the search for a doctrinal unity that could only have been achieved by imposition, and that, therefore, would not be genuine at all.

Constantius thought that he could succeed where his father had failed—but how *could* he succeed, unless there was some substantial basis for doctrinal agreement? In fact, the son stepped unwittingly into the same trap that had ensnared his father. He assumed that a consensus roughly comporting with his own ideas existed among the bishops, and that it would become manifest once the correct formula could be found to express it. As a Greek, he also assumed the superiority of his own cultural preferences (masquerading, as always, as the universal preferences of mankind) to those of a few fanatical Latins. It seemed clear to Constantius that Constantine had been too weak and changeable in dealing with clever intellectuals and ecclesiastical politicians. He would *not* cowtow to troublesome clergymen as his father had done! Surely, there must be some combination of reason and compulsion that could induce the bishops to end their destructive conflict and unite for the good of the empire. . . .

All this is reminiscent of a Greek tragedy. In attempting to surpass the father, the son replicates his most egregious errors. In attempting to vindicate his vision, he betrays his principles. If the ancient gods existed, they might well have laughed at this all-too-human demonstration of hubris and blindness to fate.

Now BEGAN a campaign of unprecedented intensity within the state-led Church to discover a generally acceptable formula of faith and the appropriate level of force needed to compel dissenters to accept it. In his efforts to end the Arian controversy and unify Christendom, Constantius convened at least nine Church councils, most of them in the West. Groups of bishops met under his watchful eye at Sirmium (351), Arles (353), Béziers (353), and Milan (355); at Sirmium three times more (357, 358, and 359); at the huge joint council of Rimini-Seleucia (359), and, finally, at Constantinople (360). Other meetings were held without his presence but with his permission; several were banned; and a few, unsanctioned, convened secretly.

It is commonly believed that the authorized meetings were dominated by Constantius, and that the Arian creeds they produced were little more than responses by frightened churchmen to state terror, but the whole truth is more complex and interesting. There *was* compulsion, no doubt, since Constantius was quite willing to exile deposed bishops and to harass their supporters severely. But so long as there were no rivals to the throne to give religious dissent the color of treason, the emperor avoided punishing doctrinal opponents as traitors. As a result, leading theologians and agitators were free most of the time to think and agitate, provided they were willing to pay a certain price in occupational insecurity and domestic discomfort. These were not pleasant or justifiable choices to impose on churchmen, but Constantius was far from the violent tyrant pictured by Athanasius and other critics. By the standards of his time (and certainly as compared with modern dictators), he was a relatively easygoing ruler.[184]

Even so, the councils of the 350s did not proceed as Constantius had hoped they would. Their final result, formally speaking, was what he intended: the adoption of a broad, simple declaration of faith by virtually all Christian bishops, Latin as well as Greek, Nicene and Arian. But the process that produced this outcome was poisoned by unresolved conflicts. Each council, as the series progressed, was attended by a larger and more diverse group of churchmen. Each tended to be stormier than the last, involving the emperor in a more active and blatantly coercive role. And each creed adopted generated more passionate and widespread dissent. This was not because the Christian world as a whole believed that Jesus Christ was God Almighty, but because the underlying consensus that Constantius sought to discover did not yet exist.

The first few councils had a wartime air about them. They were attended by relatively small numbers of bishops, many of them easterners come to Europe especially for the occasion. At Sirmium, Arles, and Milan, Constantius had two purposes: to obtain Western condemnations of Athanasius so that the bishop would be outflanked and isolated in Alexandria, and to secure the bishops' agreement to a minimalist creed that both Arians and Nicenes could sign. The First Sirmian Creed was identical to that brought to Constans ten years earlier by representatives of the Dedication Council, except that it added a series of new anathemas condemning the positions adopted by extreme Arians and Sabellians.[185] The document's middle-of-the-road intentions were obvious. Without using either the language of the Nicene Creed or the slogans of Arianism, it described Jesus as "begotten from the Father before all ages, god from God, light from light."[186]

Except for its omission of the Nicene *homoousios,* the creed was considered uncontroversial. Most of those present executed it and accepted the condemnation of Athanasius. At this early point, with a civil war still in progress, few Western bishops were willing to risk their careers for the sake of Athansius's reputation, or to avoid signing a vague statement that might be capable of an Arian interpretation. A few strong supporters of the Nicene Creed who refused to collaborate were promptly exiled by Constantius. The best known of these resistors were Bishop Julius of Rome, who was exiled for two years and then restored to office when he agreed to cooperate; old Hosius of Cordova, who was also "turned" later on by threats and pressure; and the young Gallic theologian, Hilary of Poitiers.

According to a story told by Hilary, one participant at the Council of Milan offered to condemn Athanasius if the others present would sign a copy of the Nicene Creed. When Dionysius of Milan took out his pen to sign, Valens of Mursa knocked it from his hand, saying, "You can't do that sort of thing here!" Constantius then moved the whole council to the imperial palace so that he could keep the proceedings under better control.[187] Old Hosius reacted fiercely to this interference by the emperor. "Do not intrude yourself into the affairs of the church, and do not give us advice about these matters," he lectured his sovereign, "but rather receive instruction on them from us."

> God has given you kingship, but has entrusted us with what belongs to the church. Just as the man who tries to steal your position as emperor contradicts God who has placed you there, so too you should be afraid of becoming guilty of a great offense by putting the affairs of the church under your control.[188]

Athanasius put the matter even more briefly. "If there is a decision by bishops, what concern has the emperor with it? But if it is merely a threat from the emperor, what need in that case for the so-called bishops?"[189]

Stirring words, which read today like a brief for separation of church and state, but the Nicene partisans meant nothing of the sort. They would no doubt have viewed the idea of building a "wall of separation" between the Church and the empire as absurd and immoral. Constantius considered the criticism mere rhetoric and ignored it. From his perspective the campaign was moving in the right direction. Since there was little resistance, he had not been compelled to exercise much force, and Athanasius, already isolated in the East, was now effectively abandoned by his Western allies. While the Council of Milan was meeting, Constantius gave orders to begin direct efforts to remove the troublesome Alexandrian from office.

IN THE FALL of 355 an imperial negotiator arrived in the Egyptian capital with orders to persuade Athanasius to leave the city voluntarily. Four months of discussions failed to produce the desired result. The bishop may still have banked on Constantius's unwillingness to risk replicating the disastrous riots of Constantinople in Alexandria by removing him against his will. If so, he was mistaken. On January 6, 356, a group of civil and military officials entered the city at the head of a small army. At first, Athanasius held his ground. He brandished Constantius's letter promising him perpetual enjoyment of his office and requested that the leader of the imperial troops write the emperor to confirm his orders. The official agreed, but three weeks later, perhaps after receiving fresh orders, he moved his forces by night into the Church of Theonas where Athanasius was living and attempted to arrest him. The wary bishop had again gotten advance word of the impending attack, however, and escaped to the desert.

Now all pretense of civility between Constantius and Athanasius disappeared. For the next five years Athanasius remained in hiding, sometimes daring to return to the city itself, but more often protected by the monks of the Nile valley. Constantius wrote an open letter to the Alexandrians condemning him in the strongest (and haughtiest) terms as a man from the lowest social level—"one of the multitude in power"—who had deceived the people, corrupted the state, and polluted the Church. "[Athanasius] would only suffer the punishment he deserves," thundered Constantius, "if one were to kill him ten times over."[190] Athanasius replied in kind. From various monasteries he poured out a series of written works, some primarily theological[191] and others wild diatribes against Constantius, whom he branded a persecutor worse than Saul, Ahab, Pilate, and the Jews who crucified Jesus.[192] The emperor was no Christian at all, Athanasius declared; he was the precursor of the Antichrist.[193]

Meanwhile, Alexandria became the empire's most riotous city. While the fugitive bishop moved from one hiding place to another like an outlaw hero, gangs of his supporters seized the churches, were dislodged by rival militias or imperial troops, then seized the churches again. More officials and troops were needed to protect George of Cappadocia, the Arian churchman who was brought in as Athanasius's successor. Some of the Egyptian clergy went into hiding or exile to avoid serving the new leader, but most cooperated, at least for the time being. George was given control of the city's free grain supply, but he never really gained control of the city. In 358, a riot by an Athanasian mob caught him in the Church of Dionysius and almost took his life. He left Alexandria to attend a series of major Church councils and did not return until three years had passed: an unlucky reentry, as readers may recall.

The Arians pressed their advantage. In 357 a council of bishops meeting again in Sirmium produced a creed that had enormous impact throughout the Christian world. For the first time, a distinctively Arian statement of faith was formulated by a Church council and presented as orthodox to the entire Christian community. The document began by professing belief in "one almighty God and Father . . . and his only Son Jesus Christ the Lord, our Saviour, born [or generated] from him before the ages." Nothing controversial there. But it went on to outlaw the use of the terms *homoousios* (identity of essence) and *ho-*

moiousios (similarity of essence) to describe the Father's relationship to the Son. The reason for this, said the bishops, was that the concept of "essence"

> is not included in the divine Scriptures, and it is beyond man's knowledge, nor can anyone explain the birth of the Son. . . . for it is clear that only the Father knows how he begot his Son, and the Son how he was begotten by the Father.[194]

Still, the creed asserted,

> There is no uncertainty about the Father being greater: it cannot be doubted by anyone that the Father is greater in honor, in dignity, in glory, in majesty, in the very name of "Father," for he himself witnesses . . . [that "He who sent me is greater than I"].[195]

The document concluded by affirming the basic Arian propositions that there are "two Persons of the Father and the Son" of which the Father is the greater; that Christ "took human nature from the virgin Mary, and it was through this that he suffered" (that is, God did not suffer, man did); and that the Holy Spirit "is through the Son" rather than being coequal with God.[196]

The Second Sirmian Creed was "a trumpet which was heard from one end of the empire to the other."[197] It was not *radically* Arian; it did not insist that Christ was a mere creature created from nothing or that he was capable of sinning. But it was clearly Arian in a way that previous statements intended to be more conciliatory had not been. The creed's attempt to ban the official use of "essence" doctrines generated passionate protest by the Nicenes, who denounced the "Blasphemy of Sirmium" and rallied with unexpected energy to the defense of the *homoousion*. The Latin bishops were clearly resentful of their Greek colleagues' tendency to treat them like uncultured, overzealous country bumpkins. Under pressure from Constantius and the Eastern Church, something like a regional rebellion—or, at least, a wave of self-assertion—was taking place in the West. Ironically, the backlash produced by Constantius's search for consensus unified the Latin Church but further divided the empire.

DEVELOPMENTS on the Arian side were even more explosive. Ascendant throughout the East, the Arian movement was splintering doctrinally as it approached power, just as the Christian movement as a whole had done at the accession of Constantine. Which Arianism would triumph? A large conservative group insisted that Christ was "the exact image" of God, a divine being similar in essence to the Creator, although not identical to Him.[198] To them as well as to the Nicenes, the Sirmian Creed was a blasphemy—since they believed that without a fundamental ontogenetic or "family" resemblance to the Father, Jesus could not be the Divine Son capable of saving humanity and worthy of its worship. On the opposite side, a small but growing number of radicals led by the philosopher Aetius maintained that Christ was essentially *dissimilar* in essence to God, hence, not on the same level at all.[199] Since he was more than man, some radicals concluded that he must be a sort of lesser god. "The Son is in constitution midway between the Father and the angels," said one radical leader, "and can be called the angel of the High God, as he is the god of all lesser beings."[200]

This sort of speculation was too extreme for a third group of churchmen midway in size between the first two. The second Sirmian Creed reflected the views of these moderate radicals, who believed that the most one could sensibly say of the relationship between the Father and the Son was that they were "similar." Since one could not specify this similarity without unscriptural and unprovable speculation, they called for a ban on all mention of essences. God's relationship to His Son was a topic on which Christians should be free to disagree.

Not at all, the conservatives replied. If Christians were free to reduce Jesus to the level of a superangel, they would soon consider it acceptable to consider him a mere human prophet. And who wanted to worship a superangel, anyway? Basil of Ancyra, leader of the conservative forces, convened a council on his own authority that vehemently protested the radical "coup" at Sirmium. When the radicals replied with reproaches and denunciations of their own, Constantius moved quickly to restore order in the Eastern camp. He appointed a joint committee of conservatives and moderate radicals to design a compromise creed. This statement, he declared, would be presented to the largest council of bishops in Church history—the first council universal enough to deserve the description "ecumenical."

The committee met and reported to Constantius. Pleased with its work, the emperor dispatched more than six hundred invitations summoning the empire's Christian bishops to council. In the summer of 359 about 160 Eastern bishops convened at Seleucia in Asia Minor, while more than 400 Western churchmen (many of them rounded up by Constantius's officials) gathered slightly later at Rimini on Italy's Adriatic coast. The participants in both councils were handed the joint committee's short statement of faith (the so-called Dated Creed), which included this key provision:

> Since the term essence (*ousia*) was adopted by the fathers [at Nicaea] without proper reflection [or "naively"] and, not being known by the people, causes offense because the scriptures do not contain it, it has been resolved that it should be removed and that in future there should be no mention whatever of essence in regard to God, since the divine scriptures nowhere refer to essence [when speaking] about Father and Son. *But we declare that the Son is like the Father in all things, as the holy scriptures indeed declare and teach.*[201]

"Like the Father in all things . . ." The emperor believed that the Eastern bishops would accept this as a reasonable compromise, while the westerners would subscribe either because they found it vague enough to be unobjectionable or because they feared the consequences of refusal. He proved to be wrong on both counts. Both councils were unusually stormy; it took Constantius six months to get them to affirm an even more abbreviated and controversial version of the creed.

At Rimini a substantial majority of Latin bishops rejected the proposed statement outright. To them, the statement that "The Son is like the Father in all things" was not ambiguous at all. It was pure Arianism, since similarity is *not* identity, and the creed's open-ended language made it acceptable even to the moderate radicals. The Latins defiantly reaffirmed their belief in the Nicene Creed and, adding injury to insult as far as Constantius was concerned, went on to excommunicate the leading Western Arians, including Valens of Mursa. Then they asked permission to leave Rimini.

Permission was denied. The bishops sent a delegation to Constantinople to plead the majority's case before the emperor, but they found him preparing for another military campaign; the Persians had scored important victories in Mesopotamia and were now threatening Armenia. While Constantius busied himself with war preparations, the delegates were forbidden to leave the capital. Week after week they were subjected to a steady barrage of arguments, cajolery, pressure, and threats of exile by Arian churchmen and imperial officials. Finally, after more than three months, they surrendered. They signed a creed that banned the use of the terms *ousia* and *hypostasis,* dropped the phrase, "in all things," and stated simply that the Son is "like the Father." Constantius then insisted that the bishops trapped at Rimini accept the same statement. With winter coming on they needed to return home, and they recognized that if they did not execute the creed, they would very likely have no homes to which to return. In the end, they signed, too.

Western resistance had been expected, but the meeting of Eastern bishops at Seleucia proved much more difficult than Constantius had anticipated. The moderate radicals wanted a creed like that signed at Rimini, stating simply that the Son was "like" the Father. The conservatives insisted on "likeness of essence," or at the very least, "like the Father in all things." Tempers flared; old feuds were rehearsed; and each side took to excommunicating and deposing the other. Finally, after the Latin bishops had fallen in line at Rimini, Constantius insisted that the Greeks ratify the same document. Again, he mixed strong doses of persuasion and coercion. After a debate that lasted throughout the night of December 31, 359, the last signature was obtained, and the Creed of Rimini-Seleucia was published. A few months later, to eliminate all procedural objections, the emperor convened a single council representing both Greek and Latin bishops at Constantinople and had them ratify the same creed.

At last Constantius had the result he had been seeking for almost twenty years. The Roman Church had substituted a simple, broadly inclusive statement of faith that any Arian could sign for the vexatious Nicene Creed. At least on paper, the East and West were united. Writing in Rome, St. Jerome described the situation with his customary prejudice and dramatic flair. As if after a drunken party, he said, the Roman world "awoke with a groan to find itself Arian."[202]

Ten

Old Gods and New

WHILE the Arians were triumphing at the Council of Seleucia, King Shapur of Persia was winning another kind of victory in Roman Mesopotamia. In December 359, the fortress city of Amida, gateway to Armenia, fell to his troops, and Constantius was forced to ask his nephew, the Caesar Julian, to send reinforcements from the West. This interesting young man, who treated his Gallic and ex-"barbarian" soldiers like true Romans, had won a series of spectacular victories over the Germanic tribes and was considered a great hero by both the army and the people. When he informed his men that his uncle Constantius had ordered them to fight under his command in far-off Mesopotamia, they rebelled. (One cannot help suspecting that he may have announced the news in such a way as to make rebellion inevitable.) In February 360 at Paris, his soldiers hoisted him on their shields and declared that they would no longer take orders from Constantius. Their leader was Julian, whom they proclaimed Augustus of the West.

The Eastern emperor could do nothing about this coup. In the spring he led his troops back to Mesopotamia, where they fought another series of inconclusive battles against the Persians. Meanwhile, Julian moved to challenge his uncle for leadership of the Roman world. To begin with (as if to demonstrate the connection between imperial politics and religious debate), he solidified his support among the Western bishops by permitting Hilary of Poitiers and his allies to convene a militantly pro-Nicene council in Paris. The bishops wasted little time in debate; they denounced the Creed of Constantinople, excommunicated the leading Western Arians, and proclaimed their continued adherence to the Nicene Creed, *homoousios* and all. In the summer, Julian marched his army through northern Italy and into the Balkans, gathering up pledges of loyalty from officials nominally responsible to Constantius. This time there was no one to prevent the Balkan legions from joining forces with the challenger. Arrived at last in Sirmium, Julian publicly questioned his uncle's competence to rule and offered his support to all those Constantius had persecuted.

Once more a Western general appeared as a liberator at the gates of the East. It was as if Julian was living out Constantine the Great's life and the conquest fantasy of Constans. But his own dreams were far more intoxicating than anyone suspected. Constantius, who still enjoyed substantial popular support in his own region, returned from Persia prepared to fight a civil war to retain his throne. But fate had other plans for the Arian emperor. He became seriously ill in Cilicia (malaria is suspected by some modern commentators)[203] and died at the age of forty-four. Before succumbing, he proclaimed Julian his successor for the sake of imperial unity. Whether he would have done so if he had known his nephew's true beliefs is doubtful, to say the least.

Like Constantius and Constantine, Julian dreamed of unifying the Roman Empire and restoring its lost glory. But the religion that he believed would make this renaissance posssible was not Christianity, it was paganism. Throwing off the pious Christian mask he had worn for the past decade, he revealed himself publicly to be a passionate believer in Greek mysticism and a worshiper of the ancient gods, with a particular affection for Helios, the sun god. Before his conversion, the young Constantine had also devoted himself to Helios, but Julian's real model was

not Constantine, it was Alexander the Great: pagan par excellence, student of Aristotle, and conqueror of the Persians. Julian
may or may not have believed in reincarnation, but especially
after the deaths of his wife and infant son left him without a
family, he felt the spirit of Alexander moving in his veins.

Now that it was no longer necessary to dissimulate, the
would-be Alexander announced that he had come not only to liberate the East from Arianism but the entire empire from the burdens imposed on it by "the cult of the Galilean." He cleverly
combined this religious message with edicts lowering taxes, can-
celing debts, and restoring lands to the cities. Anti-Christian
riots in some cities testified either to the strength of latent pagan
sentiment there, public gratitude for tax relief, or both.[204] No
doubt, the initial enthusiasm for Julian among some of the common people also reflected their distaste for the scandalous disunity of the Church. Christianity had conspicuously failed to
bring the empire together or to secure it from enemy attack. As
the contemporary historian Ammianus said, "no wild beasts are
such enemies to makind as are most Christians in their deadly
hatred of one another."[205] The old religion, more in harmony
with the Greco-Roman spirit, could succeed where Christianity
had failed, Julian thought, *if* it borrowed the "Galileans'" most
effective organizational innovations: their rational administrative
structure and their powerful network of social services.

First, however, this still-potent Christian organization had to
be weakened. Here Julian proved to be quite canny. It suited his
purposes to have the Christians battling each other throughout
the empire. Although too numerous and influential to be persecuted out of existence by a young pagan emperor, they seemed
quite willing to batter each other to the point of mutual extinction. The question that the Nicenes had asked of the Arians—
could they survive without state support?—he now asked of the
faith as a whole. There was every sign that, simply left to their
own devices, contending groups of Christians would split their
Church into half a dozen or more competing sects. Therefore,

while depriving the Christian clergy of the special privileges bestowed upon them by his predecessors, Julian took steps to re-
inflame the Arian controversy. He issued orders permitting
Athanasius, other pro-Nicenes, and dissident Arians to return
from exile. Then, after a brief tour of the East in which he re-
dedicated a number of pagan temples, he sat back to await the
disintegration of the "Galilean" faith.

VIOLENCE between competing Christian groups broke out
almost immediately. The first victim of Julian's new order was
the hapless George of Alexandria, who had been imprisoned
when the news of Constantius's death reached the city. After
George was killed by a mixed mob of pagans and anti-Arian
Christians, his body was paraded through the streets of Alexandria on the back of a camel and burned.[206] Julian did not seem
unduly dismayed when similar disorders ripped other major
cities including Antioch and Constantinople. Perhaps, left to its
own devices, the Church *would* self-destruct!

But the young emperor miscalculated. In fact, he made two
serious mistakes, one strategic and one tactical. Strategically, Julian did not understand that defeating Christianity would require
more than imitating its external form of organization. The religion itself was changing in response to the pressures of history
on human souls. To replace it, paganism would have to become
an inward faith, a religion offering sanctuary from the whirlwind
of earthly desire, one with a view of salvation capable of satisfying people's new spiritual ambitions, and with a vision of a City
of God that could replace the failing City of Man. In short, paganism would have to become Christianity. Or, if it wished to
avoid worshiping the man Julian called "the Galilean," it would
have to become Judaism!

Julian's response to this dilemma was logical but, at that moment, historically unfeasible: he attempted to revive the City of
Man. His vision of himself as Alexander the Great was essential

to this project. Just as he had defeated the Germans (the peace he established on the Rhine *did* last more than a half century), so he would dispose of the Persians and the rest of Rome's enemies. Fear and taxes would decline; prosperity and worldly expectations would rise. If the empire proved viable, the Christians would find a shrinking market for their otherworldly deity and their cult of self-denial. If it failed, the reign of the old gods would end with that of the Augusti. Almost as soon as he had taken power, therefore, Julian began preparing for a final war against Persia.

Meanwhile, he attempted to light the fires of an old-world cultural renaissance. Julian consulted with leading neo-Platonist intellectuals, reformed the pagan priesthood, brought the radical Arian philosopher, Aetius, to Constantinople for discussions, and promised the Jews that he would rebuild their temple at Jerusalem. Always, he assumed that the loss of state power would accelerate the pluralist tendencies within Christianity, and that multiple fractures would result. This is where he probably made his most serious tactical error. The young emperor had clearly imbibed some stereotypes of his own about Christian "fanaticism" . . . and, perhaps, about old dogs learning new tricks. As a result, he underestimated the capacity of leading Christian ideologues to alter their style of disputation and even, to an extent, the shape and content of their ideas, in order to forge alliances with former enemies.

The mistake was understandable. It was only natural to assume that Bishop Athanasius, as obstreperous as ever, would continue to attack those he called "Ariomaniacs" (one of his more civil terms for the Arians). Obviously, the old dogmatist would refuse to collaborate with anyone who did not endorse his own theology from alpha to omega. But, once returned to office in Alexandria, Athanasius surprised everyone. In a reversal of policy that caught the entire Roman world unawares, he declared that those who accept Christ's full divinity, but who still have doubts about the doctrine of *homoousion,* "must not be treated as enemies."

> Nor do we here attack them as Ariomaniacs, nor as opponents
> of the Fathers, but we discuss the matter with them as broth-
> ers with brothers, who mean what we mean, and dispute only
> about the word.[207]

Only about the word! Athanasius was talking here about
those he had previously described as heretics of the worst sort:
the large group of conservative Arians who believed that Christ
and God were essentially similar (*homoiousios*), but who did not
accept that they were essentially the same or equal (*homoousios*).
At one time, this difference seemed so important that, as the historian Gibbon facetiously remarked, the entire controversy
seemed to hang on the presence of one Greek letter.[208] It *was*
important, wasn't it? How could a passionate Nicene Christian
like Athanasius compromise with churchmen who continued to
insist that Jesus Christ was not almighty God but a separate
being inferior to the Father?

The answer is not, as one might think, that Athanasius traded
doctrinal purity for political advantage in order to block the
pagan revival. Uniting Christians against Julian's scheme was
surely one of his motives, but compromise, in his view, was neither necessary nor relevant. Athanasius advocated speaking softly
to the *homoiousians,* not cutting deals with them. For he was now
quite certain that the conservative wing of the Arian movement,
a bloc representing a substantial majority of Eastern Christians,
could be won by friendly persuasion to the Nicene faith.

THE BASIS for this optimism was Athanasius's sharp-eyed perception that a fundamental realignment of forces had recently occurred within the Christian community. The line dividing Nicenes
from Arians had shifted. The new divide separated those who denied Jesus's ultimate kinship with God—the radical and ultrarad-
ical Arians—from the Nicene Christians and conservative Arians
who affirmed it. The fate Julian had predicted for the Christians
as a whole was true for the radicals. They were doomed to shatter

as a movement, Athanasius thought, since they could agree only on a negative principle. While asserting that Jesus was *not* God, they had no agreed-upon conception of what sort of creature he *was*. The conservatives, on the other hand, knew that Christ was part of the Godhead; that is why they insisted that the Father and Son were "similar in essence." And that is what made an alliance with them justifiable as well as useful.

What does it mean, in any case, to say that two entities are "similar in essence"? To say merely that something is similar to something else, Athanasius argued, establishes no fundamental resemblance between the two entities. But to say that two things are similar *in essence* means that they share a common nature. A prejudiced Roman might say that the Goths "resemble" the Romans without meaning that they were members of the same species, but the Goths *are* similar in essence to the Romans because they are humans. The test is reproduction; if one entity can be derived from another, they must have a common nature (or, as we might say, a common genetic or molecular structure). "Thus tin is only like to silver, a wolf to a dog, and gilt brass to the true metal," Athanasius writes, "but tin is not [derived] from silver, nor could a wolf be accounted the offspring of a dog."[209]

When the conservative Arians say that Christ is like God in essence, this implies a shared nature. If Jesus exists eternally with the Father, if he is made of the very same stuff, if, in short, he is no less godly than God, what does it really mean to call him God's subordinate? In Athanasius's opinion, not much.

> For, confessing that the Son is from the essence of the Father, and not from other subsistence, and that He is not a creature or work, but His genuine and natural offspring, and that He is eternally with the father as being His Word and Wisdom, [the conservatives] are not far from accepting even the phrase, "*Homoousios*."[210]

Of course, no Nicene Christian could accept the idea that Jesus was inferior to God. "The badge of our faith," declared

Athanasius's Council of Alexandria (362), is "the Trinity of one essence (*homoousios*), true God who became man of Mary. Let all who disagree be anathema."[211] Even so, the old controversialist adopted a more understanding attitude toward the subordinationist error. For the first time he recognized that the reluctance of some Arians to equate Jesus with God sprang not from any desire to place him on a lower level, but from their fear that the doctrine of the *homoousion* would destroy him as an individual and obliterate the human aspects of his character. Therefore, in a letter produced soon after his return to Alexandria, Athanasius explained that beings sharing a common essence can still retain their individuality, and that Christ possesses a human soul, not merely a God-mind in a human body.[212]

Behind these ingenious theological arguments lay a powerful appeal to people's emotions. As debaters the radical Arians were every bit as capable as the Nicenes. Their principal thinkers, Aetius and Eunomius of Cyzicus, argued with great cogency that an uncreated or "ingenerate" God could not share that nature with any other being; hence, that Jesus could not be fully divine unless there were two Gods.[213] But the argument fell flat. If Christ wasn't on God's level, where should he be located? Christians insisted on an answer to this question. To conceive of him as some sort of superangel or lesser god was not at all ridiculous to people who believed in the existence of demons, angels, and other creatures intermediary between God and human beings. Even so, most Christians (including the Arian conservatives) considered the idea of positioning Jesus on some level closer to humanity an intolerable insult.

Did Christians really want Jesus demoted to some level far below that of Eternal God? Athanasius and his allies were certain that they did not! It was one thing to say that the Son was somewhat less than the Father, and quite another to expel him altogether from the Divine Family. Basically, the conservative Arians, like the Nicenes, wanted a strong God to worship more than they sought a semidivine friend to love or a role model to imitate. After a while, Athanasius calculated, their subordinationism would simply wither away. Meanwhile, there were enormous advantages to forming an alliance with them. Between them, the two groups represented a probable majority of all Christians. Since the conservatives were very strong in the East, the alliance would create the consensus transcending the Greek-Latin split that both sides had been seeking ever since the Arian controversy began. Best of all, a movement to unite the Church would utterly confound the brash young emperor and his utopian plans for a pagan revival.

It took Julian only eight months to reach the same conclusion. On October 24, 362, dismayed by reports of the growing solidarity among formerly opposed Christians, he issued an edict stating that the permission he had given exiled bishops to return to their cities did *not* license them to resume their bishops' thrones. Athanasius was to leave Alexandria immediately. When the city fathers resisted carrying out the order on technical grounds, Julian wrote them a furious letter demanding that the bishop be banished immediately from all Egypt. ("The infamous fellow! He has had the effrontery to baptise Greek women married to prominent citizens in my reign! Let him be hunted down!")[214] By this time, Athanasius took such reversals in stride. Terming Julian's threats "a small cloud which will soon pass,"[215] he again outwitted the soldiers sent to arrest him and headed south into the Theban desert.

SEVERAL MONTHS later, pursuing his dream of Persian conquest, the emperor came to Antioch with a vast army of soldiers and a smaller army of priests and soothsayers. After sacrificing to the gods at the temple of Apollo (the poor omens were ignored), he marched his men into Mesopotamia. At first Julian might have been forgiven for having imagined himself Alexander. The smashing victories won in his campaign down the

Tigris River recalled those of his hero.[216] City after city fell to his bold attack. Mesopotamia's large Christian and Jewish communities, as well as dissident Persians, welcomed him as a liberator. But he may have carried the parallel with the Macedonian conqueror too far. In June 363, after burning his supply ships (as Alexander had done), Julian faced a devastating Persian counterattack near the capital city of Ctesiphon. The battle went badly; Julian waded into the thick of it, and on June 26 he died while trying to rally his men, the victim of a Persian spear thrust.

Julian's dream of a pagan renaissance died with him. A persistent rumor, never proved, alleged that the thrusting weapon belonged to one of his own Christian soldiers. The Christian community, denying the calumny, preferred to consider it an instrument of God wielded by a foreign hand. According to an instant folktale, when the emperor realized he had been mortally wounded, he leaned back on his horse, opened his arms to the sky, and cried, "Galilean, you have conquered!"

An unlikely story, but it conveys a truth. Contrary to Julian's belief, Christianity did not require state power to survive. There seems, in fact, to have been an inverse relationship between the bishops' power to wield the emperor's sword against their enemies and their ability to resolve internal disputes themselves by peaceful means. Now that political instability had returned to the empire, Christian leaders and Roman rulers found themselves compelled to live without the intense, constant involvement in each other's affairs that had characterized their earlier relations. There was no possibility, of course, of divorcing church and state. But both sides were surprised to discover how useful it was to attach some limits to their intimacy.

Consider Julian's successor. The pagan emperor's defeat had not done much to inspire faith among his troops in the powers of Helios and Hercules. After his death, his officers immediately proclaimed a popular Christian general named Jovian their new commander-in-chief. Jovian withdrew the defeated army from

Mesopotamia, giving the Persians back virtually all the territory originally conquered by Diocletian and Galerius and effectively abandoning Christian Armenia. Among his first official acts as emperor were edicts reestablishing Christianity as Rome's primary religion and restoring the clergy's tax exemptions and other privileges—but at a much lower level of benefits than Constantius had maintained. Times were hard; the empire was shrinking again; taxes would have to be raised. Even the princes of Jovian's own Church would have to share the lot of their fellow citizens.

Athanasius met Jovian in Mesopotamia, where he went with churchmen representing other factions to seek the new emperor's favor. There Athanasius learned that the new ruler was a Nicene Christian who had long admired his tenacity and courage. When Jovian entered Antioch in triumph, he rode into the city with the old bishop at his side. Immediately afterward, he wrote *finis* to Athanasius's brief exile, and the prelate made another return to the Church of St. Theonas bearing a glowing letter of imperial commendation. Athanasius may have expected that the Nicene faith he had fought for so doggedly would now be recognized by Rome as the sole Christian orthodoxy. He might have been disappointed in any case, since Jovian did not seem inclined to restart the cycle of councils, creeds, depositions, and excommunications. But the matter must always remain doubtful, since after a few months in office, the soldier emperor became one of the few Roman emperors to die a purely accidental death. Jovian fell asleep in a tent in which a charcoal brazier had been left burning and was asphyxiated by the fumes.[217]

His successor, a businesslike Pannonian general named Valentinian, was a talented fighter and administrator who soon moved to the West to try to hold off the Frankish invaders. When he did so, he appointed Valens, his younger brother, Augustus of the East. Valentinian was a Nicene Christian. Valens was a committed Arian of the moderate radical type. But in the darkening atmosphere of the later fourth century, these facts no longer had vast, determinative implications. Valentinian saw himself as defender of the realm against the barbarians, not as leader of the Church. Moreover, he had not appointed his brother emperor to compete with him. While giving the Western bishops complete freedom to organize and agitate in favor of the Nicene Creed (or, for that matter, against it), he refused to approve any efforts to undermine Valens's authority in the East.

For his part Valens was somewhat more interventionist, but in comparison to earlier emperors, his efforts to favor his own party were feeble. Since he was openly pro-Arian, some Nicenes were soon accusing him of atrocious acts of persecution. But with one exception—later in his career he did oppress and harass the Egyptian clergy quite severely—Valens's policy was one of bounded but substantial toleration. Under his rule, churchmen of all schools were free to conduct vigorous campaigns in favor of their own ideas, so long as they did not openly repudiate the Creed of Constantinople or attempt to expel sitting bishops from their sees. Theological debate and ecclesiastical politics were permitted, but mob action or the scandal of mutual excommunications and depositions would not be tolerated.

Did the conservative Arians wish to hold a council? The emperor would approve it. Might the pro-Nicene bishops meet together as well? Valens saw no reason to deny their petitions, nor is it clear that his denial would have been effective. There were too many conservatives to ban without launching a major campaign of persecution, and the number of Eastern Nicenes was multiplying even more quickly, largely because of the efforts of a dynamic group of bishops centered in Cappadocia. On the other hand, when one conservative group denounced the Creed of Constantinople and called for the exile of its supporters, Valens exiled them instead. When a number of pro-Nicene bishops proposed to convene an ecumenical council in Tarsus to reaffirm the Nicene Creed and excommunicate its opponents, he banned that meeting as well. And when he saw a chance to intervene effectively in favor of the Arian candidate in a disputed election, he seized it.

Even so, without knowing it, the Arian emperor did the anti-Arians a great favor. By limiting the power of Church councils and enforcing minimal rules of civility, he created a space in which Nicene Christians and conservative Arians could communicate thoughtfully with each other. Under his relatively mild regime, a new theological school aimed at uniting these forces began to flourish in Asia Minor. Its greatest exponents were three boyhood friends from Cappadocia: Basil of Cappadocian Caesarea (Basil the Great), his younger brother, Gregory of Nyssa, and their best friend, Gregory of Nazianzus.

Years earlier, as young men, these three had traveled together to Athens to study philosophy and religion. There they made the acquaintance of an eccentric fellow student on leave from Emperor Constantius's court—the ruler's nephew, Julian. They could not have known, of course, that Julian would soon flash across the Roman sky like a strange comet, leaving little but darkness behind. Nor could young Julian have dreamed that, nearly two millennia later, Roman Catholics and Orthodox Christians around the world would rank the three Cappadocians among the greatest creators and exponents of their faith.

BASIL OF CAESAREA probably deserved the appellation "the Great" as much as any man of his time. This son of a wealthy Christian landowner was a remarkable combination of creative theologian, practical innovator, and ecclesiastical politician: a figure sometimes willful and overbearing, but a major force for change in the fourth-century Church. The form of city-based, service-oriented monasticism that he developed still inspires Christians around the world, and his letters contain statements deemed fundamental law by the Orthodox Church.[218] Initially close to the conservative Arians, then passionately pro-Nicene, Basil used his influence (and Valens's relative passivity) to obtain the appointment of pro-Nicene bishops and priests throughout Asia Minor, even going so far as to create new bishoprics in small towns so that they could be filled by cothinkers.[219]

Gregory of Nazianzus, Basil's oldest friend, was the group's best rhetorician and a strong theologian in his own right. He had political talent (he helped engineer Basil's election as bishop of Caesarea), but possibly because his father was a bishop, he was always ambivalent about holding office. He allowed Basil to talk him into becoming bishop of the tiny town of Sasima, and later, very briefly, metropolitan bishop of Constantinople, but he was never comfortable with the pomp and responsibilities of office. He would later retire to a contemplative life in the country. Gregory of Nyssa, Basil's younger brother and the only one of the trio to marry, was even less interested in Church politics, although he accepted appointment as bishop of Nyssa in order to promote the Nicene cause. Dreamy to the point of irresponsiblity (according to his brother), he was the master theologian of the group: a world-class philosopher whose ideas still seem fresh—and controversial—sixteen centuries after their formulation.

Together the three Cappadocians developed the ideas that would make it possible for conservative Arians and Nicene Christians eventually to fuse. Oddly, what triggered this burst of creative thinking was the appearance of a new issue that threatened to make divisions within the Christian community even more contentious and complex: the nature of the Holy Spirit.[220] As Basil pointed out, the growing debate about the Holy Spirit (which most Christians conceived of as some sort of person or "Him") recapitulated the controversy about the nature of the Son. The radical Arians were certain that, just as the Son was inferior to the Father, the Spirit was inferior to the Son. Even leading Nicenes, Basil admitted, were uncertain or divided.

> Of the wise men among ourselves, some have conceived of
> him [the Holy Spirit] as an activity, some as a creature, some
> as God; and some have been uncertain which to call him. . . .
> And therefore they neither worship him nor treat him with dis-
> honor, but take up a neutral position.[221]

What was needed to clear up this confusion was something that the Nicene Creed alone could not supply: a doctrine explaining how God could be One and yet consist of two or three separate entities. And the development of this doctrine, Basil recognized, could not take place without new language. It was necessary to create a new theological vocabulary capable of going beyond the bare statement that the Father and Son were of the same essence (*homoousios*). That term expressed the Oneness of God, but how to express His multiplicity as well?

The answer was to clarify or redefine key words. Even great theologians like Athanasius used "essence" (*ousia*) and "being" (*hypostasis*) interchangeably, sometimes exchanging these words with other terms like "person" (*prosopon*). The Nicene Creed itself anathematized not only those who denied that the Father and Son were one in "essence" but those who denied that they were one in "being." This was a mistake, said the Cappadocians. The corrective was to distinguish clearly between *ousia* and *hypostasis,* essence and being. The Father, the Son, and the Holy Spirit are three separate beings, each with his own individual characteristics—they are three *hypostases.* But they are one and the same in essence—they are *homoousios.* Adopting an idea of Origen's that easterners would appreciate, Basil described Jesus as a "sharer of [God's] nature, not created by fiat, but shining out continuously from his *ousia.*" And the Holy Spirit, which the Arians and some Nicenes considered a principle or person lower down the scale of divinity than either the Father or Son, shares that same divine essence. The Holy Spirit, that is, is a third individual being (or Person) "consubstantial" with the Father and the Son.[222]

Gregory of Nyssa summed up the doctrine with characteristic sharpness. God is three individuals sharing one essence. Both the unity and the tripartite division of the Godhead are real. If this seems paradoxical, so be it:

> [T]he difference of the *hypostases* does not dissolve the continuity of their nature nor does the community of their nature dissipate the particularity of their characteristics. Do not be amazed if we declare that the same thing is united and distinct, and conceive, as in a riddle, of a new and paradoxical unity in distinction and distinction in unity.[223]

The beauty of this doctrine was that it finally rid the Nicene Creed of its Sabellian overtones. Jesus could be God without being some sort of pretended man or human shell. This made it possible eventually for "similar-in-essence" Arians to come over to the "same-in-essence" side without feeling that they were reducing Christ to the level of a name or activity of God, or some temporary and less real manifestation of the Creator. In other words, the Cappadocians argued, the conservative Arians (a group with which Basil had once been associated) could stop worrying about Jesus disappearing entirely into God. The fact that he was God incarnate did not make him any less a separate individual with a human as well as a divine nature.

FOR ALL ITS elegance, this solution was not immediately accepted. It was not intended to conciliate the radical Arians who believed that Christ was unlike God, and even the conservatives were troubled at first by the tendency of the single *ousia* shared by the three *hypostases* to reduce their individuality to relative insignificance. If Jesus was really God, how important was it that he had certain individual characteristics as well? Gregory of Nyssa might insist that the Trinity's individual components were as "real" as its unity, but he also compared Jesus's humanity to his divinity by remarking that the human part was like a drop of vinegar in the sea!—not a statement designed to reassure either radicals or conservatives that his individuality mattered. The conservative Arians were placated to some extent by Gregory of Nazianzus's statement that the Father was "greater" than the Son in the sense that the Son derived his "equality and being" from Him.[224] But this sort of talk offended the old-line Nicene bishops, some of whom (particularly in the West) suspected the Cappadocians of bending too far in the direction of Eastern subordinationism.

There were other objections as well. The doctrine was too novel, too paradoxical, too mystifying, too clever by half . . . but, to many skeptics, the new theology's most troubling feature was that, in redefining the relationship of the Father to the Son, it altered the Christian understanding of God. When the Arian controversy began, one could assume that the parties to the dispute shared similar thoughts and feelings about the Father, and disagreed primarily about the Son's essential nature and relationship to Him. In fact, one could say the same thing about Christians and Jews: that is, they agreed about the identity and knowable characteristics of God, but differed about Jesus' Messiah-ship and the extent of his divinity. Christian views of God could even be said to overlap considerably with those of enlightened pagans, who had come to accept the existence of a transcendent Supreme Being not easily distinguishable from Jehovah.[225] But the Cappadocian theology changed all that (or revealed that a transformation of Christian thinking had already taken place).

It was one thing to say, as Athanasius and other early Nicenes did, that Jesus and God shared a common essence. That meant that the Son was every whit as divine as the Father, and that he was in some mysterious way united with Him. "Identity of essence," without more, was consistent with the idea that God was *really* a Father who had in some ineffable manner begotten an equally divine Son. What the Cappadocian theology did was to make it clear that if Christ was fully divine, God could not be primarily a Father, but must equally be a Son and a Spirit. As Gregory of Nyssa put it, "God is not God because he is Father nor the Son because he is the Son, but because both possess the *ousia* of Godhead."[226]

Clearly, there was some tension between this idea of a God "distributed" over three equal Persons and the notion, mentioned earlier, that God as the Father is in some sense "greater" than God as the Son and Holy Spirit. The tension, according to some commentators, was never resolved.

> Was the Lord's prayer addressed only to the hypostasis of the Father as "our Father" and the Father of the Son, or to the entire ousia of the Godhead? Basil's answer . . . was to declare that what was common to the Three and what was distinctive among them lay beyond speech and comprehension and therefore beyond either analysis or conceptualization.[227]

This vagueness may have helped bring the conservative Arians into the fold, since they could still affirm that God's Fatherhood was more powerful or causative than His Sonship. Even today, many Christians who consider themselves orthodox conceive of God "primarily" as a Father. But the real thrust of the Cappadocian doctrine was to differentiate the Christian "Godhead," which now incorporated Jesus and the Holy Spirit, from the monolithic God worshiped by Jews, radical Arians, and, later on, by Muslims, Unitarians, Bahais, and others. Restating the relationship between Father and Son, in other words, redefined both parties, not just the Son. As a result, Christians who accepted this triune God, distributed over three Persons, no longer shared Jehovah with their Jewish forebears or the Supreme Being with their pagan neighbors, nor could Jews or pagans claim to believe in the same God as that worshiped by the Christians.

Doctrinally, this is the point at which Christianity breaks decisively with its parent faith and with other forms of monotheism that, insofar as they use family metaphors, consider God a Father and the persons created in His image Sons and Daughters. For Nicene Christians, incorporating Jesus into the Godhead was a way to preserve and extend the worship of Christ without sacrificing monotheism. For others, defining Jesus as God incarnate sacrificed monotheism by definition. It was not just a question of Jesus being recognized as God, but of God becoming Jesus.

But in the 370s, when the Cappadocian Fathers produced their greatest works, it was not at all clear that their doctrine would prove triumphant. Violent conflict between radical Arians and pro-Nicene forces was on the rise, and an Arian emperor sat on the throne of Constantine. For a Nicene victory to occur—especially for the common people as well as the intellectuals to accept Jesus as God incarnate—more than theological arguments would be required. Somehow, God would have to make His own will known through history.

Eleven

When Jesus
Became God

In 373 Athanasius of Alexandria died, full of age and honors. Although he was no longer the leader of the Nicene forces—Damasus of Rome now played that role in the West and Basil the Great in the East—he was mourned as a great theologian, fighter, and statesman, the personification of the Nicene cause. Five times he had suffered exile and five times returned to his beloved city. His most passionate supporters, perhaps, were the desert monks whom he won from Arian worship to the Nicene faith. It was Athanasius's proudest boast that Antony, the founder of Egyptian monasticism, had willed him his few belongings shortly before his death. If the bishop's character had been more "saintly" (as that term is commonly used), he might not have been exiled quite so often. But a calmer, more loving personality might not have been sufficiently energized by determination and rage to endure, retaliate, and win.

Valens, the Arian emperor, was not sorry to see him go. Although he had respected the pledge of noninterference that he gave Athanasius, he was not at all inclined to honor his choice of successor. Peter, who was elected bishop at Athanasius's death exactly as the old man had planned, was said to be even more fiery and less cooperative than his former patron, if that could be imagined. Arian bishops now held the sees of Constantinople and Antioch, and Valens did not want to leave the region's largest city in the hands of the Nicene enemy. His choice for bishop was Lucius, who had been elected to that office by Alexandria's Arian clergy after the lynching of Bishop George. When Athanasius returned to the city in 362, he immediately expelled Lucius and the other Arian priests. The exiles then sought refuge in Antioch with that city's bishop—none other than Arius's old companion in exile, Euzoius. Valens was determined that Lucius the Arian, not Peter the Nicene, would be the next bishop of Alexandria.

The emperor's first move was to have Peter arrested by the prefect of Egypt. Troops surrounded Peter's church and he was duly taken into custody, but somehow he gave his captors the slip and boarded a ship for Rome. There he was welcomed by Bishop Damasus, a militant Nicene who had been named pontiff several years earlier after an election that was unusually violent even by fourth-century standards. (More than 160 men's and women's bodies were discovered in one basilica after a climactic fight between Damasus's supporters and his Arian rivals.)[228] While Peter tried unsuccessfully to interest the Western emperor in his plight, Lucius arrived in Alexandria escorted by Bishop Euzoius and a company of imperial troops. Their commander, Count Magnus, arrested and exiled some twenty priests who resisted the Arian's installation as bishop. Other clergymen who expressed sympathy for the exiles were imprisoned at hard labor in the mines, and still others who resisted Lucius's authority were deported to inhospitable foreign lands.

The reports of this persecution are all by pro-Nicene sources, but even taking their bias and exaggeration into account, the emperor seems to have behaved with unaccustomed severity toward the Egyptians.[229] There were historical and doctrinal reasons for this harshness; Egypt under Athanasius had long been a harsh oppressor of Arians, and Valens may have decided, when the opportunity presented itself, to take his revenge. But something else was afoot. Troubling reports were arriving from the region north of the Danube River. If these reports were true, the Eastern Empire was facing new dangers not only on the Persian front, but also along its long, vulnerable northeastern frontier. Especially in times of trouble, no emperor could afford to leave Egypt, the empire's chief granary and source of tax revenues, in potentially unfriendly hands.

The reports Valens was receiving were about a fierce new nation of migrants that was moving steadily west out of the Russian steppes, terrifying the Germanic tribes in their path. Huns they called themselves in their barbaric Asiatic tongue, and such was their disdain for death and love of warfare that even the Goths, with their magnificent armed horsemen, quailed before them. In the early 370s the Hunnish warriors smashed the Ukranian kingdom of the Greuthungi people (Ostrogoths), whose king thereupon committed suicide. Then they turned south, pressing hard upon the territory of the Thervingi (Visigoths). No previous migration had generated the sort of panic that now struck the once invincible Thervingi. Some two hundred thousand tribespeople, many of whom had been converted to Christianity by the Arian bishop, Ulfila, fled en masse toward the Danube.

Caught between the advancing Huns and Rome's frontier defenses, the Thervingi desperately sought permission to settle en masse in Roman territories south of the river. Although the request was unprecedented, so, Valens realized, was the situation. For one thing, keeping the panicked Visigoths out of Roman territory would be costly—and if the Huns succeeded in annihilating them, Rome would have to confront a savage new foe along the Danubian defense line. Furthermore, there was considerable vacant land in Thrace that new immigrants could settle. The Visigoths were excellent fighters and were already offering to join the Roman army—a windfall that could solve Valens's perpetual recruiting problem in one stroke. As taxpaying soldiers and farmers, they would become a source of revenue rather than a drain on the treasury. And they *were* Arian Christians. Valens therefore granted their two kings, Alavivus and Fritigern, permission to settle with their people in Roman territory.

In November and early December 376 this immense body of Gothic tribespeople was ferried across the Danube into what is now Bulgaria. Predictably, given the lack of preparation for a mass movement this large and the prejudice of Roman officials against Germanic "savages," the result was an administrative and human disaster.[230] Some of the Visigoths were dispatched immediately to the Persian frontier, where they were formed into new army units. Others were sent to spend the winter at the town of Hadrianopolis on the Thracian border. But most remained in the north, running out of food as winter approached.

Unfortunately, when it came to dealing with "barbarians"— even Christian barbarians—Roman officials and landowners often proved both racist and venal.[231] So it was with the Visigoths. The impoverished immigrants were brutally exploited and humiliated by their alleged protectors. As they began to starve, Valens's chief officials offered them dog meat to eat in exchange for their sons, whom the officials sold into slavery at a vast profit to themselves.[232] Meanwhile, the city fathers of Hadrianopolis refused to share their food supplies with the newcomers, and the tribespeople sent to that city found themselves victims of a pogrom. As if to worsen the situation further, those Ostrogoths who had survived their defeat by the Huns requested permission to settle in Roman territory as well. When their request was rejected by Valens, they crossed the Danube on their own, increasing the pressure on the region's fast vanishing resources.

Eᴀʀʟʏ ɪɴ 377 the two Visigothic kings requested an urgent meeting with Count Lupicinus, the emperor's chief military representative in Thrace, and Duke Maximus, local head of the civil administration. Both were among the leading sellers of dog meat and traders in immigrant slaves. The count agreed to meet them

at his headquarters in Marcianopolis, but not before issuing orders to his own corps of guards to surround whatever military escort the kings brought with them and watch them carefully. One
could not be too careful with these savages.

Once seated in Lupicinus's dining hall, King Fritigern
poured out an anguished, worried story. Conditions among his
people had become unbearable. Some of the minor chiefs had
organized armed bands of their own to defend themselves
against local attackers or to seize food supplies from the great
Thracian estates. The Visigoths were warriors, after all. They
could not simply sit by and watch their children starve! He and
King Alavivus were still in control of their subjects, but only
barely. Something would have to be done to avert the catastrophe. Something *must* be done to save the Theravingi people. If
not, Fritigern could not guarantee the peace. . . .

What happened next to disrupt the dinner is not clear.[233]
Count Lupicinus may have interpreted Fritigern's statement as a
direct threat (which, in a sense, it was) and taken offense. One
can easily imagine the haughty Roman, stung by barbarian inso-
lence, rising angrily to his feet. One can visualize his royal guests
rising in response, their bodyguards closing in to protect them.
We know the results, however they were provoked: the kings'
protectors run through by a forest of swords . . . the two chief-
tains themselves riding from the city gates, swept by a passion
for justice and revenge . . . Fritigern, the war leader, disappearing into the countryside . . . and then the lightning attacks on
local garrisons and food depots, the smoke rising from plundered
villas, the slaves escaping to join Fritigern's army, the cries of
grieving widows and orphaned children. . . .

The Visigoths' uprising threatened to engulf all Thrace. Elements of a class war appeared when non-Gothic slaves and prisoners left the gold mines and the rich landowners' estates to join
the Visigoth forces or to supply them with information. Roman
army units sent in to bolster the forces already on the ground

were scouted out, isolated, surrounded, and massacred. In open combat as well, Roman soldiers were no match for Fritigern's skilled and ferocious cavalry. Panic among the Romans was quickly communicated to Constantinople, less than five hundred miles east, and then to Antioch, where Valens was wintering with his army. The Visigoths' breakthrough represented the most serious military emergency to threaten Rome since the darkest days of the third century. All Thrace was open to their attack, and from Thrace Fritigern could move either toward Athens or Constantinople.

Valens prepared to move his army into Europe. Since this march of more than one thousand miles would obviously take time, the emperor requested additional troops from the West as a stopgap measure; he wanted the glory of vanquishing the Visigoths himself. If Valens's brother had still been the Western emperor, the reinforcements might have arrived, but Valentinian had died suddenly two years earlier while receiving a delegation from the Quadi people. (The Quadi had recently overrun Illyria; allegedly, their delegates addressed the emperor so rudely that in the midst of the reception he collapsed and died of a stroke.[234]) Valentinian's successor, his teenaged son, Gratian, ordered two large forces of troops sent eastward to support Valens, but almost all of them were delayed by poor leadership or diverted by the governor of Illyria to the defense of his province.

In August 378 the remnants of the divisions sent to reinforce Valens arrived in the field outside Hadrianopolis, where they had been told a great battle between the Visigoths and Romans was in progress. None who saw it would ever forget the sight of that field. The battle had been over for several days. Rotting corpses spread like a seething carpet across the fertile land. Although the dead men's weapons and standards had been taken and many of their uniforms stripped as well, it was clear that virtually all the casualties were soldiers of the Roman army. There were no Gothic corpses, no sign of the emperor or his court, no indication that any Roman, Latin or Greek, remained alive. It was as if the empire itself had suddenly ceased to exist.

Soon the story was common knowledge. Valens's senior advisors had warned him not to act precipitously. He was a reasonably competent commander and his army had extensive experience fighting the Persians, but the Persians were not the Goths. Like the Romans, they were military specialists—mercenaries—and they fought Roman-style. The Gothic fighters, on the other hand, were a people in arms. Driven from their land by the Huns, starved, enslaved, and humiliated by the Romans, they had nothing to lose. Their joy of battle was legendary; they were said to drink the blood of their enemies from their skulls. Their tactics were entirely unpredictable. And except, perhaps, for the Huns, they were the best cavalry fighters in the Western world.

Ignoring his advisors' warnings, Valens brought his huge army into northern Thrace and immediately hurled it against the rebels outside the city of Hadrianopolis. It was reported afterward that local slaves pressed into serving the Roman troops turned against them and gave the Gothic generals information about their armaments and troop dispositions. The Visigoths probably did not require this help. Their mounted warriors dealt Valens's cavalry a devastating initial blow. The Roman horsemen scattered, leaving the bulk of the foot soldiers unprotected. Led by their irresistible cavalry, the Gothic army swept through the legions like a bloody scythe, annihilating infantrymen by the thousands. Those who tried to retreat ran headlong into the Gothic foot soldiers. The Goths had no food or facilities for prisoners. They took none.

Valens himself was killed at Hadrianopolis. His body was never found. It was the worst defeat in the history of Roman arms, foreshadowing the breakdown of Rome's Rhine defenses and the sack of the Eternal City by another Visigoth army some thirty years later. The battle *was* a judgment of at least one sort. It flowed directly from the brutal mistreatment of Visigoth immigrants by corrupt and prejudiced officials. But the Arian emperor's death and the destruction of his legions were given a more abstract intereptation by partisans of the Nicene cause. In Milan, Bishop Ambrose delivered a sermon maintaining that the terrible slaughter was God's judgment on the Arian heretics, and that the safety of the Western emperor's territories was a reward for his orthodoxy.[235] God, it seems, had finally chosen sides in the Arian controversy.

THE ARIAN emperor slaughtered—the Army of the East destroyed—the immediate blow to the Arians' morale must have been crippling. But even more damaging to their cause were the long-term effects of the catastophe on popular thinking. The heart of Arianism was the idea that radical improvements in human behavior need not await the apocalypse or be limited in this world to a cadre of religious specialists. With its popular base among city artisans and workers, sailors and merchants, monks, sodalities of virgins, and young people, it represented a radical impulse in Christianity: the drive to infuse worldly existence with the spirit of Christ, and so renew human society. Hadrianopolis shocked the optimists and undermined their mass appeal by revealing that the "City of Man," as St. Augustine was soon to write, could not be secured. Only the "City of God"— the organized Church—could offer frail humanity compensation for the loss of its worldly hopes.[236]

Clearly, the crisis of the empire was endemic. The great revival of Roman power and culture begun by Diocletian and continued by Constantine was ending . . . or had it been illusory to begin with? The West was in far worse shape than the East, but no frontier was secure from attack. Valens's successor, Theodosius I, understood that to maintain the army, keep an increasingly chaotic society under control, stop the decline in food production, and guarantee the flow of tax revenues, peasants must be tied for life to their land and city workers to their professions.[237] In this world of shrinking horizons, deliberate earthly progress, whether material or moral, seemed an increasingly utopian idea. Survival, especially the survival of one's own immortal soul, was now the great desideratum.

Perhaps more than any other factor, this change of attitude—call it the "new realism"—inclined Christians to accept the new Trinitarian theology. This is not to say that the Cappadocian doctrine was false, only that it corresponded to deeply felt needs for physical and spiritual security. The same sense of vulnerability and unworthiness that inclined Romans to seek the protection of powerful patrons and the intercession of saints (a new cult practice) led them to worship a Christ who was no less mighty than God. Some believers, hoping to follow the holy monks toward a renunciation of worldly desires, required the unlimited power of such a figure to save them from their own concupiscence and willfulness. Others hoped that an all-powerful Jesus would give pious generals the victories denied to Julian, Valens, and other heterodox leaders. In any case, the vision that now seemed *less* relevant was that of Arius's Jesus: a beacon of moral progress sent not so much to rescue helpless humans as to inspire them to develop their own potential for divinity.

The man appointed by Gratian to replace the deceased Valens personified the new realism. In January 379, Theodosius, a Spanish general, became the new Augustus of the East. A practical-minded, decisive man with a violent streak, he was inured to the vicissitudes of high politics. Three years earlier his father, also a general, had been executed for treason, probably on trumped-up charges. The son understood the rewards and risks of power. Theodosius's first campaign, conducted from his headquarters in Thessalonica, demonstrated the superiority of his leadership skills to those of the unfortunate Valens. After defeating one Gothic army in the Balkans, he offered the other tribes the right to settle in designated Roman territories with their chiefs. This time, however, the immigrants were well received, food supplies were plentiful, and the tribes were not given any reason to rebel.

In January 380, with the Balkans pacified, Theodosius returned to the imperial capital at Milan. He had known Ambrose of Milan for some time, but now he asked that passionately pro-Nicene bishop to instruct him in the Catholic faith. The following month he issued an edict trumpeting the new Nicene orthodoxy. For the first time, the state adopted its own definition of orthodoxy and promulgated it as law. Theodosius declared that true Christians were those who believed in "the single divinity of the Father, Son, and Holy Spirit within an equal majesty and an orthodox Trinity." He named Damasus of Rome and Peter of Alexandria as examples of episcopal orthodoxy and labeled Arians and other dissenters heretical madmen deserving punishment.[238] Later that year, Theodosius became seriously ill and was baptized by the bishop of Thessalonica. Upon recovering, he was ready to play the role that he believed God had assigned him: defender of orthodoxy, enemy to all unbelievers, and scourge of the Arians.

The emperor's determination to outlaw Arianism was of no small importance in resolving the Arian controversy. Even so, his use of state power should not be overemphasized. Prior emperors had also played strongly partisan roles in the dispute. They had committed their prestige and, when necessary, their troops to support their Arian or Nicene allies, yet force often seemed to escalate the conflict rather than settle it. This time, although force was used, more than compulsion was involved. The Cappadocians had provided a new theology capable of uniting a large contingent of Arian Christians with most Nicenes. Valens's defeat and the deepening crisis of the empire had turned people's thoughts away from Arian ideals. Even before Theodosius made his views known, the ground was shifting under the Arians' feet, and their movement was in trouble.

As soon as Valens marched his ill-fated army into Europe, in fact, the exiled Peter of Alexandria had returned to that city to await the outcome of the emperor's struggle against the Visigoths. When news came of the Roman defeat, Peter's well-organized supporters were ready to march on the churches. The partisans of the Arian bishop, Lucius, mobilized their street fighters as well. Local troops intervened to quell the nascent riots, and Lucius remained in office . . . but not for long.

Similar scenes were played out in Antioch, where Meletius, a pro-Nicene bishop, returned from exile to challenge the radical Arian Euzoius; in Constantinople, which had been ruled for more than a decade by the Arian, Demophilus; in Ancyra, Caesarea, Tyre, Gaza, and elsewhere. While Theodosius was still in Europe negotiating with the Goths, Meletius of Antioch convened a council on his own authority that demonstrated a startling increase in the number of Greek-speaking bishops supporting the Nicene Creed. Shortly afterward in the West, Ambrose of Milan intervened in a disputed election for bishop of Sirmium, heartland of the Arian-dominated Balkans, and managed to secure the election of a Nicene bishop in that see. These were pale indications, however, of what Theodosius intended to accomplish as emperor of the East.

In NOVEMBER 380 the new Augustus came to Constantinople and immediately made his preferences known. He offered the Arian bishop, Demophilus, the choice of accepting the Nicene Creed or going into exile. A principled churchman, Demophilus chose to surrender his office and left the city. Theodosius then dispatched orders to the prefect of Egypt to expel Lucius from Alexandria and install the pro-Nicene Peter. The affairs of Antioch were settled with equal dispatch, and the emperor completed the purge by issuing another edict, called *Nullis haereticis*: No heretics. "He who professes the Nicene faith is to be thought of as the genuine worshipper in the Catholic religion," it read. Arians and other heretics were forbidden to occupy any church or meet together for worship within the walls of any town. For the first time, a substantial bloc of Christian dissenters had been denied the right of association.[239]

These decrees were lawful, but without the consent of the bishops they would not have the impact that Theodosius intended. In 381, therefore, he invited about 150 selected Eastern bishops to come to the capital to take part in the Council of Constantinople. This council plays a critical but somewhat odd role in the history of the Arian controversy. Although the creed it adopted—essentially the Nicene Creed with a few minor variations[240]—is generally considered to have terminated the controversy, attendance at the council was far from universal, it was wracked by bitter internal disputes, and its overall importance was not immediately recognized.

Using Nicene language, the Creed of Constantinople affirmed that Jesus Christ was

> the only-begotten Son of God, begotten from the Father before all ages, light from light, true God from true God, begotten not made, *homoousios* with the Father, through Whom all things came into existence.[241]

Unlike the Nicene Creed, however, which referred very briefly to the Holy Spirit, the statement of faith went on to proclaim belief in "the Holy Spirit, the Lord and life-giver, Who proceeds from the Father, Who with the Father and the Son is together worshipped and together glorified." It affirmed the Christian belief in "one holy Catholic and apostolic Church" as well, and concluded:

> We confess one baptism to the remission of sins; we look forward to the resurrection of the dead and the life of the world to come. Amen.[242]

The new statement eliminated the Nicene Creed's list of anathemas, which contained the confusing (and, in light of the new theology, erroneous) ban on belief in separate *hypostases,* but the canons adopted by the council denounced two types of Arianism,[243] among other heresies, and Theodosius left no doubt that he intended to enforce the condemnation. Immediately after the council concluded its work, he thundered,

> We now order that all churches are to be handed over to the bishops who profess Father, Son and Holy Spirit of a single majesty, of the same glory, of one splendor, who establish no difference by sacrilegious separation, but [who affirm] the order of the Trinity by recognizing the Persons and uniting the Godhead.[244]

Not long after this, the advocacy of Arian views (at least of the radical sort) and the possession of Arian writings would become crimes punishable by death.

The Council of Constantinople was an Eastern affair, but the West did not lag behind. A council held at Aquileia in 381 under Ambrose's supervision tried, excommunicated, and deposed the Balkan region's two leading Arian bishops, and the remaining Western Arians were soon dismissed as well. Since the Arian Visigoths converted the Burgundians, Vandals, and several other "barbarian" peoples to their faith, Arianism would remain for a time a significant religious movement in the lands that the tribesmen conquered. But among Romans, it disappeared fairly quickly. In 383, when Gratian was murdered by a usurper, the empress Justina, ruling the Balkans on behalf of her young son Valentinian II, came to Milan to seek the aid of Bishop Ambrose. Ambrose offered her political assistance, but when Justina—a devout Arian—asked permission to use a church outside the city walls for worship with members of her court, he refused. "A bishop cannot give up a temple of God," he is reported to have replied.[245]

Arians below the rank of empress met together at their peril. A law of Theodosius of 389 describes them as "eunuchs" and threatens them with the gravest punishments for advocating their faith. Another decree appoints inquisitors to inquire into the orthodoxy of various groups, and still another makes landowners, imperial bailiffs, and tenants responsible for heretical acts that take place on their lands.[246] Theodosius was an enthusiastic persecutor; under his regime, for the first time, pagans were strictly forbidden to sacrifice to their gods or participate in other traditional rites, and Manicheans were hunted down and killed. He had a bloody temper, too; he invited some seven thousand citizens of Thessalonica to a special show in that city's arena, only to massacre them as punishment for a riot that had killed one of his officials.[247] But there does not seem to have been a need to use intense violence to suppress the Arians. The historian Theodoret, writing in the late 440s, recalls that their suppression was accomplished "without tumult or bloodshed in all the provinces of the East."[248]

Theodoret may have overstated his point, but it still reveals an important truth. State power was effective against the Arians—it did not produce many counterattacks or martyrs—because the Arian view of the world was by now generally recognized as obsolescent. Nicene Christianity, with its majestic Christ incorporated into the Godhead, its pessimistic view of human nature, and its bishops and saints playing dominant roles, was better suited to express the hopes and fears of Christians in an age of unpredictable change and lowered social expectations. After seventy years of internal struggle culminating in the shocking disaster at Hadrianopolis, Theodosius appears on history's stage like a Roman Cromwell, Napoleon, or Stalin: an authoritarian figure whose mission was to consolidate the Christian revolution by conservatizing it, adapting it to existing social realities, and incorporating it into the structure of state power.

One year after he banned Arianism, Theodosius officially declared Christianity the religion of the Roman Empire, thus bringing the movement begun by Constantine the Great full circle. The formerly persecuted sect now became a state church with the power (and, according to some, the duty) to suppress or control its rivals. A religious community once harboring diverse strains of belief became an orthodoxy committed to doctrinal unity and the extinction of heresy. And the loose, decentralized organization of the earlier Church gave way to a more hierarchical structure, with power concentrating in the hands of a few great bishops. With the elevation of Jesus to God, orthodox Christianity broke the intellectual links that had bound it to both Judaism and Greco-Roman paganism. Increasingly autonomous both as a faith and as an organization, the Roman Church was now positioned to survive even the collapse of the Roman Empire.

NOT LONG after the emperor outlawed Arian religious worship, a violent and revealing incident occurred in Callinicum, a Roman frontier town in Mesopotamia. A Christian mob led by monks burned both a Jewish synagogue and a chapel used by the Valentinians, a tiny sect of heretical Christians. It is not clear whether there were worshipers in these buildings at the time; such "details" were seldom reported. Theodosius responded as one would expect a responsible ruler to respond: he ordered the local bishop to make restitution to the injured parties and to punish the mob's ringleaders. But before the order could be carried out, Ambrose of Milan, the self-appointed guardian of Western orthodoxy, objected strongly.

Why should Christians be penalized for attacking Jews and heretics? Ambrose complained. Had the pagan emperor, Julian, punished his people when Christians were attacked? Theodosius's intervention against Christ's faithful servants was nothing less than sacrilegious. The fact that imperial officials in Mesopotamia were calling for the protection of Jews and heretics was irrelevant. Unless the emperor repented, Ambrose warned, he could hardly offer him Holy Communion in good conscience. . . .

The threat of possible excommunication struck home.

Theodosius revoked his command.

It is not clear whether this reversal acted as a signal, or whether Christian zealots would have gone on a rampage against unbelievers in any event, but a long wave of religious violence followed. Bands of wandering monks attacked synagogues, pagan temples, heretics' meeting places, and the homes of wealthy unbelievers in Mesopotamia, Syria, Egypt, Palestine, and North Africa.[249] Theophilus, the fire-breathing bishop of Alexandria, incited local vigilantes to destroy the Temple of Serapis, one of the largest and most beautiful buildings in the ancient world, with a library donated by Cleopatra. Alexandrian Christians whipped up by Bishop Cyril rioted against the Jews in 415, and then murdered Hypatia, a wise and beloved Platonic philosopher. Since Arianism was now identified with the "barbarians" who were its main advocates, the remaining Arians within the empire, now split into small, powerless sects, were also fair game for Christian avengers.[250] And the struggle to uproot paganism, conducted sporadically ever since the days of Constantine the Great, now resumed in earnest.

It is not surprising that the triumph of Nicene Christianity was followed by a violent campaign to impose the new order on outsiders. Other revolutionary movements, once consolidated internally, have turned aggressively against unbelievers still "outside the walls." The mood that motivates such crusades is almost always a mix of triumphalism and insecurity, as if success itself somehow intensified hidden feelings of vulnerability on the part of the victors. Clearly, Theodosius and the Nicene movement had little to fear from Jews, Valentinians, or pagans. But uniting against the infidels may have been their way of denying or suppressing persistent tendencies toward internal disunity. They may well have sensed that the settlement of the Arian controversy left important subsurface issues unresolved, and that their victory might not be as final as they hoped.

Was the Arian controversy resolved? Roman Catholic and Orthodox Christians who today recite the Nicene Creed (as amended at Constantinople) would doubtless answer, "Of course." With the adoption of the Cappadocian Fathers' theology, the Catholic Church recognized Jesus as God incarnate, the Second Person of the Holy Trinity. Arianism in its original form disappeared rapidly as a living force within the Roman Empire,[251] and by the seventh century the last of the Arian tribes in Western Europe had been converted to Catholicism. About one thousand years later, Arian beliefs would be espoused by a number of well-known English Protestants, some of whom would go on to create Unitarianism.[252] But for most Christians the question of Jesus Christ's divinity was settled at Constantinople in 381.

Yet there is a sense in which unresolved issues, appearing in changed form, continued to produce serious religious conflicts. Oddly enough, the Council of Constantinople itself became a cause of contention between the Latin and Greek churches. Led by Damasus of Rome, the Western bishops objected to the additions made by the easterners to the Nicene Creed. The element of regional competition is unmistakable. The Roman pontiff was particularly incensed by a canon of the council that declared, "The bishop of Constantinople is to enjoy precedence in honor next after the bishop of Rome because it is the New Rome."[253] In Damasus's view, Rome was unique because of its apostolic foundation, and should be followed by Alexandria and then Antioch. The upstart Constantinople, whose new bishop was a recently baptized civic official, should not even be considered a major see!

But the Latin reaction had a serious doctrinal basis as well. Led by Damasus, the Western bishops objected strongly to the new creed's statement that the Holy Spirit "proceeds from the Father." They insisted on adding the words "and the Son," and this additional clause, known as the *Filioque*, became a major item of controversy in the series of disputes that ended in the Great Schism separating the Roman Catholic and Orthodox churches.[254] The difference of three words may seem trivial, but it exposed a continuing disagreement between Latins and Greeks about Jesus' relationship to God. What the Nicene faith meant to Westerners was that the Father and Son were equal in all things.[255] The Eastern bishops, on the other hand, obeyed a powerful impulse to assert that, in some ways at least, the divine Father was greater than the divine Son.

The contrast between Christian thinking in the two worlds of Christianity became progressively more marked after the Council of Constantinople. So far as the West was concerned, the triumph of the Nicene Creed meant that Christ was God, and that the "Christological" controversy was over. The great theological question now was to determine how fallen humanity could be saved by God's sovereign grace through the sacraments of the Church. And the great practical question was how to convert and integrate the Germanic tribes into the Catholic community. To the extent that Latin Christians felt the need for a heavenly mediator between man and God, that role was played by the cults of the saints and especially the cult of the Virgin Mary, which was greatly strengthened by the triumph of Nicene orthodoxy.[256] Mary was exactly the sort of liminal figure, combining human characteristics with a divine mission and certain more-than-human features, that many Arians had imagined when they glorified Christ. As he was uniquely favored among men, so was she among women. And her function as a protective, inspiring, saving friend was very much that of the Arian Jesus.

In the East, however, Mary would become a subject of violent debate before she became an object of veneration. Was it correct to call her *Theotokos,* the God-bearer, or was she the mother of the man, Jesus, in whom God dwelt?[257] In other words, were Christ's divine and human natures totally fused, so that one could rightly say that God had once been an infant and had suffered on the Cross? Or were there two separate natures, divine and human, somehow integrated in one Person? In the Greek-speaking lands, the end of the Arian controversy triggered more than two centuries of intense conflict over the question, with the Alexandrians taking the view that there was one nature only in Christ, and the Antiochenes insisting that there were two.[258] Once again, bishops met in council to proclaim the orthodoxy of their views and to excommunicate their opponents. Once more the East knew depositions and exiles, riots and assassinations. Each side accused the other of Arianism. The Second Council of Ephesus (449) condemned the school of Antioch; the Great Council of Chalcedon (451) condemned the Alexandrians; numerous emperors intervened on one side or the other; and the controversy did not end until the one-nature "Monophysites" were driven to form their own churches, many of which exist to this day.

One may be tempted to call this conflict unhealthy and to see it as a product of religious fanaticism on the part of the Greek bishops and their flocks. That the parties to the struggle could be violent and overly impassioned is indisputable. But their continuing debate can also be considered evidence of the continuing vitality of Eastern Christendom as a diverse community and a questing faith. While Roman authority collapsed in the West, giving way to a Church-dominated society that struggled bravely to preserve the sparks of learning and kindness in an increasingly violent environment, the East remained urban, relatively prosperous, and, until the great wave of Muslim conquests began in the seventh century, reasonably secure. Hope for humanity's moral progress—for a City of Man that could also be a City of God—did not go underground, as it did in the West. The correlative of this ethical optimism, as in the Arian controversy, was an affirmation of Jesus' humanity and his relevance to society as a model of loving, righteous, transformative behavior.

The East accepted the Trinitarian premises of Nicaea and Constantinople, but the Greeks—now inhabitants of the Byzantine Empire—clung tenaciously to the idea that ordinary men and women could become as God through the imitation of

Christ. That is why they continued to struggle for so long with the question of the relationship between the human element in Jesus and the humanity of God's other children. This same emphasis on the Son's human nature tended to elevate the entirely transhuman Father to a position of supremacy and unknowability that resonated with traditional Eastern values, although to Western theologians any inequality between Father and Son smacked of Arianism.

Like other issues allegedly put to rest at the Council of Constantinople, the issue of Jesus' relationship to God remained alive, although its context had been altered. Greek and Latin Christians agreed that Jesus was fully divine, but there was no consensus about what it meant for someone to be fully divine *and* fully human. This would long remain a cause of contention, not only because alternative Christologies were possible, but because the doctrinal differences between the two Christian worlds had become entangled with their increasing social and cultural separation. At Rome the pope took to excommunicating Eastern emperors whom he considered heretics. In Constantinople, Rome's decrees were ignored. The periods lengthened during which Eastern and Western Christians ceased communicating altogether. Sadly, but perhaps inevitably, the two branches of Christianity were on the way to becoming separate religious confessions.

Soon, most of the Eastern world would come under the domination of a new religion offering another interpretation of Jesus' nature and mission. The Islamic Jesus was not the incarnate God of Nicene Christianity or the superangelic Son of the Arians. In the view of the Muslim conquerors, he was a divinely inspired man: a spiritual genius ranking with the greatest prophets, Moses and Muhammad himself. Apparently, this teaching struck a chord among large numbers of easterners who still thought of God as unitary, and who had not fully accepted Jesus' incorporation into the Godhead. This may explain why, in the Middle

East and North Africa, "the whole [Christian] structure was swept away in a few decades by the Arab tribes and their clear Moslem doctrine of One God."[259]

With the ascension of Islam, Arianism as a discrete religious philosophy disappeared in the East as well as in the West. But the great questions that had generated the controversy over Jesus' divinity remained—and remain yet—to haunt the imagination and provoke the conscience of humankind.

Principal Characters

Constans: youngest son of Constantine and Fausta; Augustus of Italy and North Africa from 337; killed while attempting to escape the forces of Magnentius (350).

Constantia: sister of Constantine; married to Licinius (313).

Constantine the Great: first Christian emperor; Augustus of the West (306–324); sole emperor (324–337); convenor of the Council of Nicaea (325).

Constantine II: eldest son of Constantine and Fausta; Augustus of the West from 337; killed in the war against Constans (340).

Constantius II: middle son of Constantine and Fausta; Augustus of the East (337–353); sole emperor (353–361); Arian sympathizer; convenor of numerous councils leading to the Joint Council of Rimini-Seleucia (359) and the Council of Constantinople (360).

Crispus: son of Constantine and Minervina; executed by Constantine (326).

Diocletian: sole emperor (284–305); reformer; founder of the College of Emperors (Tetrarchy); initiated the Great Persecution (303); abdicated (305).

Fausta: second wife of Constantine; accuser of Crispus; suicided or executed by Constantine (326).

Fritigern: war leader of the Visigoths, victor of the Battle of Hadrianopolis (378).

Galerius: Caesar of the East (293–304); Augustus of the East (304–311); halted the Great Persecution on his deathbed.

Gallus: Julian's half brother; Caesar of the East (351–354); executed by Constantius for malfeasance in office.

Gratian: Augustus of the West (376–383); killed in uprising.

Helena: mother of Constantine; pilgrim, benefactor, and founder of churches.

Jovian: sole emperor (363–364); killed accidentally.

Julian (Julian the Apostate): nephew of Constantius; Caesar of the West (355–361); sole emperor (361–363); pagan; killed in battle against the Persians.

Licinius: Augustus of the East (307–324); defeated in civil war against Constantine; murdered, probably by Constantine (325).

Magnentius: rose against Constans (350); defeated by Constantius and suicided (353).

Theodosius I: Augustus of the East (368–383); sole emperor (379–395); convenor of the Council of Constantinople (381); outlawed Arianism.

Valentinian I: Augustus of the West (364–375).

Valens: brother of Valentinian; Augustus of the East (364–378); Arian; killed at the Battle of Hadrianopolis.

CLERGY

Alexander of Alexandria: Bishop of Alexandria from 313; convenor of the first council of bishops to condemn Arius (318).

Alexander of Constantinople: Bishop of Byzantium and first Bishop of Constantinople, pro-Nicene.

Antony: Christian hermit; founder of Egyptian monasticism.

Arius of Alexandria: presbyter at Church of Baucalis; founder of Arianism; condemned at Council of Nicaea (325) and exiled by Constantine; rehabilitated at Councils of Nicomedia (327), Tyre (335), and Jerusalem (335); died in Constantinople on eve of his readmission to communion.

Athanasius of Alexandria: Bishop of Alexandria from 328; theologian of the Incarnation and leader of the Nicene party; condemned by Council of Tyre (335), *inter alia;* exiled five times; proposed common front with conservative Arians.

Basil of Ancyra: Bishop of Ancyra from 336; leader of the conservative Arians.

Basil "the Great" of Caesarea: Bishop of Cappadocian Caesarea from 356; leader of the Cappadocian theologians; theorist of Eastern Christian monasticism.

Donatus of Carthage: schismatic Bishop of Carthage following the Great Persecution; leader of Donatist sect in North Africa.

Eusebius of Caesarea: Bishop of Caesarea; Origenist theologian friendly to Arianism; first great historian of the Catholic Church.

Eusebius of Nicomedia: Bishop of Nicomedia from 317; deposed and exiled by Constantine (325–327); Bishop of Constantinople from 337; leader and chief strategist of the Arian party.

Eustathius of Antioch: pro-Nicene Bishop of Antioch; deposed and exiled for heresy and misbehavior in office by the Council of Antioch (330).

George of Cappadocia (George of Alexandria): Arian Bishop of Alexandria from 356; imprisoned and lynched by Alexandrian mob (361).

Gregory of Nazianzus: Bishop of Sasima; Cappadocian theologian.

Gregory of Nyssa: brother of Basil the Great; Bishop of Nyssa; Cappadocian theologian.

Hosius of Cordova: Bishop of Cordova; Constantine's earliest Christian advisor; president of the Council of Nicaea.

Ischyras: Egyptian priest allegedly attacked by Macarius at the instigation of Athanasius.

Julius of Rome (Julius I): pro-Nicene Bishop of Rome (337–351); convenor of the Council of Rome (341); advocate of Roman pontiff's right to adjudge between conflicting Church councils.

Macarius: Egyptian priest charged with attacking Ischyras on Athanasius's orders and breaking a sacred chalice.

Marcellus of Ancyra: pro-Nicene Bishop of Ancyra; deposed and exiled for heresy (336).

Melitius of Lycopolis: Egyptian bishop who acted as Bishop of Alexandria (303–305); imprisoned during the Great Persecution; leader of the schismatic Melitian clergy thereafter.

Origen of Alexandria: Christian teacher; outstanding theologian of the third century.

Paul of Constantinople: pro-Nicene Bishop of Constantinople intermittently from 337; imprisoned and executed on orders of Constantius.

Peter of Alexandria: Bishop of Alexandria from 300; fled city during the Great Persecution (303); returned 305 or 306; martyred by Galerius.

Ulfila: Arian Bishop of the Visigoths; consecrated by Eusebius of Nicomedia; translated the Bible into Gothic; converted Goths and other tribes to Arian Christianity.

Selective Bibliography of Works in English

Armstrong, Karen. *A History of God: The 4000-Year Quest of Judaism, Christianity and Islam.* New York: Ballantine Books, 1993.

Athanasius. *The Life of Antony and The Letter to Marcellinus.* Trans. and intro. Robert C. Gregg. New York: Paulist Press, 1980.

Augustine of Hippo. *The Confessions of St. Augustine.* Trans. Rex Warner. New York: Mentor Books, 1963.

Augustine of Hippo. *The City of God.* Trans. Marcus Dods. New York: Modern Library, 1950.

Barnes, Timothy D. *Constantine and Eusebius.* Cambridge, MA: Harvard University Press, 1981.

Barnes, Timothy D. *Athanasius and Constantius: Theology and Politics in the Constantinian Empire.* Cambridge: Harvard University Press, 1993.

Bettenson, Henry, ed. *Documents of the Christian Church.* 2d ed. London: Oxford University Press, 1963.

Brown, Harold O. *Heresies: The Image of Christ in the Mirror of Heresy and Orthodoxy from the Apostles to the Present.* Garden City, NY: Doubleday, 1984.

Brown, Peter. *Augustine of Hippo.* London: Faber & Faber, 1976.

Brown, Peter. *The Making of Late Antiquity.* Cambridge: Harvard University Press, 1978.

Brown, Peter. *The Body and Society: Men, Women, and Sexual Renunciation in Early Christianity.* New York: Columbia University Press, 1988.

Brown, Peter. *Power and Persuasion in Late Antiquity: Towards a Christian Empire* (Curti Lectures). Madison, WI: University of Wisconsin Press, 1992.

Brox, Norbert. *A Concise History of the Early Church.* New York: Continuum, 1995.

Chadwick, Henry. *The Early Church.* Rev. ed. Vol. I, *Penguin History of the Church.* London: Penguin Books, 1993.

Coakley, Sarah, and David A. Pailin, eds. *The Making and Remaking of Christian Doctrine: Essays in Honour of Maurice Wiles.* Oxford: Clarendon Press, 1993.

Davies, J. G. *The Early Christian Church: A History of Its First Five Centuries.* Grand Rapids, MI: Baker Book House, 1965.

Eusebius. *The History of the Church from Christ to Constantine.* Trans. G. A. Williamson. Rev. and ed. Andrew Louth. London: Penguin Books, 1989.

Fox, Robin Lane. *Pagans and Christians.* San Francisco: Harper & Row, 1988.

Fromm, Erich. *The Dogma of Christ.* New York: Holt, Rinehart and Winston, 1963.

Gibbon, Edward. *The Decline and Fall of the Roman Empire,* Vols. I–III. New York: Modern Library, 1932.

Grant, Michael. *The Fall of the Roman Empire.* New York: Macmillan (Collier Books), 1990.

Grant, Michael. *Constantine the Great: The Man and His Times.* New York: Charles Scribner's Sons, 1993.

Gregg, Robert C., and Dennis E. Groh. *Early Arianism—A View of Salvation.* Philadelphia: Fortress Press, 1981.

Gwatkin, H. M. *Studies of Arianism.* 2d ed. Cambridge: Cambridge University Press, 1900.

Hanson, R. P. C. *The Search for the Christian Doctrine of God: The Arian Controversy, 318–381 A.D.* Edinburgh: T. & T. Clark, 1988.

Harnack, Adolph. *History of Dogma.* Vol. 4. Trans. from 3d German ed. by Neil Buchanan. New York: Dover Publications, 1961.

Hughes, Philip. *The Church in Crisis: A History of the General Councils, 325–1870.* Garden City, NY: Doubleday (Hanover House), 1961.

Jocz, Jakob. *The Jewish People and Jesus Christ.* London: S.P.C.K., 1949.

Johnson, Paul. *A History of Christianity.* New York: Atheneum, 1976.

Jones, A. H. M. *The Later Roman Empire 284–602: A Social Economic and Administrative Survey.* Vols. I and II. Norman, OK: University of Oklahoma Press, 1963.

Jurgens, W. A., ed. and trans. *The Faith of the Early Fathers: A Sourcebook of Theological and Historical Passages from the Christian Writings of the Pre-Nicene and Nicene Eras.* Collegeville, MN: The Liturgical Press, 1970.

Kannengiesser, Charles. *Arius and Athanasius: Two Alexandrian Theologians.* Brookfield, VT: Gower Publishing Company, 1991.

Kelly, J. N. D. *Early Christian Creeds.* 3d ed. London: Longman, 1972.

Maier, Harry O. "Private Space as the Social Context of Arianism in Ambrose's Milan." *The Journal of Theological Studies* 45:1, (April 1994): 72 *et seq.*

Nigg, Walter. *The Heretics.* Ed. and trans. Richard and Clara Winston. New York: Knopf, 1962.

Quasten, Johannes. *Patrology. Vol. III, The Golden Age of Greek Patristic Literature from the Council of Nicaea to the Council of Chalcedon.* Utrecht/Antwerp: Spectrum Publishers, 1960.

Pattison, Robert. *The Great Dissent: John Henry Newman and the Liberal Heresy.* New York: Oxford University Press, 1991.

Payne, Robert. *The Fathers of the Eastern Church.* New York: Dorset Press, 1989.

Pelikan, Jaroslav. *The Christian Tradition: A History of the Development of Doctrine.* Vol. 1, *The Emergence of the Catholic Tradition (100–600).* Chicago: University of Chicago Press, 1971.

Pelikan, Jaroslav. *The Excellent Empire: The Fall of Rome and the Triumph of the Church.* Rauschenbusch Lectures, New Series, I. San Francisco: Harper & Row, 1987.

Pelikan, Jaroslav. *Jesus through the Centuries: His Place in the History of Culture.* New Haven: Yale University Press, 1985.

Sanders, E. P. *The Historical Figure of Jesus.* London: Penguin Books, 1993.

Schaff, Philip, and Henry Wace, eds. (original editor Archibald Robertson). *Nicene and Post-Nicene Fathers.* Second series, vol. 4, *Athanasius: Select Works and Letters.* Peabody, MA: Hendrickson Publishers, 1994.

Schatz, Klaus. *Papal Primacy: From Its Origins to the Present.* Trans. John A. Otto and Linda M. Maloney. Collegeville, MN: Liturgical Press, 1996.

Scullard, H. H., and A. A. M. van der Heyden. *Shorter Atlas of the Classical World.* New York: E. P. Dutton, 1967.

Smith, John Holland. *Constantine the Great.* London: Hamish Hamilton, 1971.

Tomlinson, Richard. *From Mycenae to Constantinople: The Evolution of the Ancient City*. London: Routledge, 1992.

Veyne, Paul, ed. *A History of Private Life*. Vol. I, *From Pagan Rome to Byzantium*. Trans. Arthur Goldhammer. London: 1987.

Vidal, Gore. *Julian*. New York: Ballantine Books, 1964.

Wiles, Maurice. *Archetypal Heresy: Arianism through the Centuries*. Oxford: Clarendon Press, 1996.

Wiles, Maurice, and Mark Santer, eds. *Documents in Early Christian Thought*. Cambridge: Cambridge University Press, 1975.

Williams, Daniel H. *Ambrose of Milan and the End of the Nicene-Arian Conflicts*. Oxford: Clarendon Press, 1995.

Williams, Rowan. *Arius: Heresy and Tradition*. London: Darton, Longman and Todd, 1987.

Williams, Rowan, ed. *The Making of Orthodoxy: Essays in Honour of Henry Chadwick*. Cambridge: Cambridge University Press, 1989.

Wolfson, Harry Austryn. *The Philosophy of the Church Fathers*. Vol. I, *Faith, Trinity, Incarnation*. 3d ed., rev. Cambridge: Harvard University Press, 1970.

Notes

CHAPTER I

1   Christopher Haas, "The Alexandrian Riots of 356 and George of
    Cappadocia," *Greek, Roman, and Byzantine Studies*, 32:3 (au-
    tumn 1991): 281, 292–93.

2   Quote from the *Historia Akephala* in R. P. C. Hanson, *The Search
    for the Christian Doctrine of God: The Arian Controversy,
    318–381* (Edinburgh: T&T Clark, 1988), 386.

3   Timothy D. Barnes, *Athanasius and Constantius: Theology and
    Politics in the Constantinian Empire* (Cambridge: Harvard Uni-
    versity Press, 1993), 155.

4   Peter Brown, *Power and Persuasion in Late Antiquity: Towards a
    Christian Empire* (Curti Lectures) (Madison, WI: University of
    Wisconsin Press, 1992).

5   Charles Kannengiesser, *Arius and Athanasius: Two Alexandrian
    Theologians* (Variorum: Hampshire, UK, and Brookfield, Vermont,
    1991), XII, 209.

6   Kannengiesser, "Holy Scripture and Hellenistic Hermeneutics in
    Alexandrian Christology: The Arian Crisis," *Arius and Athanasius*,
    I, i.

7   W. H. C. Frend, *The Rise of Christianity* (Philadelphia: Fortress
    Press, 1984), 636. I have altered the translation slightly.

8   This interpretation of Arianism owes much to Robert C. Gregg
    and Dennis E. Groh, *Early Arianism—A View of Salvation*
    (Philadelphia: Fortress Press, 1981).

9   The doctrine of the "pre-existent Christ" was accepted by Arian
    and non-Arian theologians. Arius insisted, however, that Jesus

was a created being: "a perfect creature of God, but not like one of the creatures, a product, but not like one of the things produced. . . ." Hanson, *Search*, 7; and see the discussion in Rowan Williams, *Arius: Heresy and Tradition* (London: Darton, Longman and Todd, 1987), 95–116. Some commentators think that the doctrine of pre-existence refers mainly to God's foreknowledge of future events. According to Gregg, God named Christ Son "on account of works he performed (works foreknown by God). . . ." *The Life of Antony and The Letter to Marcellinus*, trans. by Robert C. Gregg (New York: Paulist Press, 1980), 12. And see Gregg and Groh, *Early Arianism*, 22–24.

10   Matthew 27:46, *The Holy Bible, Revised Standard Version, The New Testament* (New York: Thomas Nelson and Sons, 1953), 37.

11   Matthew 24:36 RSV, 31.

12   John 14:28 RSV, 123.

13   Athanasius, "On the Incarnation of the Word," in Philip Schaff and Henry Wace, eds. (original editor Archibald Robertson), *Nicene and Post-Nicene Fathers, Second Series*, vol. 4, *Athanasius: Select Works and Letters* (Peabody, Mass.: Hendrickson Publishers, 1994), 36–67.

14   John 5:30 RSV, 109.

15   The heresy of Apollinaris, on the other hand, pictured Christ as a soulless human body occupied by the Divine Spirit. See Hanson, *Search*, 642–647.

16   The Second Creed of Antioch (Dedication Creed) of 341 declared the bishops' belief in Jesus as the "exact Image of the Godhead." J. N. D. Kelly, *Early Christian Creeds*, 3d ed. (Essex: Longman, 1972), 268. And see the discussion of images in Jaroslav Pelikan, *Jesus Through the Centuries: His Place in the History of Culture* (New Haven: Yale University Press, 1985), 83–94.

17   For readable short summaries of these doctrines, see Robert Payne, *The Fathers of the Eastern Church* (New York: Dorset Press, 1989); Henry Chadwick, *The Early Christian Church*, Rev. ed. (London: Penguin Books, 1993). See also Johannes Quasten, *Patrology*, vol. III, *The Golden Age of Greek Patristic Literature from the Council of Nicaea to the Council of Chalcedon* (Utrecht/Antwerp: Spectrum Publishers, 1960).

18   Robin Lane Fox, *Pagans and Christians* (San Francisco: Harper & Row, 1986), 30–31. Fox notes that another possible meaning of *pagani* is "civilians" and opts for this translation on the ground

that the pagans were not soldiers in the army of Christ. "Rustics" makes more sense, in my view, since the Christians were highly concentrated in the cities and may well have considered paganism a product of rural backwardness.

19 See Athanasius, *The Life of Antony and the Letter to Marcellinus,* trans. Robert C. Gregg (New York: Paulist Press, 1980). Athanasius claimed that Antony supported the Nicene position in the Arian Controversy and brought him to Alexandria to testify to his good character (11–13).

20 The division of opinion was exceptionally close in Antioch and Constantinople, where religious rioting became almost a way of life. Alexandria, long dominated by the figure of Athanasius, was exceptional.

21 "And now one George, a Cappadocian, who was contractor of stores at Constantinople, and having embezzled all monies that he received, was obliged to fly, [Constantius] commanded to enter Alexandria with military pomp, and supported by the authority of the General." Athanasius, "History of the Arians," in Schaff and Wace, *Athanasius: Select Works and Letters,* 298.

22 Edward Gibbon, *The Decline and Fall of the Roman Empire,* vol. 1 (New York: Modern Library, 1932), 70.

23 The crisis of the third century is described by numerous historians; see, e.g., A. H. M. Jones, *The Later Roman Empire, 284–602,* vol. I (Norman, OK: University of Oklahoma Press, 1964), 21–36. See, more generally, Michael Grant, *The Fall of the Roman Empire* (New York: Macmillan [Collier Books], 1990).

24 *Sayings of the Fathers,* trans. Rabbi Joseph H. Hertz (New York: Behrman House, 1945), 13, 79.

25 Romans 8:16–17 RSV, 176.

26 Peter Brown, *The Body and Society: Men, Women, and Sexual Renunciation in Early Christianity* (New York: Columbia University Press, 1988), 160 et seq.

27 See Frend, *The Rise of Christianity,* 179: "Nothing suggests, however, that Christianity was a formidable movement before the reign of Marcus Aurelius (161–180)."

28 Ibid., 320. "Practically collapsed" seems somewhat overstated.

29 J. G. Davies, *The Early Christian Church: A History of Its First Five Centuries* (Grand Rapids, MI: Baker Book House, 1965), 115–118.

30 Quoted in Eusebius, *The History of the Church from Christ to*

Constantine, rev. ed., trans. G. A. Williamson (London: Penguin Books, 1989), 211.

31 Fox, *Pagans and Christians,* 310. On this subject in general, see Peter Brown, *The Body and Society,* esp. 145–154.

32 Fox, *Pagans and Christians,* 309.

33 See A. N. Wilson, *Paul: The Mind of the Apostle* (New York: W. W. Norton), 23–35, passim.

34 Peter Brown, *The Making of Late Antiquity* (Cambridge: Harvard University Press, 1978), 51–52.

CHAPTER 2

35 Frend, *Rise of Christianity,* 308.

36 H. H. Scullard and A. A. M. van der Heyden, *Shorter Atlas of the Classical World* (New York: E. P. Dutton, 1967), 101.

37 It is not clear exactly when this ceremony of sacrifice took place, but I have imagined it occurring at the end of the emperors' triumph. For descriptions of the ceremony and accounts of the Great Persecution, see Timothy D. Barnes, *Constantine and Eusebius* (Cambridge: Harvard University Press, 1981), 18–27; Jones, *The Later Roman Empire,* vol. I, 71–76; Fox, *Pagans and Christians,* 592–601; Frend, *Rise of Christianity,* 456–463.

38 The subject of supernatural powers is discussed extensively in Peter Brown, *The Making of Late Antiquity* (Cambridge: Harvard University Press, 1978).

39 Exodus 20:3 RSV, 76. *The Jerusalem Bible, Readers Edition* (Garden City, NY: Doubleday, 1968), 81, translates "before" as "except," which is perhaps clearer to modern readers.

40 The incident is described in Henry Chadwick, *The Early Church,* rev. ed. (London: Penguin Books, 1993), 121; Frend, *Rise of Christianity,* 457; Fox, *Pagans and Christians,* 595; and elsewhere.

41 Barnes, *Constantine and Eusebius,* 22.

42 Eusebius, *History of the Church,* 261–262.

43 Barnes, *Constantine and Eusebius,* 201; Frend, *Rise of Christianity,* 493.

44 The great modern explanation of the distinction between "charismatic" and "rational-legal" authority was made by the German sociologist Max Weber. See Weber's *Theory of Social and Economic Organizations* (New York: Free Press, 1964).

45 This account of Galerius's letter is from Barnes, *Constantine and Eusebius*, 39.

CHAPTER 3

46 Fox, *Pagans and Christians*, 638.

47 Frend, *Rise of Christianity*, 497.

48 Ibid.

49 The facts of Arius's early career are not well documented. This account relies on Barnes, *Constantine and Eusebius*, 202, and *Athanasius and Constantius*, 14; Rowan Williams, *Arius: Heresy and Tradition*, 29–47; and Hanson, *Search for the Christian Doctrine of God*, 3–5. While performing the duties of bishop in Alexandria, Melitius did ordain a priest named Arius, but most scholars deny that this was the same Arius whose theology later set the Roman world aflame. Frend's treatment of the subject in *Rise of Christianity*, 493, may be unduly speculative.

50 See, e.g., Jaroslav Pelikan, *The Christian Tradition: A History of the Development of Doctrine*, vol. I, *The Emergence of the Catholic Tradition, 100–600* (Chicago: University of Chicago Press, 1971), 191.

51 Quoted in Frend, *Rise of Christianity*, 381.

52 Barnes, *Constantine and Eusebius*, 198–199.

53 Hanson, *Search for the Christian Doctrine of God*, 5–8. Since Arius's writings were lost or destroyed, the accounts of his teachings are based on reports by others—most of them his theological enemies.

54 Robert C. Gregg and Dennis E. Groh, *Early Arianism—A View of Salvation* (Philadelphia: Fortress Press, 1981).

55 Pelikan, *Emergence of the Catholic Tradition*, 194–196.

56 See, e.g., Hanson, *Search for the Christian Doctrine of God*, 13; Pelikan, *Emergence*, 198.

57 The *Thalia* is quoted (from Athanasius's no doubt biased version in the *Oration Against the Arians*) by Quasten, *Patrology*, 12. I have replaced several antique words with modern synonyms and changed the order of quotations for clarity.

58 Pelikan views Arianism as a form of "angelology": *Emergence*, 197. But only a few radical Arians later went this far.

59 See Pelikan, *Emergence*, 194–95.

60   Arius's response to the excommunication and the general chronology of events prior to the Council of Nicaea are from Hanson, *Search*, 134–136.

61   Barnes, *Constantine and Eusebius*, 205.

62   Quasten, *Patrology*, 10.

63   The council of Bythnia is briefly described in Barnes, *Constantine and Eusebius*, 205; and Hanson, *Search*, 135.

64   Quasten, *Patrology*, vol. III, 14.

65   Barnes, *Athanasius and Constantius*, 16.

66   Athanasius's works are collected in Philip Schaff and Henry Wace, eds. (original editor Archibald Robertson), *Nicene and Post-Nicene Fathers*, second series, vol. 4, *Athanasius: Select Works and Letters* (Peabody, MA: Hendrickson Publishers, 1994). His views are conveniently summarized in Hanson, *Search*, 415–458.

67   Eusebius, *History of the Church*, 329.

68   Hanson, *Search*, 149.

69   Ibid., 150.

70   Barnes, *Constantine and Eusebius*, 213–214.

CHAPTER 4

71   Eusebius, *Life of Constantine*, quoted in Fox, *Pagans*, 655.

72   Frend, *Rise of Christianity*, 499.

73   Descriptions of the council and its work are to be found, *inter alia*, in Kelly, *Early Christian Creeds*, 3d ed., 205–262; Hanson, *Search*, 152–207; Barnes, *Constantine and Eusebius*, 208–223; and Philip Hughes, *The Church in Crisis: A History of the General Councils, 325–1870* (Garden City, NY: Doubleday [Hanover House], 1961).

74   The setting and Constantine's speech are described in Barnes, *Constantine and Eusebius*, 215.

75   Kelly, *Early Christian Creeds*, 182.

76   Hanson, *Search*, 13.

77   Ibid., 16.

78   Ibid., 160. This account follows that of Hanson, 160–162.

79   Quoted and discussed in Kelly, *Early Christian Creeds*, 214.

80   Kelly, *Early Christian Creeds*, 243.

81   Ibid., 244. And see Hanson, *Search*, 181–202.

82   This argument is made by Barnes, *Constantine and Eusebius*, 216, citing Opitz, *Urkunde*, 22.7.

83 The creed recited by Christians today, although based in large part on the Nicene Creed, is actually an altered version of that creed adopted at the Council of Constantinople in 381. See the discussion in Chapter XI, infra.

84 Kelly, *Early Christian Creeds,* 215–216. Kelly translates *ousia* as "substance" here, and the creed as recited today translates *homoousios* as "consubstantial"—of the same substance.

85 Ibid., 216.

CHAPTER 5

86 Barnes, *Constantine and Eusebius,* 219.

87 Quoted in Frend, *Rise of Christianity,* 500.

88 Barnes, *Constantine and Eusebius,* 220–221. See, more generally, A. H. M. Jones, *The Later Roman Empire, 284–602,* vol. II (Norman, OK: University of Oklahoma Press, 1964), 972–979; Peter Brown, *The Body and Society: Men, Women, and Sexual Renunciation in Early Christianity* (New York: Columbia University Press, 1988). This is the best source of information and insight on this subject overall.

89 Hanson, *Search,* 210, believes that the trip was not a "pilgrimage of reparation," since that would have "multipl[ied] the bad publicity already gained for the imperial house."

90 On this subject generally, see Paul Veyne, ed., *A History of Private Life,* vol. I, *From Pagan Rome to Byzantium,* trans. Arthur Goldhammer (London, 1987).

91 Matthew 19:12 RSV, 23.

92 Quoted in Peter Brown, *The Body and Society,* 205.

93 Ibid., 256.

94 Ibid., 292–293.

95 Ibid., 224–235.

96 Cited in ibid., 31.

97 *The Confessions of St. Augustine,* trans. Rex Warner (New York: Mentor Books, 1963), 176–177.

98 See *The Confessions of St. Augustine,* Book XI, 257–284.

99 See the extensive discussion of *hypostasis* and *ousia* by Hanson, *Search,* 181–207.

100 This doctrine was associated with the Arian thinker, Asterius. Ibid., 226.

101   Ibid., 211–217.

102   Barnes, *Constantine and Eusebius,* 228.

103   Ibid., citing various sources, including the Arian historian Philostorgius.

104   Although a council did meet in Nicomedia, it is unclear how large and representative it was. Barnes (*Constantine and Eusebius,* 229) and certain other scholars think it was a "second Council of Nicaea" on the scale of the first, while Hanson (*Search,* 174–178) thinks it was much smaller.

105   Thus, Barnes, *Constantine and Eusebius,* 230; Hanson, *Search,* 248–249.

106   Hanson, although a supporter of Athanasius's theology, accepts the truth of at least some of these charges. See his *Search,* 249–255.

107   Barnes, *Constantine and Eusebius,* 230–231.

CHAPTER 6

108   On cultural life in Constantinople and other ancient cities see Richard Tomlinson, *From Mycenae to Constantinople: The Evolution of the Ancient City* (London: Routledge, 1992). See also Paul Veyne, ed., *A History of Private Life,* vol. I, *From Pagan Rome to Byzantium,* trans. Arthur Goldhammer (London: 1987).

109   Jaroslav Pelikan, *Jesus through the Centuries: His Place in the History of Culture* (New Haven: Yale, 1985), 85–86.

110   This charge is somewhat inconsistently described in Barnes, *Constantine and Eusebius,* 231–232; Barnes, *Athanasius and Constantius,* 21; and Hanson, *Search,* 255–256.

111   See Athanasius, *The Life of Antony and the Letter to Marcellinus,* op. cit.

112   Barnes, *Constantine and Eusebius,* 232.

113   Hanson, *Search,* 257.

114   Barnes, *Constantine and Eusebius,* 233.

115   Hanson, *Search,* 9.

116   Schaff and Wace, *Athanasius: Select Works and Letters,* 303–447.

117   John 10:30 RSV, 117.

118   John 14:9 RSV, 123.

119   At the Council of Tyre in 335 the Melitians produced evidence that Plusianus, an Athanasian bishop, had committed these acts

of violence, allegedly on Athanasius's orders. Barnes, *Constantine and Eusebius*, 336.

120 See Hanson's extensive discussion in *Search*, 246–273. At the Council of Tyre such anti-Arians as Paul of Constantinople voted against Athanasius.

121 The letters, published by H. I. Bell in *Jews and Christians in Egypt*, vol. VI (London, 1924), are described in Hanson, *Search*, 252–254.

122 Ibid., 253.

123 Hanson says the number was "about 60" (*Search*, 259), but this is probably incorrect, since there were forty-eight Egyptian bishops in Athanasius's camp, and they were a minority of the council (Barnes, *Constantine and Eusebius*, 237).

124 Hanson, *Search*, 255.

CHAPTER 7

125 The incident is described in Barnes, *Constantine and Eusebius*, 239–240.

126 Ibid. See also Athanasius, "Defence Against the Arians," in Schaff and Wace, *Athanasius: Select Works and Letters*, 146.

127 There are differing accounts of this charge against Athanasius. Barnes, *Athanasius and Constantius*, 178–179, thinks that the charge was that Athanasius, who had legal access to the grain supply for purposes of supporting widows and orphans, was threatening "to divert to his own purposes grain needed to prevent riots in the imperial city [Constantinople]." Others (e.g., Chadwick, *The Early Church*, 135) believe that he was charged with threatening to delay the grain ships by calling a dock strike. Hanson, *Search*, 263, doubts that Athanasius ever made such a threat.

128 Barnes, *Constantine and Eusebius*, 240.

129 There is some disagreement about the succession of bishops in Constantinople, but the best opinion is that Alexander died in 337 and was then replaced by Paul.

130 See the extensive discussion in Hanson, *Search*, 217–235.

131 Athanasius, "To Serapion, concerning the death of Arius," in Schaff and Wace, *Athanasius: Select Works and Letters*, 564–565.

132 Ibid.

133 Ibid.

134   Ibid.

135   Barnes, *Constantine and Eusebius,* 137, puts this very strongly, stating that Arius's death was "by the standards of the age, damning," and that afterward not even those sympathetic to his views would defend him. This may be somewhat overstated; there were other reasons, discussed in the text, for the Arians to avoid identifying themselves as such and defending Arius by name.

136   For example, Frend, *Rise of Christianity,* 528.

137   Chadwick, *The Early Church,* 136.

138   There is no evidence of which I am aware that Arius was "painfully" aware of any such negligibility.

139   Document quoted by Athanasius and translated by Hanson in *Search,* 285.

140   Barnes, *Athanasius and Constantius,* 34, gives Constantine II "the initiative" in issuing the decree.

141   This statement by the bishops at the Council of Serdica (343) is translated by Barnes in *Athanasius and Constantius,* 35.

142   Ibid., 49.

143   Athanasius, "Circular Letter," in Schaff and Wace, *Athanasius: Select Works and Letters,* 94.

144   See, e.g., Michael Grant, *The Fall of the Roman Empire* (New York: Collier Books/Macmillan, 1990), esp. 51–68.

145   Hanson, *Search,* 268.

146   See Peter Brown's discussion of the relationship between worldly and "invisible" patronage in *The Making of Late Antiquity,* 63 et seq.

147   Kelly, *Early Christian Creeds,* 268–269.

148   Ibid., 268. The Second Creed of Antioch was a moderate Arian creed.

149   Discussed in Hanson, *Search,* 450.

CHAPTER 8

150   Barnes, *Athanasius and Constantius,* 52, considers the allegation that Athanasius urged Constantine II to attack his brother "plausible." I disagree; Athanasius was not usually that rash.

151   Barnes speculates that Marcellus went to Constans's court before coming to Rome (Ibid., 57). If so, this would support the idea that Constans backed the exiles for reasons of his own.

152   Ibid.

153 Metropolitan bishops held the sees of Alexandria, Antioch, Caesarea, and Constantinople. Later Jerusalem would be added to this list.

154 Ibid., 137.

155 A typical declaration of the Second Creed of Antioch, the so-called Dedication Creed, states that the terms Father, Son, and Holy Spirit denote "accurately the particular subsistence [*hypostasis*] *rank* and glory of each that is named, so that they are three in subsistence but one in agreement." Kelly, *Early Christian Creeds*, 269. Kelly remarks accurately that while the creed abandons certain "hard" Arian positions (e.g., that the Son is changeable), its "main drift" is "resolutely anti-Sabellian, anti-Marcellan" (270).

156 Summarized in Barnes, *Athanasius and Constantius*, 58–59.

157 Reproduced by Athanasius in his "Defence Against the Arians," Schaff and Wace, *Athanasius: Select Works and Letters*, 110–119.

158 Ibid., 111.

159 See the divergent interpretations by Hanson, *Search*, 271, n. 136, and Barnes, *Athanasius and Constantius*, 61.

160 Kelly, *Early Christian Creeds*, 272. See also discussion at 273.

161 The Eastern creed condemned "those who say that there are three Gods, or that Christ is not God." Kelly, *Early Christian Creeds*, 276.

162 The creed also condemned those who say "that before the ages he is neither Christ nor Son of God, or that Father and Son and Holy Spirit are one and the same, or that the Son is unbegotten, or that the Father did not beget the Son by His choice or will." Ibid.

163 Quoted in Barnes, *Athanasius and Constantius*, 75.

164 See the discussion in Hanson, *Search*, 300–305.

165 Barnes, *Athanasius*, 80–81.

166 In North Africa, however, Constans intervened ferociously against the Donatists, who were still challenging the authority of the mainstream Church.

167 Kelly, *Early Christian Creeds*, 279.

168 Ibid., 280.

169 The document submitted to the Eastern bishops has not been preserved. Several scholars (e.g., Barnes, 89; Hanson, 312) assert that their refusal to sign was based on objection to the manner in which it was presented, not to its content. Kelly (280–281) believes that they refused because the document required them to renounce the doctrine of the "three hypostases." The latter view

seems preferable. Valens of Mursa and Ursacius of Singidunum did sign, apparently in order to keep their sees in Pannonia.

170 Translated by Barnes in *Athanasius and Constantius,* 89. Hanson questions the letter's authenticity on the ground that Constans would not have been willing "to plunge the Empire into civil war, no matter how irresponsible he may have been, for the sake of the restoration of a few bishops" (Search, 307). Hanson seems to underestimate the extent to which Constans was willing to take calculated risks in order to strengthen his own position and weaken that of his brother.

171 Barnes, *Athanasius and Constantius,* 90.

172 Frend, *Rise of Christianity,* 532.

CHAPTER 9

173 Ibid., 533.

174 On Ulfila, see Hagith Sivan, "Ulfila's Own Conversion," *Harvard Theological Review* 89:4 (October 1996): 14 et seq.

175 Heinrich Graetz, *History of the Jews,* vol. II (1893; reprint, Philadelphia: Jewish Publication Society of America, 1949), 567.

176 The deposition and imprisonment of Paul are discussed at some length in Barnes, *Athanasius and Constantius,* 214–217.

177 Ibid., 103.

178 Ibid., 104.

179 Schaff and Wace, *Athanasius: Select Works and Letters,* 240.

180 Ibid., 242.

181 The story as told by Sulpicius Severus is related by Hanson, *Search,* 317.

182 This is one of the first known instances of the use of a tactic allegedly employed by Baron Rothschild to obtain early news of Napoleon's defeat at Waterloo, which permitted him to make a killing on the bond market.

183 Karl Marx, "The Eighteenth Brumaire of Louis Bonaparte," in David McLellan, ed., *Karl Marx: Selected Writings* (Oxford: Oxford University Press, 1977), 300.

184 Hanson, *Search,* 321, and see his general discussion at 315–325. To similar effect, see Barnes, *Athanasius and Constantius,* 168–175.

185 For the text, see Hanson, *Search,* 325–329; and see the discussion in Kelly, *Early Christian Creeds,* 281–281.

186 Kelly, 272, 272–283.

187 Hanson tells this story at 333.

188 In Barnes, *Constantine and Eusebius,* 174–175.

189 Ibid., 132.

190 Athanasius reproduces the letter in his "Defense Before Constantius." Schaff and Wace, *Athanasius: Select Works and Letters,* 249–250.

191 "Four Discourses Against the Arians," in Schaff and Wace, *Athanasius: Select Works and Letters,* 303–447.

192 In "History of the Arians," ibid., 295.

193 Ibid., 298–299.

194 Hanson, 344–345. I have replaced Hanson's "declare" with the clearer term, "explain." Note that the issue of the Father's and Son's birth-relationship is "genetic" (from the Greek *gennetos*) but not in the materialistic sense.

195 Ibid., 345.

196 Ibid.

197 H. M. Gwatkin, *Studies of Arianism,* 2d ed. (Cambridge: Cambridge University Press, 1900), 162.

198 See the extended discussion in Hanson, *Search,* 557–597.

199 The most complete discussion of Aetius's career and doctrine is to be found in Hanson, 598–611. On those he calls "neo-Arians" in general, see 598–636.

200 Ibid., 626. The quotations are from Gregory of Nyssa's critical work, *Against Eunomius.*

201 Emphasis supplied. The "Dated Creed" is so called because the committee of bishops took the unusual step of dating it: May 22, 359. The translation is Barnes's in *Athanasius and Constantius,* 144. "Naively" is Hanson's version of Barnes's "without proper reflection." *Search,* 364.

202 Frend, *The Rise of Christianity,* 541.

CHAPTER 10

203 For example, Frend, *Rise of Christianity,* 600.

204 Ibid., 602.

205 Ibid., 601.

206 Description quoted in Hanson, *Search,* 386.

207 Athanasius, "On the Councils of Ariminium and Seleucia," in Schaff and Wace, *Athanasius: Select Works and Letters,* 472.

208 Gibbon, *Decline and Fall of the Roman Empire,* 670.

209 Athanasius, "On the Councils of Ariminium and Seleucia," 472.

210 Ibid.

211 Translated in Barnes, *Athanasius and Constantius*, 156. I have omitted two elliptical additions of "is" that seem unnecessary.

212 Athanasius, "Letter from the Council of Alexandria" (*Tomus ad Antiochenos*), discussed in Hanson, *Search*, 639–645.

213 Ibid., 607. To the same effect, Eunomius, discussed at 622–626.

214 Barnes, *Athanasius and Constantius*, 159.

215 Ibid.

216 See Gore Vidal's brilliant fictionalization, *Julian* (New York: Ballantine Books, 1964).

217 Frend, *Rise of Christianity*, 617.

218 Hanson, *Search*, 685.

219 See Hanson, *Search*, 676–737. Basil made his brother bishop of Nyssa. Gregory of Nazianzus was made bishop of the village of Sasima (680–682).

220 The controversy over the Holy Spirit is discussed, inter alia, in Jaroslav Pelikan, *The Christian Tradition: A History of the Development of Doctrine*, vol. I, *The Emergence of the Catholic Tradition (100–600)* (Chicago: University of Chicago Press, 1971), 211–225. See also Hanson, 738–790.

221 Pelikan, *Emergence*, 213.

222 Hanson, *Search*, 687–688.

223 Ibid., 723–724. See also Gregory of Nyssa, "On the Holy Trinity" and "On 'Not Three Gods,'" in Schaff and Wace, eds., *Nicene and Post-Nicene Fathers*, second series, vol. 5, *Gregory of Nyssa, Dogmatic Treatises, Etc.* (Peabody, Mass.: Hendrickson Publishers, 1994), 326–336.

224 Pelikan, *Emergence*, 222–223.

225 Both Constantine, before his conversion, and Julian worshiped an all-powerful God that they identified in a purely symbolic way with the sun.

226 These quotations from Gregory of Nyssa are cited and discussed in Hanson, *Search*, 724–726.

227 See Pelikan, *Emergence*, 223.

CHAPTER 11

228 Barnes, *Athanasius and Constantius*, 118, n. 62, 276.

229 Somewhat earlier, Valens was said to have received a delegation

of pro-Nicene clergy from Constantinople at Nicomedia, rebuffed them, and put them on a ship to transport them back across the Bosporus. The ship caught fire and the priests died. Valens was accused of ordering the blaze, but it was very likely accidental. See, e.g., Hanson, 791.

230 See A. H. M. Jones, *The Later Roman Empire, 284–602: A Social and Administrative Survey,* vol. I (Norman, Oklahoma: University of Oklahoma Press, 1964), 152–153.

231 The Battle of Hadrianopolis (Adrianople) and its causes are discussed in Michael Grant, *The Fall of the Roman Empire,* 7 et passim.

232 Ibid., 131.

233 See the brief account in Jones, *Later Roman Empire,* 153, citing the contemporary historian Ammianus.

234 Jones, *Later Roman Empire,* 140.

235 Frend, *Rise of Christianity,* 620. See also Daniel H. Williams, *Ambrose of Milan and the End of the Nicene-Arian Conflicts* (Oxford: Clarendon Press, 1995).

236 St. Augustine of Hippo, *The City of God,* trans. Marcus Dods (New York: Modern Library, 1950).

237 The institution of serfdom may therefore be said to begin in the fourth century.

238 Hanson, 804; see also Barnes, *Athanasius and Constantius,* 182.

239 Hanson quotes the decree at 805.

240 There has been a great deal of discussion of the meaning of these variations, whether they are minor, etc. See Hanson, *Search,* 812–820, and the definitive study of Kelly in *Early Christian Creeds,* 296–367. Kelly concludes that the council's "sincere intention, perfectly understood by contemporary churchmen, was simply to confirm the Nicene faith" (325).

241 Kelly, *Early Christian Creeds,* 297. Kelly translates *homoousios* as "of one substance."

242 Ibid., 298.

243 Arianism of the extreme radical (Eunomian) and moderate radical (Eudoxian) types was denounced. Basil of Ancyra's conservative Arianism was not named, suggesting that conservative Arians who could accept the language of the creed were not to be harassed or persecuted.

244 Hanson, *Search,* 821. This is the edict of Theodosius I called *Episcopis tradi.*

245 Quoted in Frend, *Rise of Christianity,* 622.

246 Ibid., 639–640.

247 The massacre at Thessalonica produced a famous confrontation with Ambrose of Milan, who refused to communicate with Theodosius until he had repented. See Frend, *Rise of Christianity,* 624–625; Williams, *Ambrose of Milan.*

248 Frend, *Rise of Christianity,* 637.

249 Peter Brown, *The World of Late Antiquity,* 104–106.

250 On the weakness of the surviving Arian sects, see J. G. Davies, *The Early Christian Church,* 182. On the spread of Arianism from the Visigoths to the Ostrogoths, Burgundians, Vandals, and other peoples in the fifth century, see ibid., 229–230.

251 There is evidence that Arianism went "underground" for a decade or more in the form of private observances. See Harry O. Maier, "Private Space as the Social Context of Arianism in Ambrose's Milan," *The Journal of Theological Studies,* 45:1 (April 1994), 72 et seq.

252 Sir Isaac Newton was one of them. On this subject, see Maurice Wiles, *Archetypal Heresy: Arianism through the Centuries* (Oxford: Clarendon Press, 1996).

253 Hanson (*Search,* 808) remarks that this provision was probably "intended to reduce the pretensions of the archbishop of Alexandria," which seems a reasonable interpretation.

254 See the discussion in Kelly, *Early Christian Creeds,* 358–367.

255 See, e.g., Karen Amstrong, *A History of God: The 4000-Year Quest of Judaism, Christianity and Islam* (New York: Ballantine Books, 1993), 119–123.

256 Paul Johnson, *A History of Christianity* (New York: Atheneum, 1976), 108.

257 Pelikan, *The Christian Tradition,* 241–243.

258 See, for example, Pelikan, *Emergence,* 226–277. For a shorter treatment, see Chadwick, *The Early Church,* 192–212.

259 Johnson, *A History of Christianity,* 93.

Index